InterVarsity Press
P.O. Box 1400, Downers Grove, IL 60515-1426
ivpress.com
email@ivpress.com

Based on Window on the World, 2001 edition, by Daphne Spraggett with Jill Johnstone.

InterVarsity Press® is the book-publishing division of InterVarsity Christian Fellowship/USA®, a movement of students and faculty active on campus at hundreds of universities, colleges, and schools of nursing in the United States of America, and a member movement of the International Fellowship of Evangelical Students. For information about local and regional activities, visit intervarsity.org.

While stories in this book may be true or based on true events, some names and identifying information may have been changed to protect the privacy of individuals.

World map and people group map work: Joshua Project (Mark L. Reichel)
Additional cartography consulting: Bryan Nicholson of cartoMission
Cover design: David Fassett
Interior design: Tim Dowley Associates, Ltd.
Images: African children: © Bartosz Hadyniak / E+ / Getty Images
              Balinese dancer: © Cahaya_Images / iStock / Getty Images Plus
              blue sky: © czekma13 / iStock / Getty Images Plus
              Earth: © cundra / iStock / Getty Images Plus
              eye icon: illustration by David Fassett
              globe and plane icons: © macrovector / iStock / Getty Images Plus
              Indian teen girl: © VikramRaghuvanshi / E+ / Getty Images
              light bulb: © ihorzigor / iStock / Getty Images Plus
              location marker: illustration by David Fasset
              mountain: © filizbbr / iStock / Getty Images Plus
              palm tree: © alenaohneva / iStock / Getty Images
              Vietnam landscape: © Chaiyaporn11441144 / iStock / Getty Images Plus
              Grand Palace Thailand: © AleksandarGeorgiev / E+ / Getty Image
              Pakistani girl: © Ahmad Abdul-Karim Photography / Getty Images
              World map: © switchpipipi / iStock / Getty Images Plus

ISBN 978-0-8308-5783-8 (print)
ISBN 978-0-8308-7410-1 (digital)

Printed in the United States of America ∞

InterVarsity Press is committed to ecological stewardship and to the conservation of natural resources in all our operations. This book was printed using sustainably sourced paper.

Library of Congress Cataloging-in-Publication Data
A catalog record for this book is available from the Library of Congress.

P	24	23	22	21	20	19	18	17	16	15	14	13	12	11	10	9	8	7
Y	38	37	36	35	34	33	32	31	30	29	28	27	26	25	24	23	22	

REVISED EDITION

Window on the World

An Operation World Prayer Resource

Edited by JASON MANDRYK and MOLLY WALL

IVP Books

An imprint of InterVarsity Press
Downers Grove, Illinois

WEC International

CONTENTS

INTRODUCTION

Did you know there are about two hundred thirty different countries in our world? The people who live in them belong to many thousands of smaller groups, who speak different languages and have different customs. Sometimes they have come from other places and settled in a new country that they now call home.

We call these PEOPLE GROUPS, and there may be as many as sixteen thousand people groups making up the world's population. One example of a PEOPLE GROUP you may have heard of is the Kurds. They don't have their own country (see page 86). But they have their own languages and customs, which are very different from those of the other peoples around them.

ABOUT THIS BOOK

This book will tell you something about some COUNTRIES and PEOPLE GROUPS. In some of these places, little is known about God's love shown to us in Jesus. The book will help you to pray that this good news will become more widely known there.

There are ninety-two entries in this book—fifty-two COUNTRIES, thirty-four PEOPLE GROUPS, and a handful of special topics and regions. These sections are arranged in alphabetical order to make them easy to find.

You can read these sections alone or with your family or friends. You could even start a "Pray for the World" prayer club. That's what the children did who helped put the first version of this book together.

At the end of each section are prayers for you to use for the COUNTRY or PEOPLE GROUP you've been reading about—some to thank God, some to ask God. You can pray them all at once, or maybe one each on different days of the week. Remember, all the stories and information, maps and flags, pictures and prayers are there for a bigger reason—to help you change the world by prayer. But perhaps you are wondering how that can happen?

CHANGING THE WORLD

During winter a lot of snow falls in the mountains of Switzerland. When spring comes there is often a danger of avalanches. Sometimes avalanches have been started by a skier just shouting a few words. It only needs a small amount of snow to be disturbed by that shout, and thousands of tons of snow will soon be thundering down the mountainside.

In the same way, a few words spoken to God our Father in Jesus' name can set off an "avalanche" of God's power in any part of the world. Even when we think our prayers are small and weak, God can use them if we trust in him—because he is so powerful.

A missionary named Jill Johnstone met many children all over the world during her lifetime. Many of them didn't know Jesus—so she started a prayer club for kids who did know Jesus. She wrote the first edition of this book. It was called *You Can Change the World* because she knew God would use the prayers of children like them—and like you—to change the world. And she was right!

CHANGED BY PRAYER

Jill started by writing about the country of Albania. The children in the prayer club were sad because, at that time, the Albanians were not allowed to worship God, to pray to him, or to have any books about him. The kids in the club prayed hard for change in Albania, and soon the men who ruled Albania were removed from power. Today people in Albania are free to follow Jesus. The children's prayers, and those of other Christians around the world, changed Albania, so much so that Jill had to rewrite that chapter!

Since that first book came out, God has answered other prayers like this. Jill prepared a new set of COUNTRIES and PEOPLE GROUPS that she knew needed our prayers. She also knew she didn't have long to live, so she asked her friend and colleague Daphne Spraggett to finish a second book, using this material. It was titled *You Too Can Change the World*. Later, Daphne also wrote the first edition of *Window on the World*.

and Molly have enjoyed working on the different versions of it across the last twenty-five years. Let's change the world together through our prayers!

Some of the countries in this book have been changed, or are being changed, because families prayed and went on praying—sometimes for years and years. Albania, China, Mongolia, Russia, and Vietnam are just a few of them.

Will your prayers help change other countries too? Follow the news about other countries, look at books or magazines for information about places and people in this book, and you will see answers to your prayers. The answers may not come right away, but we should never give up praying for the good things we know God wants to happen.

TO HELP YOU PRAY

Whether you want to pray for the things in this book, or for your family or friends, here are some important things to remember. If you find the Bible verses hard to understand, ask an older Christian to help you.

- Prayer is simply talking with God. As we do this, we get to know him better, to understand his ways, to love him, and become his friends. When we pray, we are working together with God—and he wants to change the world.
- We don't have to shut our eyes and put our hands together for God to hear us, although sometimes this can help us to concentrate better. We can pray at any time and in any place— when we're walking, or sitting on the

bus, or when we wake up in the middle of the night.

- God knows everything—but we certainly don't. When we pray to him about something that troubles us, we are sharing with him in what he wants to do in that situation. Jesus talked to his special followers about this. Read what he said in John 15:14-15.
- Evil spiritual powers are trying to prevent God's will from being done in the world. This is why sometimes we must keep on praying for a long time until our prayers are answered. Daniel discovered this for himself; read about it in Daniel 10:10-14. So don't give up!
- God wants us to pray with a clean, pure heart (Psalm 24:3-4). Our prayers might be hindered by these kinds of problems:
  - Our own selfishness (James 4:3).
  - Not being willing to say sorry to God, or to others, for things we have done wrong (Psalm 66:18; Matthew 5:23-24).
  - Ignoring the needs of someone we could help (Proverbs 21:13).

Finally, remember that the best way to learn more about prayer is to pray. We hope this book helps you to do that more and more, and that you will enjoy using it as much as Jill, Daphne, and now Jason

TO HELP YOU USE THIS BOOK

- On pages 194 to 205 there are short chapters telling you a little about Animism, Buddhism, Christianity, Hinduism, Islam, and Judaism.
- You will find the meanings of difficult words in this book in the Word List on pages 208 to 211.
- There is a map of the world on pages 6 to 7.
- On pages 206 to 207 you will find some ideas to help you, your family, your friends, and your church begin to get involved with God's work around the world.

WORLD MAP

Countries and regions featured in this book are shown in orange. People groups are shown in green.

GREENLAND

ICELAND

NAVAJO

SPAIN

MEXICO

CUBA

ATLANTIC
OCEAN

HAITI

GARIFUNA

MANDINKA

DOGON

BIJAGOS

GUINEA

LOBI

PACIFIC
OCEAN

TRINIDAD

VENEZUELA

YANOMAMI

BRAZIL

SAMOANS

QUECHUA

URUGUAY

ARCTIC OCEAN

RUSSIA

UKRAINE

BULGARIA

ALBANIA
GREECE

KABYLE

TURKEY

KAZAKHSTAN

NORTH
CAUCASUS

UZBEKISTAN

KURDS

AZERBAIJANI

YAZIDIS

SYRIA

ISRAEL

IRAQ

DRUZE

PERSIANS

EGYPT

QATAR

UAE

SAUDI
ARABIA

OMAN

BALOCH

BEJA

TUAREG

CHAD

WODAABE

YEMEN

DJIBOUTI

SOUTH
SUDAN

ETHIOPIA

SOMALIS

PYGMIES

AFGHANISTAN

PAKISTAN

MONGOLIA

BURYATS

CHINA

HUI

XINJIANG

HUI

HAZARA

NEPAL

TIBETANS

BHUTAN

BANGLADESH

GONDS

INDIA

ROHINGYA

HUI

NORTH
KOREA

JAPAN

IU-MIEN

PACIFIC
OCEAN

TAI LUE

VIETNAM

MALDIVES

SRI LANKA

MINANGKABAU

PAPUA NEW GUINEA

SUNDANESE

INDONESIA

BALINESE

INDIAN OCEAN

ZIMBABWE

MADAGASCAR

FIJI

SAN

SOUTH
AFRICA

LESOTHO

NEW
ZEALAND

7

AFGHANISTAN
A Land That Longs for Peace

UZBEKISTAN

TURKMENISTAN

TAJIKISTAN

Mazar-i-Sharif

KABUL

AFGHANISTAN

IRAN

Kandahar

PAKISTAN

MOUNTAINS AND DESERTS

Afghanistan, a land of great mountains and scorching deserts, is at the heart of Central Asia. Its climate is harsh with hot, dry summers and cold winters. But its people are warm, and they hope for a better future for their beloved country.

For thousands of years, fierce wars were fought in Afghanistan by the ancient Persians, Greeks, and Mongols. In more recent times, the British, Russians, and Americans have all invaded Afghanistan. There's also been continual fighting between the many different tribes and ethnic groups inside the country. Its main peoples are the Pashtun, the Tajiks, Hazara (see page 62), Uzbeks, and Turkmen.

AFGHANISTAN

NO PEACE

In 1978, the Soviet Union invaded Afghanistan, and many Afghans fled to Iran and Pakistan. The Communist Russians retreated in 1989, and many more Afghans fled the fighting that followed. Although some returned to their own country, many remain in Pakistan.

"Why can't we have peace? What's life like without fighting?" Samir asked his father.

"Sadly, I don't know," his dad replied. "When I was a child, we fought a holy war—or jihad—against the Communists until finally they left. But groups of Afghans went on fighting each other, to get control of the country.

"Eventually the group called the Taliban took over. There was less fighting for a while, but we had to follow their strict Islamic rules. Your mother could not keep her job or even go out of the house without covering herself completely. And there was always supposed to be a man from our family with her. Girls could not attend school at all. Life changed for us and all our neighbors here in Mazar-i-Sharif."

"Is that why some families are scared to send their girls to school now?" Samir asked.

"Yes. Many people fear attacks on girls' schools, which happen from time to time. If we kept *all* the Taliban rules, we wouldn't watch television or listen to music. Men would all have to grow beards and wear only traditional long shirts and baggy trousers—the *shalwar kameez*," said Samir's father. "Things are slowly changing back to a freer way of life, but the Taliban's influence is still very strong.

"Western forces helped overthrow the Taliban and begin a new constitution and government for our country. We started

FACT FILE

AREA: 251,800 square miles

POPULATION: 36.4 million

CAPITAL: Kabul

MAIN LANGUAGES: Dari, Pashto

MAIN RELIGION: Islam

CHIEF EXPORTS: Carpets, fruit, gemstones, opium

to vote for our leaders and laws. But the Taliban remain active, especially now that most foreign troops have left. And in recent years the so-called Islamic State has been causing a lot of problems. Son, I hope you and your friends will come to know a peaceful Afghanistan—one that I have dreamt of, but may never see."

NONSTOP VIOLENCE

Continuous violence has had a terrible effect on people's lives. In most of the country, there's no clean water or sanitation, nor enough food. Hospitals have been badly damaged, and many doctors have left the country. Healthcare and education are limited, and many of the people in Afghanistan have short lives. Children—especially in rural areas—often die from preventable illnesses such as diarrhea and pneumonia. Most Afghans alive today have never known a time without war.

Although farmers raise animals and crops for food, it is difficult because of the violence. Landmines have been left all across the countryside, so walking in the fields is dangerous.

One crop that earns a lot of money is poppies, which people use to make the dangerous drug opium. Although opium is mostly sold to other countries, there are now more than one million opium addicts in Afghanistan.

DREAMS OF JESUS

Fifty years ago, probably fewer than fifty Afghans followed Jesus. Today, there are many hundreds of Afghan Christians. But they often keep their faith secret to protect themselves from the opposition of their Muslim family or community. Afghans hear about Jesus through Christian radio, from refugees returning home, and sometimes in their dreams, or through seeing visions of Jesus. There is now a complete Bible in Dari, and parts of the Bible have been translated into Hazaragi and Pashto. None of the other language groups has a complete Bible. Only twenty percent of women can read, and many men can't read either. Afghans need to have a Bible they can listen to, as well as one they can read.

Christians from abroad are trying to show Jesus' love to Afghans by helping blind, disabled, ill, and needy people. Others provide films, radio programs, apps, websites, and other media resources to teach about Jesus.

TO HELP YOU PRAY FOR AFGHANISTAN

YOU CAN THANK GOD FOR:

- secret Christian believers in Afghanistan, and Afghans who meet Jesus when they flee to other countries.

- the Bible in Dari, and parts of Scripture available in some other languages.

- aid workers who care for the injured, blind, poor, ill, and needy. Many risk their own lives.

YOU CAN ASK GOD:

- to bring peace to this land. People are weary from war and the problems it causes the country, but fighting continues.

- to help people translate the Bible into all the languages of Afghanistan, and to make recordings so that people who can't read can hear the Word of God.

- that people listening secretly to Christian radio will find Jesus and help others find the hope and peace he brings.

- to protect the lives of Afghan and foreign workers who care for people in need.

ALBANIA
Land of the Eagle

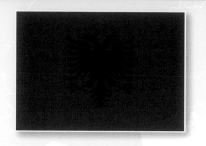

Albanians call their country "the land of the eagle," or *Shqipëri* (she-pur-ee). On their flag, they have a double-headed eagle. That's not surprising, because more than two-thirds of Albania is mountainous, and eagles love mountains. Transport through the mountains is difficult because the roads are poor, so most of Albania's people live near the coast. Because of the mountains, only one-quarter of the land can be used to grow crops.

Albania has many natural resources, including chrome, oil, natural gas, copper, and iron—so it could be a rich country. But it's one of Europe's poorest countries. Why is this?

DARK DAYS

In 1944, Albania became a Communist country. For the next forty-one years, a man named Enver Hoxha ruled Albania. He didn't allow Albanians to travel abroad or to buy things such as cars and fridges. People had little food and no luxuries. In 1967 the Communist government declared Albania "the world's first officially atheistic state," and even made an atheist museum. Muslims and Christians were no longer allowed to worship in their mosques or churches, to pray, or to have religious books. Parents were even forbidden to give their children Muslim or Christian names. The country was difficult to enter, so it became almost completely closed off from the outside world and the Christian good news.

During those difficult times, Christians around the world prayed for Albania. Finally, in 1991, Enver Hoxha's Communist government was forced out. The country became more open, both for its own people to travel outside and for foreigners to enter.

The world was shocked to discover the terrible conditions in Albania. Hospitals were poorly equipped. Many people didn't have enough money to buy food. Starving children filled the orphanages and children's homes, with too few adults to care for them. In the capital, Tirana, there were more donkey-carts and

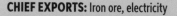

FACT FILE

AREA: 11,100 square miles

POPULATION: 2.9 million

CAPITAL: Tirana

MAIN LANGUAGE: Albanian

MAIN RELIGIONS: Muslim majority, Christian minority, some nonreligious

CHIEF EXPORTS: Iron ore, electricity

bicycles than cars. Villages had neither electricity nor running water.

LIGHT SHINES IN THE DARKNESS

Christians abroad wanted to share Jesus' love with Albanians and started to take in food and medical supplies. The new government allowed both Albanian Christians and Muslims to worship again and to talk about their faith. It is now more than twenty-five years since the end of the Communist rule, and the number of Albanians who want to follow Jesus has increased. Today there are many churches led by Albanian pastors in the cities, and some in smaller towns and villages too. But there are still many towns and villages without a church. Sometimes this is because church leaders or members have moved away. Albanian evangelists and foreign missionaries are trying to share the gospel throughout the country, but much work and prayer is needed.

Because the Bible had been forbidden for such a long time, many Christians knew little about its stories and teaching. But soon after Communist rule ended, Christians worked hard to make modern translations that many Albanians are now reading.

Because Albania has so many poor and needy people, Christians not only tell others about Jesus, but also put love into action with practical help and care for people. Christians from many countries help look after children in the orphanages and share the good news of Jesus with Albanians. Several thousand Albanians, many of them young people, now follow Jesus.

FAR FROM HOME

"When will my mom come to get me, Aunt Marjeta?" Dritan asked. Marjeta looked down with compassion at her neighbor's little boy, who had come to live with her three months earlier. His mother had gone away to Italy to find work. There were no more jobs in their town, and she needed money to care for herself and Dritan.

"I miss her so much," said Dritan, starting to cry. Marjeta took the young boy into her arms to comfort him. "Your mom loves you very much, and misses you dearly. She will be back once she finds a good life for you with her in Italy. Times in Albania are hard. We must love one another and pray to God for help to make it through," she said.

More than half of the Albanian people now live outside of Albania. Nearby Kosovo and Macedonia have large Albanian populations, and most of them do not know about Jesus. Many Albanians have gone to find work in Italy, Greece, and many other countries. Some women, like Dritan's mom, work as cleaners, waitresses, or caregivers for the elderly. They try to send money back home to their families.

TO HELP YOU PRAY FOR ALBANIA

YOU CAN THANK GOD FOR:

- answering the prayers of Christians to open Albania to the gospel.
- every Albanian who follows Jesus.
- the translation of the Bible into modern Albanian.

YOU CAN ASK GOD:

- to help Christians share his love with everyone in Albania and to care for people in practical, helpful ways.
- for the Albanians in Kosovo and Macedonia to hear the truth about Jesus.
- to protect and encourage families who are living apart while one or both parents work abroad.
- for Albania to create more jobs so that families can stay together and the country can improve.
- to help Christian leaders care for their congregations and teach them to follow God's Word.

AZERBAIJANI
The Fire Guardians

Farzali lives in the city of Baku, the capital of Azerbaijan, a country on the Caspian Sea. His people, the Azerbaijani, are almost all Muslims. They live mainly in Azerbaijan and Iran, with some in nearby countries, such as Iraq, Turkey, and Russia. A few smaller groups of Azerbaijani live in countries even farther away. But more live in Iran than in any other country, including Azerbaijan.

A few Christian people also live in Azerbaijan alongside the Muslim Azerbaijani. One part of Azerbaijan—Nagorno-Karabakh—is also claimed by their neighbor, Armenia. The Armenians are traditionally Orthodox Christians. The Azerbaijanis and Armenians fight over who should have control of that land. During the 1990s, there was a war between the Azerbaijani and the Armenians, and many people fled the country.

ARE WE MUSLIMS?

Farzali was excited when his friend Babek invited him to his house after school. "I'll ask my mother, but I'm sure I can come," he said.

"I used to love going to Johan's house to play," Babek said. "But my mother doesn't let me go there any longer, because his family are Dutch Christians. His father is a pastor at an international church. My mother said they would try to make me a Christian too. But Johan is a great friend. Do you think it's really so bad to be a Christian?"

Farzali frowned. "I think it would be terrible. My great-grandfather says it's unforgivable for an Azerbaijani to become a Christian," he said.

"Why do they make such a fuss?" Babek asked. "My family all say we're Muslims, but we never go to the mosque."

Farzali wasn't sure whether his family were Muslims or not. His great-grandfather certainly was. He read the Qur'an every evening. But his father talked mostly about politics and money, not about being a Muslim. He said

that, because of all the oil, a few people were very rich here in Baku—but most Azerbaijanis remained poor.

The next day, Farzali went with his father and great-grandfather to visit his uncle's farm. Farzali loved his great-grandfather. He was more than a hundred years old, but still very active.

"Today's a special day, when we jump over a bonfire three times. We imagine that our sicknesses are falling into the fire, and that it gives us strength for the next year," explained Farzali's uncle. "Before the Azerbaijani became Muslim, we used to worship fire and our ancestors. For this reason, the ancient Greeks called our ancestors 'fire

FACT FILE

NUMBERS: Around 40 million

MAIN COUNTRIES: Iran (more than 20 million) and Azerbaijan (Azerbaijani make up much of the population); also Iraq, Turkey, Russia, and Georgia

MAIN LANGUAGE: Azerbaijani

MAIN RELIGION: Islam

MAIN OCCUPATIONS: Oil and natural gas industries

Baku

DO YOU KNOW?

There is a site on a hillside near Baku called Fire Mountain, where a wall of fire has been burning for more than sixty-five years. Natural gas seeps out from the ground, so the flames never go out.

guardians.' Now, we still keep up some of the old ceremonies in our holidays."

Farzali took a running start and leaped over the small fire. Even his great-grandfather hopped over the flames. Farzali wondered if the fire could really take away their sickness and pain.

PURE

Farzali's cousin wore a traditional fire-red dress for the first part of her wedding celebrations. Farzali felt confused. He wondered which was best to follow: the old Azerbaijani religion, Islam, or Christianity? Surely they couldn't all be true?

The Azerbaijani want their souls to be made clean and pure. But only Jesus can do that for them. Few Azerbaijani people have heard about Jesus, but now the Bible is available in their language, in print and online. The Azerbaijani can also listen to Christian radio programs in their language. Some Azerbaijani Christians have composed special music, literature, and poetry so they can worship Jesus in the Azerbaijani language and style.

During the last thirty years, the number of Azerbaijani Christians has increased. Today there are Azerbaijani Christians in Azerbaijan, mainly in the capital, Baku. They usually meet in house churches and hope one day to see churches in every town and village in Azerbaijan. There are perhaps even more Azerbaijani Christians in Iraq, and a few in Iran. But it's very difficult for churches to register and meet together legally in public places or in church buildings, and Azerbaijanis often face persecution for following Jesus.

Mud volcanoes, Azerbaijan

TO HELP YOU PRAY FOR THE AZERBAIJANI

YOU CAN THANK GOD FOR:

- Azerbaijani Christians and the few Azerbaijani churches, meeting mostly in homes.

- the Bible and other Christian resources in the Azerbaijani language.

- the chance for Azerbaijani in Azerbaijan to hear about Jesus more openly there than in some nearby countries.

YOU CAN ASK GOD:

- to send Christians to Azerbaijanis, wherever they live, to share what the Bible says.

- for every Azerbaijani to meet Jesus and follow him.

- to show the Azerbaijani that only Jesus can make them pure and clean.

- to help Azerbaijani Christians share their Christian music, poetry, and literature with more people.

BALINESE
From the Island of the Gods

Bali Sea

BALI

Denpasar

INDIAN OCEAN

PHILIPPINES

MALAYSIA

INDONESIA

A BEAUTIFUL ISLAND

Anne thought Bali was the most beautiful place she'd ever seen. It had sandy beaches, brightly colored flowers, rice fields of green and gold, and thousands of temples. She could see the mountains in the distance—some of them were volcanoes.

Anne had even seen a performance of the graceful *Legong* dances, which tell the stories of gods and demons, witches, and kidnapped princesses. The dancers wore dresses of gold, scarlet, and green, with headdresses glittering with gold, and bright, tropical flowers in their shiny black hair. All the Balinese people she met had such gentle, smiling faces.

No wonder that every year more than four million tourists visit Bali, a small island in the long necklace of Indonesian islands. Visitors often call it "the island of the gods" or "the island of a thousand temples."

MANY GODS

There are thousands of Hindu temples on Bali. The Balinese had many gods before they became Hindu. In Bali, Hindus say they worship one god (Brahman, or Hyang Widhi) who takes many forms.

Once a year, the Balinese have a religious festival called Nyepi: a day of silence, fasting, and meditation. They bring out statues of their gods to be washed clean in the sacred waters of the sea. They also make bamboo statues called *ogoh-ogoh* that look like evil spirits, parade them around, and then burn them to get rid of evil influences.

SPIRITS OF THE ANCESTORS

The Balinese believe the spirits of their gods and ancestors live in the mountains. Each family builds a little temple; its altar faces one of the sacred directions—north or east. Every day they make little offerings to the spirits of their ancestors. They believe it's important to be on the good side of these spirits.

The Balinese are very concerned about what happens when they die. Sometimes a family saves money for several years so they can build an elaborate funeral tower and hold a cremation ceremony, when the body of the dead relative is burnt to

FACT FILE

HOMELAND: Indonesia

LOCATION: Most live on Bali, an island just east of Java

NUMBERS: About 4 million

MAIN LANGUAGES: Balinese, Indonesian

MAIN RELIGIONS: Hinduism, animism

OCCUPATIONS: Tourist industry; also farming (rice and coffee), fishing, and handicrafts (weaving and wood carving)

Young Balinese boy in the town of Ubud

Rice, Bali's staple crop, growing in a paddy

DO YOU KNOW?

The Balinese have a legend that says that their beautiful island was once flat. Nothing would grow there. When the island of Java became Muslim, the Hindu gods moved a short distance to Bali. These gods needed mountains where they could live, so they created some. Water from these mountains made the island fertile.

Traditional Balinese temple dancer

ashes. They believe the soul of a dead person isn't free to reincarnate (be reborn) until this ceremony has taken place.

JESUS' POWER

There aren't yet many Balinese Christians. Sometimes Hindu family members or neighbors treat Christians badly. They're afraid the gods will be angry if people leave them and follow only Jesus instead.

Eight-year-old Nyoman was frightened. Some people in his village had done mean things to his family because they were Christians. "Why won't they let us have water for our fields? What did we do wrong?" he asked his parents. "The other kids said that one night when I'm asleep, the gods will come and punish me because I don't follow them."

"Don't be afraid, Nyoman!" said his father. "Jesus promised he'll always be with us. He's more powerful than anyone who wants to harm us. People in the village think the gods are angry because we've become Christians. They

want us to turn back to our old gods. But we know that, with Jesus, we don't have to fear those gods. Jesus will look after us—even when we're asleep. Let's pray, Nyoman, and ask Jesus to take away your fears."

Christians often try to show Jesus' love to their Hindu neighbors by helping them in practical ways. Christians are starting to tell Bible stories the Balinese way, using dance and gamelan music.

They want them to know Christianity isn't a religion that belongs just to foreigners. Some tourists give Balinese people a wrong impression about Christians when they come from countries that are Christian, but behave badly.

One by one, Balinese are coming to know Jesus as the friend who is always with them. They find the Holy Spirit can heal when the other spirits can't. Those who follow Jesus are praying that many more Balinese will come to know that Jesus is far greater and more powerful than the thousands of gods they keep in their shrines.

Hindu statue, Ubud, Bali

TO HELP YOU PRAY FOR THE BALINESE

YOU CAN THANK GOD FOR:

- Balinese who are coming to know Jesus as the one true living God and as their friend.

- a Bible translation in Balinese.

- Balinese Christian groups caring for poor people in villages and housing homeless children in Denpasar.

YOU CAN ASK GOD:

- to help Christians show Jesus' love to their Hindu friends and neighbors.

- to show the Balinese that Jesus is so much more powerful than all the gods they worship.

- to help Christians like Nyoman know that evil spirits can't harm them if they trust in Jesus.

- for whole families to come to know Jesus so children learn about Jesus when they're young.

BALOCH
Carpet Weavers of Pakistan

HARD WORK

Abdullah tossed some freshly cut wheat onto the bullock cart. *Not a bad harvest this year!* he thought. He looked over at his grandfather, with his wrinkled face and white beard, wearing his turban and long, homespun shirt over baggy trousers. His grandfather was glad Abdullah was there to help because he couldn't manage the little farm on his own any more.

Abdullah's father and his brother, Ghaus, had gone to the city of Karachi to find work. Although Abdullah was only twelve years old, they had left him to do most of the farm work. It was very difficult: the weather was burning hot in summer and bitterly cold in winter.

The old bull plodded into the high-walled courtyard leading to the house Abdullah's father had built. It was much better than the shack made of reeds where they used to live, or the goat-hair tent where his grandfather grew up.

Abdullah's sisters were sitting at the carpet looms where they worked most of the day. Their quick fingers tied thousands of knots as they wove beautiful carpets. The intricate carpet designs had been passed down through their family. When he smelled the *naan* (wheat bread) and curry

that his mother was cooking for dinner, Abdullah realized how hungry he was feeling.

Meanwhile, on a busy street in Karachi, Abdullah's father finished up his work at the kebab stall and set out searching for his son, just as he did at the end of every day. Abdullah hadn't seen his son Ghaus for months now, but he didn't want the rest of the family to know this. Like thousands of other young people,

FACT FILE

NUMBERS: About 13 million

COUNTRIES: 5 million live in Pakistan, and 6 million in Iran; others live in Afghanistan, the United Arab Emirates, Oman, and Turkmenistan

MAIN LANGUAGES: Balochi; many Baloch use Urdu, Pashtu, and Arabic to communicate with other groups

MAIN RELIGION: Islam

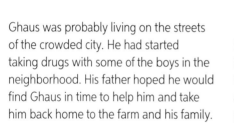

Ghaus was probably living on the streets of the crowded city. He had started taking drugs with some of the boys in the neighborhood. His father hoped he would find Ghaus in time to help him and take him back home to the farm and his family.

A RICH PROVINCE

Abdullah's farm is in Balochistan, the largest of the four provinces of Pakistan. Balochistan has natural gas, copper, iron ore, and coal, and there are lots of fish in the sea. It is Pakistan's richest province in terms of resources, but most of its people live in the greatest poverty. Water is difficult to get, and jobs are few. Many Baloch people think the Pakistani government neglects them. "The other three provinces use most of our gas," they complain. Balochistan needs better roads and railways, clean water supplies, and good health care and schools. Some Baloch people want their province to become an independent country together with the Baloch areas of Iran and Afghanistan.

Many Baloch have left the rural areas to find work in Karachi—the biggest city in Pakistan—or abroad. There aren't many schools in the mountainous countryside, so few Baloch children learn to read.

HEARING THE GOOD NEWS

Missionaries used to work among the Baloch people, who live in very dangerous areas. Because of war, violence, and persecution, the missionaries had to flee.

The Baloch like listening to programs in their own language on the radio and internet. There are even some Christian programs. They can also read or listen to the New Testament online in the Balochi language. There are only a few hundred Baloch Christians in the world, but more and more are interested in learning about Jesus.

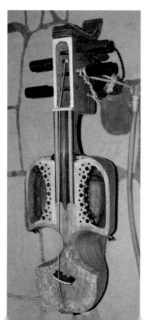

Suroz, the national instrument of the Baloch

TO HELP YOU PRAY FOR THE BALOCH

YOU CAN THANK GOD FOR:

- the New Testament in Balochi.
- the hundreds of Baloch who now follow Jesus.

YOU CAN ASK GOD:

- for people who will go and share the love and message of Jesus with the Baloch and pray regularly for them.
- to send Christians to care for drug addicts in Karachi and show Jesus' love for them.
- that the Baloch who now follow Christ will find boldness to tell others about Jesus. Pray for the church to grow in number and in wisdom.
- that many Baloch will listen to Christian radio broadcasts and encounter Jesus through the programs.
- for a better future for the Baloch: clean water to drink, jobs to earn a living, education, peace from the ongoing conflict in the region, and to know Jesus.

BANGLADESH
Land of Mighty Rivers and Floods

HOMELESS

"What are we going to do now?" Ali cried. Feeling very scared, he clung to his father on a pile of mud where their house used to stand. He clutched a squawking chicken that was struggling to escape. Aziz, his father, gripped a little basket of rice. It was all he'd managed to save when pounding rain, strong winds, and floodwaters from the great Brahmaputra River destroyed their home.

"We'll start again, somehow," Aziz said. "The floods bring fresh soil that helps us grow good crops. But this time the winds and heavy rains have destroyed everything. They've killed people and taken our homes and cattle. If only we knew what's happened to your mother and little sister. We must hope they're safe." Aziz tried to reassure Ali, fighting back his own tears.

FLOODS AND CYCLONES

Every year, water comes rushing down the mighty Ganges, Brahmaputra, and Meghna rivers, running through Bangladesh to the Bay of Bengal. This usually happens from June to August as the snows on the Himalayan mountains melt and the mighty north Indian monsoon brings its heavy rains. Every year, the rivers burst their banks and flood the countryside. Every year, homes and fields are washed away, and animals and people die. Every year, the floods carry fresh soil onto the land, creating some of the best farming land in the world for the coming year.

When a cyclone hits the country, the chaos and destruction are terrible. The worst cyclone in history happened here in 1970, killing 300,000 people. And the world's deadliest tornado struck here too, in 1989, killing 1,300. No wonder Bangladesh has been one of the poorest countries in the world. There are so many rivers, so little land, and so many people, making it one of the most crowded countries on earth. Everyone—from the smallest child to the oldest grandfather—has to work hard just to live.

Because there aren't enough jobs to go around, at least one million Bangladeshis go abroad each year to find work. Many travel to the oil-rich countries around the Persian Gulf, and others to India. Wherever they go, these migrants send money home to support their families.

But change has been coming to Bangladesh. In recent years, it has become one of the main countries supplying the world with clothes—check the labels of your clothes for "Made in Bangladesh." Bangladesh

BANGLADESH

FACT FILE

AREA: 55,600 square miles

POPULATION: 166.4 million

CAPITAL: Dhaka

MAIN LANGUAGE: Bangla or Bengali; English also used

MAIN RELIGIONS: Large Muslim majority, Hindu minority

MAIN EXPORTS: Clothing is the largest export by far; also cloth for garments, jute, and tea

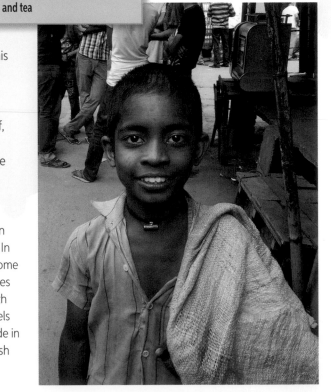

Bangladeshi bride

also supplies the cloth for the garments, so many of those who were once very poor now have jobs. The government has worked to improve education, so more children can finish at least primary school. New bridges and ongoing improvements to the roads both help to lessen the flood damage year by year.

A NEW NATION

The country we call Bangladesh was once part of India—one of the richest, most fertile parts, with rivers full of fish. In 1947, it became the eastern part of a new Muslim nation called Pakistan. West Pakistan and East Pakistan were a thousand miles apart, separated by India. But the people of East Pakistan thought the government wasn't fair to them, and in 1971 a civil war broke out. More than a million people died as a result. In the end, East Pakistan separated and became Bangladesh, the "land of the Bengalis."

Most Bangladeshis are Muslims, but some are Hindus. Christian missionaries have worked among the Bengali people for at least two hundred years. An English missionary named William Carey came to India, learned the Bangla (Bengali) language, and wrote their first grammar book. He also translated the Bible into the Hindu form of Bengali. That remained the only Bible in Bengali for nearly 200 years. Today, updated translations are available in print, audio, and online. And a translation for Bengali Muslims has led to many Muslims following Jesus. Christian workers have shown God's love in Bangladesh, teaching children, giving healthcare, and setting up hospitals and schools. They've also helped people suffering from natural disasters, like Ali and Aziz.

A NEW CHURCH

Praise God that the church in Bangladesh is growing, even though Christians are sometimes persecuted in this mainly Muslim land. Most Christians come from a Hindu background, but recently some tribal groups have also come to know Jesus. In most Muslim countries, very few people follow Jesus; but in Bangladesh, tens of thousands of people from a Muslim background worship Jesus as their Lord.

But many Bangladeshis have still never met a Christian, read Bible stories, or heard about Jesus and his love for them. Bengalis (the majority in Bangladesh) are the world's largest unreached people group. Many more Christians will need to share about Jesus with the Bengalis before that changes.

TO HELP YOU PRAY FOR BANGLADESH

YOU CAN THANK GOD FOR:

- every Christian who is showing God's love to others in Bangladesh.

- the many believers from Muslim backgrounds who now love and follow Jesus.

- improvements in education and working conditions, making life better for the struggling people of Bangladesh.

YOU CAN ASK GOD:

- to help the leaders of Bangladesh be fair to all its people, rich and poor.

- to help Christians show God's love to the people of Bangladesh, especially to homeless children and the disabled.

- for more Christians to come to Bangladesh and show God's love to the millions of needy people.

- for Christians in other countries to welcome Bangladeshis who are living abroad, far from their families, and to share Jesus with them.

Buriganga River, Dhaka

19

BEJA
Frightened by the Evil Eye

EGYPT

Red Sea

SUDAN

ERITREA

WHAT ABOUT THE FUTURE?

Amna watched her grandmother carefully. She hoped that one day she would be as wise as her grandmother. They sat together on the matting outside their tent made from palm fronds. Her grandmother dropped five cowrie shells and looked closely at the pattern they made on the ground. Then she shook her head and scooped them up again.

"What's the matter?" Amna asked anxiously. "What do the shells say?" She knew her family needed some good luck right now because her older sister, Khadija, was getting married after the Muslim festival of Eid. Khadija felt worried. She was only twelve, but her parents had already arranged for her to be married to her cousin Ahmed.

"What's Ahmed like?" Amna asked Khadija, who was sitting behind her on the mat, patiently braiding Amna's frizzy hair.

"He's been here to talk about our marriage and to drink *jabana* (coffee) with our brothers—but I've never met him," Khadija replied. "He must be really old, though. He's been working for uncle for a long time. It'll be strange to go and live with his mother and sisters on the other side of town. I'll be so lonely without you, Amna."

After the wedding, Khadija had to stay with Ahmed's family. But she wouldn't meet Ahmed face to face for another year because of Beja marriage customs.

Sometimes Khadija and Amna sat and listened to their brothers talking around the fire, usually about their frustrations with the government or problems with their herd. Her brothers used a lot of Arabic words, and Amna wished they would speak their own language, Bedawi, so she could understand what they were saying. She preferred the nights when they relaxed and sang traditional songs together—her favorite song was about a Beja camel.

EVIL SPIRITS

The Beja (*bay-juh*) are a group of tribes living in the northeastern part of Africa bordering the Red Sea that stretches from southern Egypt through northern Sudan to Eritrea. There are about three and a half million Beja. They have lived as nomads in this hot, dry, desert land and the windy Red Sea hills for more than four thousand years. They are always looking for pasture for their herds of

FACT FILE

COUNTRIES: Most Beja live in northeastern Sudan, and some in nearby Egypt and Eritrea

NUMBERS: Between three and four million

MAIN LANGUAGES: Beja (also called Bedawi, or Badawiyet); many can also speak Tigre

OCCUPATIONS: Most Beja are nomadic herdsmen, but some farm or take jobs as laborers in villages or towns

Beja tent

DO YOU KNOW?

Bedawi is a difficult language to learn. It is sometimes written with Arabic letters, and sometimes with our Roman alphabet. Only a few parts of the Bible have been translated into Bedawi.

camels, cattle, sheep, and goats. But it's a harsh place to live, and some Beja settle in towns and villages. They are not Arabs, like many people in the region, so they keep to themselves and don't easily trust outsiders.

The Beja are Muslims, but few of them fully follow the Muslim faith, or pray and fast according to Muslim laws. They mix many traditional superstitions and practices together with Islamic teachings. They're afraid of the "evil eye"—they believe some people can curse others with it—and of evil spirits (*jinns*) that they believe want to harm them. They have many superstitions about what brings good and bad luck. Life is very hard for the Beja. They face drought, famine, political conflict—and many live in fear of evil spirits.

Only around fifty Beja people have become Christian so far.

A NEW FRIEND

One day, when she was buying goat milk from the milkman, Amna made a new friend. Nora came with her mom and younger brother from Eritrea. Her father had found asylum in Europe after escaping Eritrea, and now Nora helped her mother sell tea by the roadside. They hoped one day to join him. They needed to earn money to buy food for the family and to pay for her brothers to go to school.

Amna missed Khadija so much that she was very glad to have a new friend. "Nora," she asked, "what do the shells say about your future? Will you have to get married soon? Will our brothers be safe?"

Nora squeezed her hand. "Amna, don't worry. God loves us all. We can trust him to take care of us. We don't have to be scared of the spirits all the time. You're my friend, and I want you to know Jesus, who is a true friend to all— even to young girls like us."

Jesus died for the Beja people, as well as for you and me. Will you pray for the Beja to hear the message God has for their people?

Beja shield

TO HELP YOU PRAY FOR THE BEJA

YOU CAN THANK GOD FOR:

- Christians from Sudan and nearby countries who want to tell others about Jesus.

- Christian resources in Arabic and Bedawi such as Christian radio broadcasts and parts of the Bible.

- the Beja who have decided to follow Jesus after reading the Bible in Arabic.

YOU CAN ASK GOD:

- to send help to the Beja, who live on difficult land and often don't have enough food or water.

- that the Beja will find release from the constant fear of evil and know the power of Jesus to overcome it.

- to reveal his love to the Beja through Jesus and his followers.

- for Beja children—girls as well as boys—to have an education.

BHUTAN
Land of the Thunder Dragon

CHINA

THIMPHU

BHUTAN

INDIA

BHUTAN

THE THUNDER DRAGON

Sangay had been looking forward to attending his first Buddhist festival—but now that he was there, he felt scared. Monks were dancing around wearing big masks with scary, bulging eyes and sharp teeth. He didn't want them to get too close. "Why is there a picture of a dragon on the flag and on the temple walls?" he asked.

Sangay's mother leaned down and told him the story of the thunder dragon. "Have you heard the dragon roar when there's a storm?" she asked. "A very long time ago, there was a monk who wanted to build a monastery. When he found a good place to build this monastery, he heard thunder. He thought the thunder was a dragon roaring, so he named his monastery 'Druk,' which means 'thunder dragon'. So our country is called Druk Yul, the 'Land of the Thunder Dragon', and we are called Drukpas, 'the dragon people.'"

Sangay's parents are farmers. Because Bhutan is covered with mountains and hills, they grow their rice and wheat in terraced fields—flat areas cut into the sides of the hills. Sangay helps his parents in the fields and with their goats. Sangay's big brother lives away from home in the town where he goes to school. Sangay would also like to go to school, but it would cost too much money for them both to go. So Sangay stays home to help on the farm. He's learning to read and write at a little school in the local monastery.

SNOW LEOPARDS

Bhutan is a small country in the Himalaya mountains nestled between two large countries: China and India. The southern part of Bhutan is warm and humid, while the northern part is very cold. The Himalayas are the highest mountains in the world; snow and ice always cover them. In the valleys between the mountains are forests and mighty rivers. Black bears, tigers, red pandas, and snow leopards are just a few of the rare animals found in Bhutan.

FACT FILE

AREA: 14,800 square miles

POPULATION: 817,000

CAPITAL: Thimphu

MAIN LANGUAGE: Dzongkha (Bhutanese)

MAIN RELIGION: Buddhism

CHIEF EXPORTS: Timber and electricity

Bhutan is a Buddhist kingdom, and religion, culture, and traditions play a big part in peoples' daily lives. Buddhist religious ceremonies are held for many different occasions. Bhutan is also home to many Hindus, as well as very small groups of other religions.

Although it's not common, some men in Bhutan have several wives, and some women have several husbands. The former king of Bhutan, Jigme Singye Wangchuck, married four sisters on the same day. He was succeeded by his son, Jigme Khesar Namgyel Wangchuck, in 2006.

The king of Bhutan is expected to care for his people. They can contact him with their requests. The current king tours around his country so that even the people in far-off villages can talk to him.

Bhutanese men traditionally wear a knee-length tunic called a *gho*. The women wear the *kira*, a dress made from one piece of cloth, fastened at the shoulders, and with a wide belt. Traditional dress was once required for everyone. Today it is required only in certain buildings, such as government offices or monasteries, or for certain jobs or festivals. But many people still wear it proudly.

TALKING ABOUT JESUS

When the last king saw how much crime was happening around the world, he decided to try to protect his people from seeing bad things. So until 1999, no one was allowed to watch television. The king realized that what we watch and hear affects what we do, the way we treat others, and the way we think. But it also meant that Bhutan was mostly cut off from the gospel for many years.

Taktsang monastery

Eventually, the laws were relaxed, and the people of Bhutan can now go online and connect to the rest of the world. But Bhutan is still isolated and mysterious. It has fewer outside visitors than most countries. It's very expensive to travel in Bhutan, and only a few people are allowed to visit the country each year. It is easier for Indians to travel in Bhutan, and Indian Christians have taken the gospel there over the years.

Experts from other countries help Bhutan with medical care, farming, engineering, and in other areas. Some of the people who come to help are Christians, but they aren't allowed to ask people to follow Christ. No one knows exactly how many Christians there are in Bhutan, but most people there haven't heard about Jesus. In the southern part of the country, small groups of Christians have come together. Some of these groups are made up of refugees from Nepal. In Thimphu, the capital, there are house churches where people meet to worship in secret—church buildings are forbidden. There is a New Testament in Dzongkha (Bhutanese), but most of the other languages of Bhutan do not have any part of the Bible to read or listen to in their language. Bhutan needs Christians who can stay in the country, sharing Jesus with their words and their lifestyle.

BIJAGOS
Who Believe in a Spirit Who Punishes

The Bissagos Islands (or Bijagos) belong to Guinea-Bissau, a small West African country, and are home to the Bijago people. Many still live there today, although Bijagos also live in other parts of Guinea-Bissau. Some have migrated to Portugal, Brazil, and Spain for study or work. Like most of us, Bijagos are grateful for mobile phones to help them stay in touch with loved ones in other parts of the world.

The Bijagos once struggled to find clean water—poverty, hunger, and disease were big problems. But bore holes have provided clean water to most villages, and Bijagos living in Bissau (the mainland) send supplies back to their families on the islands.

GUINEA-BISSAU

GUINEA-BISSAU

Bissau

BISSAGOS
ISLANDS

FACT FILE

NUMBERS: About 35,000

HOMELAND: Bissagos Islands (Guinea-Bissau)

MAIN LANGUAGE: Bidyogo

MAIN RELIGIONS: Animism, Islam, Christianity

MAIN OCCUPATIONS: Farming, fishing

The Bijagos are traditionally animists. They believe in a great spirit who made them, but who won't help them. Instead, he sends punishment and disaster. They build temples of mud and thatch, with an altar in the middle. The altar is surrounded by fetishes (charms or magic items) and carved idols that they worship. The Bijagos are afraid of evil spirits called *iran*. They sacrifice animals and take part in special ceremonies in the hope that these spirits won't harm them. Some Bijagos are Muslim; some are Christian. Others—especially young people—have left behind their traditional beliefs and don't follow any particular religion.

MOVING HOUSE AGAIN
Carlos lived on the island of Bubaque in the village of Bijante. Every other year, the villagers moved to the nearby island of Rubane to cultivate their rice crops there—a kind of farming called crop rotation. During the six months they were away, Bijante became overgrown with forest while they lived in temporary shelters on Rubane.

"Why do we have to move to Rubane every other rainy season?" Carlos

complained. "Why can't we just stay in Bijante? I like it here in our cozy house with the thatched roof. And why do we sacrifice an animal before we cut down the forest?"

Carlos asked his parents question after question. His mother was collecting pots, basins, and everything else the family would need for the next six months. His father had been busy sharpening his machete for clearing the forest away. But now he was catching their chickens and putting them into a woven palm branch basket.

![lightbulb icon]

DO YOU KNOW?

The Bijago islands, with their white, sandy beaches, palm trees, and brightly colored birds, are a beautiful tropical paradise. The islands are home to many sea turtles, as well as the rare saltwater hippo. Altogether there are eighty-eight islands, but only about twenty of them are populated year-round.

Everyone in the village was packing their belongings, gathering everything up.

"It's our tradition, Carlos," his dad said. "Rubane is a sacred island that belongs to our village. Before we start cutting down the forest to prepare our lands for planting, the witch doctor sacrifices an animal. Do you remember last time? The witch doctor gave us a piece of the meat to cook where we made our fields. That's called 'paying the ground.' The *iran* will punish us if we don't."

Before long, Bijante was empty. People scrambled to find places for themselves and their things in the dugout canoes. They had to paddle across the water to Rubane.

CLEAN WATER

Many years ago, the village of Ancarave, on the island of Uno, was just like any other Bijago village. Even though it grew very good rice, its people and animals often became sick—they got their water from a filthy pool. The witch doctors made offerings to the *iran*, but nothing got better.

One day some Christians visited the island. "You don't have to be frightened of the *iran*," they said. "We see your priests and witch doctors make sacrifices, but your children and animals are still dying. The God we worship loves you so much that he sent his only son, Jesus, as a sacrifice for you. You never need to make sacrifices again. If you trust Jesus, he will help you."

Missionaries came to the island. They helped to translate the New Testament into the Bijago language and dug the first well on Uno island. What a difference clean water made! The village chief became certain that God had sent these people to the island. He and all the villagers became Christians and burned all the idols. The Bijago Christians danced and sang for joy. When other villages on Uno saw the change in Ancarave, they wanted to follow Jesus too.

Today there are more than four hundred Bijago Christians spread across a number of the islands. When a civil war broke out on the mainland of Guinea-Bissau, many Bijagos living there returned to their home islands. Some were Christians who helped lead the churches. More Bijagos hear about Jesus now, but many more still need to hear of his love.

TO HELP YOU PRAY FOR THE BIJAGOS

YOU CAN THANK GOD FOR:

■ Bijago people—on the islands, in Bissau, or around the world—who have trusted in Jesus.

■ churches led by pastors from Guinea-Bissau, including some Bijago pastors.

■ the practical help missionaries brought, such as wells for clean water and schools for education.

YOU CAN ASK GOD:

■ to reveal his love for the Bijagos and the good news of Jesus.

■ to help Bijago Christians break free from the power of the *iran*.

■ to show Bijagos how to follow Jesus faithfully but also keep the good parts of their culture.

BRAZIL
A Land Full of Life

Brazil is big! It's the biggest country in South America. And it has the second largest population of Christians in the world. It makes a big impact on other countries through its music, culture, sports, and even its missionaries—Brazil sends many. Its regions are big too: the Amazon rainforest in the north, the ranchlands of the south, the miles of beaches, and the Pantanal wetlands to the west.

FOLLOWING JESUS, OBEYING PARENTS

Claudia begged her mother, "Please can't I go just once? All my friends from camp will be there!"

Claudia loved her time at Christian camp—playing games, singing around the campfire, and giggling with the girls after lights out. During that week, she had prayed, confessed her sins, and believed in Jesus.

"No, Claudia. Our family is Catholic. Your friends are *evangélicos*—we are not like them," her mother scolded her. "You can go to youth meetings, but not to church. Honor our family and its traditions." Claudia didn't understand what the big deal was. Weren't they all Christians?

One Thursday after youth meeting, Claudia talked to the pastor about it. He said, "I know this is difficult. But until your mother says it's okay, I think Jesus would

want you to obey your parents."

"One more thing," the pastor said. "You can ask God to take away your angry feelings and replace them with love and patience."

She did feel angry, so she confessed that to God on her way home and asked him to change her heart.

LEAVING THE SPIRITS

Antonio felt as if his life had been turned upside down. His mother still sold street food from Bahia every day at the beach. But now she wore normal clothes—not the white clothes and jewelry of their religion, *Candomblé*. She'd stopped going to their meetings. She'd even put away the drum she loved playing there. Lots

Map Labels

VENEZUELA
GUYANA
SURINAME
FRENCH GUIANA
COLOMBIA
ECUADOR
North Atlantic Ocean
Manaus
Fortaleza
Recife
BRAZIL
Salvador
BOLIVIA
BRASÍLIA
Belo Horizonte
PARAGUAY
São Paulo
Rio de Janeiro
Curitiba
ARGENTINA
Porto Alegre
South Atlantic Ocean
URUGUAY

FACT FILE

AREA: 3.3 million square miles

POPULATION: 210.9 million

CAPITAL: Brasília

MAIN LANGUAGE: Portuguese

MAIN RELIGION: Christianity—Catholic majority, but also Protestants and other Christian groups

ECONOMY: Many wealthy people, but many poor; good natural resources, rich agriculture

CHIEF EXPORTS: Soybeans, iron ore, sugar, oil, and poultry meat

PEOPLES: More than 275 indigenous people groups, speaking 185 languages. Also descendants of Europeans, descendants of African slaves, Romani, river dwellers (*ribeirinhos*), and immigrants—especially Japanese, Chinese, and Lebanese.

Rio de Janeiro

DO YOU KNOW?

Brazil is best known for *futebol* (*soccer* in the United States). Brazil, with players in bright yellow shirts, has won the World Cup more times than any other country.

of people in Salvador follow *Candomblé*, and lately they all seemed angry with his mother.

Antonio's ancestors arrived from West Africa as slaves, and over time they had mixed African witchcraft and ancestor worship with Catholic rituals. In northeast Brazil, many *Candomblé* houses exist alongside Catholic and evangelical churches.

"You are bringing shame on us," Antonio heard his uncle tell his mom, "by leaving the religion of our family and our people to follow Jesus with the *evangélicos*."

On the days that he preached at the beach, Marcos bought food from Antonio's mother. When Marcos talked to her about Jesus, her spirit felt alive and clean. She knew Jesus was real. When she gave her life to Jesus, she felt his love. He was more powerful than any spirit in *Candomblé*.

But life, religion, family, and work were all tied together. Leaving *Candomblé* wasn't simple. Antonio's mother would earn less money, and her family might cut off communication with them.

"I don't know how we'll manage," she said. "But I know this is what God wants me to do."

WEAK OR STRONG?

Carlos went along to the new Christian youth club. *Why not? They give away free food and play futebol,* he thought. He wasn't interested in God, though. What had God ever done for him?

Drugs, gangs, street fighting, and unjust raids by the police have become common in Brazil. Carlos' father and grandfather were both in prison. With his habits of stealing and lying, he'd probably end up in prison too.

If our politicians and police can get away with it, why shouldn't I? he thought. *I just need to be more careful than my papa, and not get caught!*

The Christian center was okay. It was fun playing *futebol* against the staff. Carlos liked pushing himself hard to win. The leaders at the center told stories from the Bible. In the stories, Jesus was always forgiving someone, saving someone, healing someone, or giving them hope for the future.

"Stay away from drugs, from gangs, and from violence," the center staff urged the kids. Carlos sat at the back, pretending not to listen.

But Jesus was different from any person Carlos had ever met. He taught people to turn the other cheek instead of fighting back. And he spoke out fearlessly against the religious and political leaders. You had to be strong to do that.

TO HELP YOU PRAY FOR BRAZIL

YOU CAN THANK GOD FOR:

- millions in Brazil who follow Christ.

- the many Brazilian missionaries who go to other parts of their country and abroad to talk about Jesus.

- the spiritual passion of Brazilians— when they find Christ, they are active in prayer, and experience the power of the Holy Spirit.

YOU CAN ASK GOD:

- for people to tell the truth and act fairly in government, in business, and in churches, schools, and families.

- for kids living on the streets or in the *favelas* (slum communities) to meet Jesus, flee temptations, and find hope.

- to free the many people who live in fear of evil spirits and practice magic.

- for groups with few or no Christians— especially in more remote regions—to meet Jesus.

BULGARIA
Life-Giving Water

If you look at a map, you will find Bulgaria in the southeast corner of Europe, beside the Black Sea. If you look in a history book, you will discover that Bulgaria was a Communist country between 1944 and 1989. But a whole generation has grown up since Communism ended there; only their parents and grandparents remember those days.

ROMANIA

SERBIA

BULGARIA

Varna

SOFIA

Burgas

MACEDONIA

Plovdiv

TURKEY

GREECE

BULGARIA

Black Sea

TIMES CHANGE

"Todor, let me remind you of the times before you were born." Uncle Stanislav is a pastor and likes to tell stories about the old days. "The government was atheist and tried to stop Christians from going to church. Even the traditional Bulgarian religion—the Orthodox Church—felt the persecution. Some of the members of our Pentecostal church were actually spies for the government. Because of one of those spies, I spent almost a year in prison. But I've long since forgiven that spy and the government," he said.

"It's really different these days!" Todor exclaimed.

"So much is different," Stanislav agreed. "But not all of it is better. Schools and hospitals are not as well run as they used to be. Some people have gotten rich, but a lot of them are corrupt—or even criminals. A lot of people are poorer than before. At least under Communism, the government took care of the poorest people. That's why our church is so busy with programs. We try to help look after the elderly, the orphans, the poor, and the sick—no one else seems to care much for them."

OLD AND NEW

"Now we have new challenges. So many people are leaving Bulgaria—especially the younger generation. They move to other European countries to find a better job. Bulgarians are not having many babies, so our population is getting smaller and smaller," he said.

FACT FILE

AREA: 42,800 square miles

POPULATION: 7 million

CAPITAL: Sofia

MAIN LANGUAGE: Bulgarian

MAIN RELIGIONS: Christianity (mostly Orthodox), nonreligious, Islam

CHIEF EXPORTS: Machinery, food, wine, iron, roses, rose oil, textiles, and chemicals

Traditional Bulgarian salad

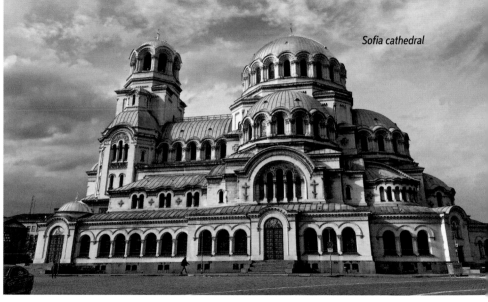
Sofia cathedral

"But our population is not only thing going down," Stanislav added. "Did you know that in the 2000s, Bulgarian schoolchildren had the best reading levels in the world? It's gone down since then.

"Bulgaria became a Christian country well over a thousand years ago. Today, most Bulgarians couldn't tell you a thing about the gospel. We need a revival from the Holy Spirit!"

DREAMS

Ahmed is a Bulgarian Turk. As a boy, he was taught it was important to serve Allah. So he learned to read Arabic and studied the Qur'an, where he read about Jesus. When he was about eleven years old, Ahmed had a dream about Jesus.

"Jesus came to my house," he remembers. "He offered me a jar of water, but I wouldn't take it until he promised he would never leave me."

When Ahmed was around twenty, a man gave him an old Turkish Bible. Ahmed read it but couldn't understand it.

"I wanted to know about Jesus, but there was no one to help me," he said. "Then I prayed and opened my Bible. I read a story in John chapter 4 about a woman who met Jesus at a village well in Samaria. He offered her life-giving water.

"At last I understood my dream from all those years before. From then on, I wasn't thirsty inside, and I followed Jesus."

A MIRACLE

Florika is a Romani girl who lives with her family in a city slum. Every day she has to clean and cook and look after her little brother and sister while their mother goes out to work. Florika was born mute. She didn't speak a word for the first nine years of her life. Her family often prayed and took her to healers. But Florika still couldn't talk.

Some Christians visited the slum where Florika lived. She squeezed into a crowded room and listened to them tell about Jesus healing the blind, the deaf, and the mute. She wondered if Jesus could heal her.

The Christians prayed for Florika—and God worked a miracle.

"May I please have a drink of water?" she asked. It was the first time in her life that Florika had spoken.

Florika ran to her mother, calling, "I can talk. Jesus healed me!" Her mother couldn't believe her ears. Her whole family was amazed and happy. They wanted to learn about this God who had healed Florika. They decided to follow Jesus too.

God doesn't always do miracles when we pray. But miracles show people who don't know God how powerful and loving he is. All around the country, Bulgarians, Turks, and Romani are coming to know Jesus as their friend. But they don't always understand the Bible well enough to put into practice what it teaches.

TO HELP YOU PRAY FOR BULGARIA

YOU CAN THANK GOD FOR:

- every person who follows Jesus, and the long history of the Christian faith in Bulgaria.

- dreams and miracles that bring healing and help people understand who God is.

- Christian groups that visit the slums and other poor areas to speak about Jesus.

YOU CAN ASK GOD:

- to help the different people groups of Bulgaria love, understand, forgive, and respect each other after long years of conflict and distrust.

- to show churches and Christian groups how to work together to reach their people, and to send missionaries to other parts of the world.

- for church leaders and pastors to know the Bible well.

- for the Holy Spirit to breathe new life in to the large Orthodox church, and for many to encounter Jesus.

BURYATS
Buddhists of Siberia

Lake Baikal

RUSSIA

Ulan-Ude

MONGOLIA

CHINA

PRAYING WITH BEADS AND WHEELS

"What a great film!" Bator exclaimed. "I've never seen anything like it. Do you think it's true? That there's a Creator who loves the whole world and wants everyone to know him? Imagine—God sending his own son to earth as a tiny baby."

"I felt really sad when they put God's son, Jesus, on that cross," said Temudjin.

Bator and Temudjin sat on a bench outside a Buddhist temple. Brightly colored prayer flags fluttered over the monastery. The boys could hear the sound of gongs and the chanting of monks inside the temple.

Temudjin let his prayer beads slip through his fingers one by one. Earlier that morning, he and his uncle had gone to the temple to set the prayer wheels spinning.

"It's so different from our Buddhist ways," Temudjin said. "My uncle says if we do bad things, we have to be punished. We'll go on suffering for our sins every time we're reborn."

"I'm going to read the book about Jesus that the teacher gave me," said Bator. "I want to know more about him. Come on—I'll race you home."

HORSE BREEDERS

Bator and Temudjin are Buryats. They live in Buryatia, southeastern Siberia, northern Mongolia, and the part of China called Inner Mongolia. They are probably descended from the Mongols of Genghis Khan's time. For hundreds of years the Buryats were nomads. They bred horses and cattle in wide valleys between forest-covered mountains. Like the Mongols, they lived in traditional round felt tents called yurts, moving with their herds several times a year.

Today, most Buryats live in villages and cities, like their Russian neighbors. Many are still farming and raising cows, pigs, and chickens. In Ulan-Ude, the capital city of Buryatia, many work in the big factory that makes carriages for the Trans-Siberian Railway. But many others don't have any job.

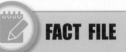

FACT FILE

COUNTRIES: Russia (Buryat Republic), Mongolia, and China

NUMBERS: 460,000 Russia, 50,000 Mongolia, China (estimates vary)

MAIN LANGUAGE: Buryat; Buryats in Russia, Mongolia, and China usually also speak the local language

MAIN RELIGIONS: Buddhism, shamanism

OCCUPATIONS: Once nomadic herders; now many work in industry

Sacred poles by Lake Baikal

DO YOU KNOW?

Lake Baikal contains as much water as all the Great Lakes of North America together. It's the biggest freshwater lake in the world—and the deepest. Experts think it's the oldest too.

Five hundred years ago many Buryats became Buddhists—especially those living east of the vast Lake Baikal. Before Buddhism arrived, all the Buryats followed their shamans, tribal priests who could communicate with the spirit world.

Things changed a lot for the Buryats after 1917, following the Russian Revolution. By the end of the 1930s, the new Communist government had forced many of them to settle in villages. The authorities closed the monasteries and set up government schools for the children. The Communists did not allow Buddhism and destroyed many Buddhist shrines and religious books.

In 1989, the Communists lost power and Russia had a new government. Soon after, the Dalai Lama—the Buddhists' spiritual leader—visited Ulan-Ude, the capital of Buryatia. He told the people to put atheism and Communism behind them and return to Buddhist beliefs. Many Buryats did so. Today, some Buryat boys go to school at a Buddhist monastery. A few go on to become monks, taking their religion around the world.

But even for Buryat Buddhists, the influence of shamanism is very strong. Many Buryats have also kept their old animist beliefs. They are very aware of the spirit world, and they ask their shamans to use magic and astrology to protect them.

BURYAT BIBLE

In 1817, the czar of Russia permitted three English missionaries to travel to Siberia.

"Why do you want to help the Buryats? We don't think much of them," said Russians living in the region.

The Buryats were also puzzled why the missionaries had come. Only twenty Buryats became Christians. The missionaries translated the Bible into the Buryat language. But since then, the way that Buryats write down their language has changed. Today, no one can read the old translation. Thankfully, there is a recent translation of the New Testament into Buryat that they can read, and some Christians are working hard to finish translating the Old Testament. The *JESUS* film was also translated into Buryat and has been shown in many places.

Only a few Buryats believe in Jesus, but their numbers are growing. Who will the Buryats decide to follow? Their shamans, the Buddhist monks, or Jesus?

TO HELP YOU PRAY FOR THE BURYATS

YOU CAN THANK GOD FOR:

- Mongolian Christians who go as missionaries to the Buryat people.

- the New Testament in the Buryat language.

- the growing number of Buryats who follow Jesus.

YOU CAN ASK GOD:

- to show Buryats that only Jesus can take away sin and bring spiritual peace.

- for Christians to reach out to the Buryats with God's love in practical ways, such as helping in schools, farming, and health care.

- to help workers finish the Old Testament translation into Buryat.

- that many Buryats will believe in Jesus.

- that Buryats will find a way to follow Jesus, but still be Buryat.

Temple of the Pure Land, Ivolginsky Datsan Buddhist Monastery

CHAD
Land of Refuge

A DISAPPEARING LAKE

Chad is a country in the middle of Africa, hundreds of miles from the sea. It can be divided into three zones. In the north is the Sahara Desert and the windy Tibesti Mountains. In the center is vast grassland called the Sahel, where nomadic herdsmen keep their camels, goats, sheep, and cows. In the south is greener savannah, which gets more rain, and where crops can be grown.

Chad's name comes from Lake Chad in the southwest of the country. *Chad* is a local word meaning "a large expanse of water." But in the last hundred years, Lake Chad has largely disappeared. Where there used to be water and lots of fish, there are now mainly swamps and wetlands. Almost seventy million people—and their millions of animals—depended on these waters for farming and to water their herds. Without rain to refill the lake, the region has suffered terribly. And in recent years, a terrorist group called Boko Haram has been active in the area, so it's unsafe for people to access the lake for water, fishing, farming, or to travel to school.

SCHOOL IS CANCELLED!

Chad is one of the poorest countries in the world. It doesn't have a coast or many good roads, so it's hard to move food, water, or important equipment around the country. Chad does have oil underground, but money from the oil doesn't reach the poor people—it mostly makes the rich people richer. Corruption like this happens in a lot of countries.

It's very hard to find a job in Chad. And even people with jobs face challenges. For example, school teachers have a tough time. Schools have hardly any supplies or equipment. The government didn't pay teachers their wages for so long that they protested by stopping work. School was cancelled for a year. That might sound like fun—but if your future depends on your education, it's a disaster to miss a whole year of school.

A SAFE PLACE

Chad is surrounded on all sides by troubled countries: Libya is to the north, Nigeria to the southwest, the Central African Republic to the south, and Sudan to the east. From all sides, violence spills over into Chad. Refugees spill across the borders, too—more than 550,000 of them. How can Chad look after all these people when it's one of the world's poorest nations? There isn't enough food in the country for everyone.

MISSION TO CHAD

In the south of Chad there are quite a lot of Christians. But in the north and central

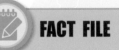

DO YOU KNOW?

When the rains come, children run into the streets, laughing and splashing in the puddles. Frogs come out to catch termites—and people collect them too. Fried termites make a delicious snack.

parts of Chad, most people are Muslims or follow their own traditional religions. Many wear charms or little bags with bits of bark, hair, and other "magic" things inside to protect them from illness and other troubles. Muslims wear charms with verses from the Qur'an inside.

When people become Christians, they often burn these charms. Jesus is stronger than any other power, so they no longer need to be afraid. But Muslims who become Christians sometimes suffer a lot. Their friends and family often treat them badly until they return to Islam. It's a hard choice to follow Jesus.

Missionaries look after children in orphanages, sick people, and the many refugees. Christian radio programs in French and Arabic spread the good news about Jesus. Christians are translating the Bible into some of the tribal languages, but very few of Chad's many languages have any Scripture. Only about one in four people in Chad can read, so it's important to produce Scriptures that people can listen to rather than read. Many can now get resources through their mobile phones and on micro SD cards.

UNCLEAN?

Brahim and his family had just moved to the city. The drought made it too hard to keep animals. They sold their few goats and cows and moved into a crowded area in town to find work. Brahim made new friends—mostly Muslim, but some were Christian. The Christians pointed out a building they said was their church where they worshiped God. Brahim's family worshiped Allah but also used charms to protect themselves.

One afternoon, Brahim went with the Christian boys to their church. People were singing happy songs about someone called Jesus. Then they read from a book called the Bible. Although he was nine, Brahim hadn't yet learned to read. Suddenly Brahim remembered that his father had told him Christians were unclean. He quickly left the church and ran home—he didn't want to get beaten.

Street market, N'Djamena

TO HELP YOU PRAY FOR CHAD

YOU CAN THANK GOD FOR:

- the peace in Chad that makes it a safe place for refugees.

- missionaries and Christians in Chad who translate the Bible and tell people about Jesus' love.

- the growing number of Christians in Chad. Many are children.

YOU CAN ASK GOD:

- to send enough rain every year for crops to grow well so people have enough food.

- to protect Chad from the terror attacks in neighboring countries.

- to help keep the schools open so every child can have an education.

- for more missionaries to help care for refugees and to share about Jesus.

- for Bible translators to work on the remaining languages of Chad.

CHINA
A Growing Church

SO MANY PEOPLE

Almost one out of every five people on earth lives in China. It has more people than any other country.

China has around five hundred people groups. By far the largest of these is the Han: more than one billion. The Han are the largest ethnic group in the world. You can read about a few other people groups in China: the Hui (page 64), the Tai Lue (page 158), the Iu Mien (page 78), and the Tibetans (page 162). You can also learn more about Xinjiang (a region of China) on page 184.

In recent years, China has experienced the biggest migration in human history. Several hundred million people have moved from the countryside to the cities in search of work and a better life. China now has more than one hundred cities with a population of more than one million people. They're busy with round-the-clock activity. Impressive skyscrapers, expensive shopping malls, shipping ports, high-speed trains, subways, elevated freeways—the rich live in luxury, and masses of workers crowd into apartment towers that seem to spring up overnight.

Many new factories, cars, trucks, and trains helped bring China and many of its people out of poverty. But progress came so fast that now much of the air, land, and water is badly polluted. The government is trying to solve this problem, but meanwhile, millions are getting sick from the pollution.

Many Chinese still live in the countryside, working as traditional farmers. Rice is the most important crop, but the Chinese also grow fruit, vegetables, tea, and cotton. People in these poorer, rural areas have many needs such as better health care, education, and clean water.

NO RELIGION

In 1949, the Communist Party took control over China. They wanted to get rid of all religion. In 1950, they forced foreign Christian missionaries to leave China. Missionaries had shared the good news of Jesus with people in China for hundreds of years. What would happen to all the Chinese Christians they left behind?

The door into China slammed shut.

FACT FILE

AREA: 3.7 million square miles

POPULATION: 1.42 billion

CAPITAL: Beijing

MAIN LANGUAGE: Mandarin Chinese

MAIN RELIGIONS: China officially recognizes Taoism, Buddhism, Protestant and Catholic Christianity, and Islam. Many Chinese don't follow any religion.

CHIEF EXPORTS: Electronics, computer parts, machinery, clothing and shoes, iron and steel products, vehicle parts, and toys

The Temple of Heaven, Beijing

Shanghai

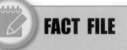

For the next thirty years, it was almost impossible to get news about the Christians in China. Around the world, Christians prayed for the Chinese. God answered their prayers in an amazing way.

STANDING FOR JESUS

During that time, churches were closed down and many Christians were killed, jailed, or sent to work in prison camps. Life was easier if they said they no longer believed in Jesus. But most refused to deny him.

Instead, Christians relied on Jesus and on the strength that he gave. They encouraged one another and shared his love with others, especially the poor and sick. They even shared Jesus with other prisoners. Instead of disappearing, the church in China grew! When China opened its borders again, we discovered the Chinese church was much larger than before, and spreading rapidly.

God had protected his church and blessed it with its own leaders, its own Chinese praise songs, and a bold passion to share about Jesus with everyone, whatever the cost.

UNKNOWN NUMBERS

No one knows exactly how many Christians there are in China today. Some think there are more than a hundred million. There are Christians in many different walks of life: teachers, doctors, farmers, business people, restaurant owners, shopkeepers, and even some government officials.

There are also all sorts of church groups in China. Some worship in churches officially recognized by the government. Others worship in independent churches. Many Christians traditionally met in homes; but as their numbers grew, churches began meeting in larger and larger congregations. Even though China enjoys more freedom now, Christians often still face restrictions and pressure from the government. Bibles are available in Chinese, but it is not always easy for everyone who would like a Bible to get one. This is changing as more and more people have Bible apps on their phones.

CHINESE MISSIONARIES

Yang is nine years old. His parents are Christian leaders, and he loves to listen as they read the Bible and pray. When his father reads the Bible, it's as if the stories come alive!

"Can I have some of my friends over to hear the stories?" he asks.

"It their parents say it's okay," his father says.

Yang knows it's important to respect parents and elders, Christian or not.

Next year, Yang and his family are moving to a country in Central Asia to be missionaries. His parents will transfer to new jobs with their company, and he will go to a new school and learn in a new language. But he only talks about these plans with friends from church. Being a missionary is not something the Chinese government favors. Thousands more Chinese Christians like Yang's family are taking the gospel to people who haven't yet heard about Jesus.

TO HELP YOU PRAY FOR CHINA

YOU CAN THANK GOD FOR:

- the faithfulness of the Chinese church during the years of persecution.

- millions of Chinese people who share God's love with others, even when they suffer for doing so.

- the Chinese Christians who go as missionaries so that others can hear about Jesus.

YOU CAN ASK GOD:

- that many children will hear about Jesus from Christian friends.

- to help Christians show Jesus' love by caring for those in need, especially the disabled, elderly, and unwanted babies.

- to send many Chinese missionaries. Pray for them to learn the best ways to share about Jesus with people from other cultures.

- to give every person in China the chance to hear about Jesus in their own language.

- that Chinese leaders will rule the country wisely and fairly.

CUBA
A New Day

MANY FACES

Cuba is a beautiful island in the Caribbean Sea. Cubans are descended from the people originally living on the island, from Spanish settlers, and from Africans brought here centuries ago to work as slaves, but later freed.

Many people today have parents or grandparents from different groups, as marriage has mixed peoples together. Cuba is famous for its lively music and dance—centered around a mix of vibrant West African and Spanish rhythms and styles.

In the early years, sugar plantations made Spanish landowners in Cuba very wealthy. By 1959, Cuba was one of the richest countries in Latin America. Beautiful beaches, and luxury hotels in cities such as Havana attracted many tourists. But most people weren't rich. Many couldn't even afford to send their children to school.

REVOLUTION AND EDUCATION

On January 1, 1959, Fidel Castro and his supporters overthrew the government. They wanted to make Cuba a better country for all. They made sure every child went to school and that adults learned to read too. They set up the first Communist government in the Western hemisphere.

Roberto was eight when this revolution took place.

"We went to school in a little hut," he told his grandson, Federico. "My family was very poor. We had no shoes, our clothes were ragged, and I was hungry most of the time. But I was excited because they told me that—if I learned to read—I'd get a good job."

"Everyone goes to school now, Papa," his grandson said.

"Yes, that's true. There are more doctor too. And many of us have been able to buy houses. The Communists solved a lot of problems, but created others. Life still isn't easy—and I'm still poor. Medicine is hard to find, there are still food rations, and my children—your father and uncles—were often hungry, growing up. After the revolution, many people—rich and poor—left Cuba and went to live in the United States.

But Cuba is my home, and I love it. I always wanted to stay, but it's never been easy here," he said.

CHANGE

Fidel Castro died in 2016 after ruling Cuba for more than fifty years. The Communist Party controlled almost every part of life. It still remains in power, but big changes have come.

Tourism has become important again. Relations with the United States have started to improve, so trade should start to grow. More people are allowed to run their own businesses. Prices have gone up, although most Cubans still earn low wages. The internet is connecting Cubans

Bible distribution

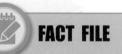

FACT FILE

AREA: 42,800 square miles

POPULATION: 11.5 million

CAPITAL: Havana

MAIN LANGUAGE: Spanish

MAIN RELIGIONS: Christianity; some Cubans follow no religion

CHIEF EXPORTS: Sugar, tobacco, and oil

Havana Cathedral

DO YOU KNOW?

After 1959, few new cars could be imported, so Cubans kept their old American cars running for decades. For people who love classic cars, Cuba is a living museum.

to the outside world, but the cost is still too high for most Cubans. Even so, there is growing hope for the future.

CUBA FOR CHRIST

Although the Communist government has strictly controlled the churches, Cuba is not an atheist state. Almost half the people are Christian. Most of these are Roman Catholic, but there are also Protestants and other Christian groups.

In the past, the government tried to suppress Christianity. Christians were persecuted, arrested, imprisoned, and even tortured. Yet many Christians stood firm for Jesus. There are still restrictions, and Christians are still persecuted. But there's more freedom than in a long time.

Just as many parts of Cuban culture are a mix of African and Spanish traditions, so too is religion. Many people mix their Catholic beliefs with spiritism. Millions of Cubans practice a kind of spiritism called *Santería*, visit mediums who contact the spirit world for guidance, and mix worship rituals for other gods with worship of Catholic saints.

Maria, a young Cuban believer, says, "Evangelical churches get bigger every year, and we keep hearing about new ones starting. Many of us—especially young people and children—have discovered Jesus as our friend and future hope. Christians all over Cuba meet in churches and in homes. We're excited to share the good news about Jesus and connect with other Christians around the world. I love finding new Christian music from other countries and listening to sermons by preachers from elsewhere. It feels like a great new day for Cuba."

Norlen was only seven years old when God called him to be an evangelist, and only sixteen when he started a small church. He is passionate to give every Cuban the chance to read the Bible and know the love of Jesus. Because the Communist Party put a strong emphasis on education, most Cubans can read well. But there are not enough Bibles in the country. Whenever Norlen travels to Cuban towns and villages passing out Bibles, crowds gather. People are hungry for the Word of God!

TO HELP YOU PRAY FOR CUBA

YOU CAN THANK GOD FOR:

- the survival of the church in Cuba through many years of persecution and isolation.

- more freedom for Bibles to be printed in Cuba and brought in from abroad.

- many Cubans—especially young people—who are coming to know Jesus.

YOU CAN ASK GOD:

- to give his strength to those who suffer for their faith in Jesus.

- for more Bibles, books, and teachers for the new churches and Christians.

- to help the many Cubans who don't have enough food.

- that the Cuban government will rule wisely as the country changes.

DJIBOUTI
One of the Hottest Places on Earth

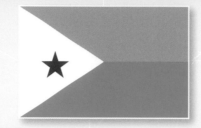

A DRY AND DESERT LAND

Djibouti is one of the world's hottest countries. It's usually much too hot to sleep at night, especially as you have to sleep under a mosquito net. Almost no one has air conditioning, and most people don't even have fans. It hardly ever rains, and the ground is so rocky that it's very hard for farmers to grow food. Many people are very poor and don't get enough to eat.

Djibouti is a tiny African country on the Gulf of Aden across from Yemen. It forms part of the Horn of Africa. You can see why it's known by this name if you look at a map of the African continent.

Gulf of Aden

DJIBOUTI

NOMADS AND NAVIES

The two main groups of people that live in Djibouti used to be enemies. The Afars are Ethiopian in origin and live in the north. The Issas are Somalis and live in the south. When Djibouti was a colony of France, it was actually called the "French Territory of Afars and the Issas." Because France controlled Djibouti for almost a hundred years, French became a common language between the two groups.

Djibouti has been an independent country since 1977.

In the past, almost all Djiboutian people were nomads, moving around the harsh desert and mountains with their herds of camels, sheep, goats, and cattle, looking for pasture—a hard way of life. Many still live as nomads today, but others have moved into the capital,

which is also called Djibouti. It's a major seaport, and people hoped to find work there. Refugees from wars in Ethiopia, Yemen, Eritrea, and Somalia have also settled there. Djibouti is a peaceful place to start a new life.

FACT FILE

AREA: 9,000 square miles

POPULATION: 971,000

CAPITAL: Djibouti

MAIN LANGUAGES: Arabic and French (official); Somali, Afar

MAIN RELIGION: Almost all Muslim; small Christian minority

MAIN INCOME SOURCES: The deep-sea port, Djibouti, which is near one of the world's busiest shipping routes. Also, foreign military bases.

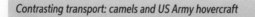

Contrasting transport: camels and US Army hovercraft

DO YOU KNOW?

Lake Assal, in the center of Djibouti, is 509 feet below sea level, and the lowest place in Africa. Water in the lake is ten times saltier than seawater. You can float on top of the water without even swimming. Salt is harvested from deposits that collect on the shores or by men wading into the water to collect it in crystallized form. This lake has long been an important source for salt, which can be sold or traded.

About two-thirds of the country's population lives in the capital city, but most of them have no work. Djibouti may be peaceful, but it is poor, and the life expectancy for Djiboutians is short.

Djibouti is a tiny country, but it has become a strategic place for the world's biggest military powers. France has a base here, and the US's largest base in Africa is in Djibouti. Japan and Italy have bases here too. More recently, China opened a base here—the first overseas military base for modern China. Why is Djibouti so strategic? It is a peaceful, stable country on some of the world's busiest shipping routes in the middle of a troubled region.

CHEWING ON LEAVES

Most Djiboutian men like chewing an addictive drug called *qat*, or *khat*, which comes from the green leaves of a flowering plant. It's so popular that the daily stash—brought in from nearby Ethiopia—is always sold out by the end of the day. In the heat of the afternoon, most of the men sit around chewing *khat*, talking, and taking naps. Many people spend most of their spare money buying *khat* to chew every day.

NEW LIFE IN THE DESERT

Almost all Djiboutians are Muslims. Islam came to this area soon after it started to spread. But a few people here have heard about Jesus and decided to follow him. If Issas or Afars become Christians, life can be very difficult for them. Their family usually rejects them, beats them, and sometimes even tries to kill them for going against the traditional religion of their people. Those who follow Jesus in Djibouti can feel alone. It is best when whole families decide together to follow Jesus. Sadly, even when they come to trust Jesus, people from the rival Afar and Issa groups often don't want to meet with each other because of the bad history between them.

Some of the refugees in Djibouti are Christians. They come from Ethiopia, Madagascar, Eritrea, and the Democratic Republic of Congo—even as far as countries in Asia. Some pray—sometimes all night long—for their own people and for the people of Djibouti. They ask God that these people will one day follow Jesus. But it's difficult—and dangerous—to talk with others about Jesus in Djibouti.

TO HELP YOU PRAY FOR DJIBOUTI

YOU CAN THANK GOD FOR:

- every Christian who is praying for, and working with, Djiboutian people.

- the body of Christ in Djibouti: local Afars and Issas, together with foreigners who live and work in Djibouti or who have come as refugees.

YOU CAN ASK GOD:

- for trust to grow among all Jesus' followers in Djibouti, especially between Afars and Issas who were once enemies, so the church can grow here.

- to provide food for the people of Djibouti who do not have enough.

- to help people get rid of their *khat* habit.

- that Djiboutians who start to follow Jesus will stay faithful, even when friends and family persecute them.

- for families to share about Jesus with other families so that every Djiboutian will have the chance to hear about Jesus in a way they can understand.

Street tailors, Djibouti

DOGON
Sharing the Good News

MALI

BURKINA FASO

MALI

BURKINA FASO

PIGEON DUNG!

If you gaze straight up the cliff face, you can see a tiny moving figure. It's Oumar, swinging dangerously on a rope. He dare not look down! He climbs hundreds of feet to reach caves hollowed out of the cliff. He's collecting pigeon dung to sell as fertilizer at the market.

Oumar's people are called the Dogon. They live in a part of Mali in West Africa that is very rocky. The fertilizer helps them grow as much food as possible in the few fields they have. Some Dogon villages are actually embedded in the cliffs. Facing the cliffs is the Sahara Desert, where nothing grows. So every bit of soil is precious to the Dogon.

Oumar loves all the ceremonies that are part of Dogon life. He can't wait till he's old enough to learn to dance on colorful stilts and wear a mask of cowrie shells and hibiscus. The fantastic masks and unique dances are a very important part of Dogon culture. Both are famous around the world.

HOW COULD YOU TELL OUMAR ABOUT JESUS?

Oumar has been learning Dogon traditional beliefs ever since he can remember. He probably wouldn't understand at first if you told him about Jesus. But there are some truths in the Bible that could help.

If a Dogon person does something wrong, the elders may make that person leave the village. This is a terrible punishment, because it means they have to start life again alone without the support of their close community. But if they admit they were wrong and want to be forgiven, they bring a goat or sheep to the edge of the village. The elders kill the animal and make a trail of blood to the door of this person's home. Then the people of the village accept back the person who did wrong.

In the Bible, God teaches us that sin makes us unfit to go to heaven—just as Oumar's people believe that doing wrong

Dogon mask dance

makes a person unfit to live in their village. But killing a goat or sheep is not enough to get us into heaven. God's son, Jesus—who the Bible calls "the Lamb of God"—gave himself on the cross so we can be forgiven for all the bad things we've done and be accepted by God. All we need to do is believe in him and be truly sorry. Then God will accept us into heaven to live with him.

IT'S HARD TO FORGIVE

After decades of missionary work, quite a few Dogon villages now have churches. In some of them, the number of Christians is increasing rapidly. Christians are busy building bigger churches or expanding their old ones to make room for the new brothers and sisters!

The nomadic Fulani people are cattle-herders who live in the same part of Mali as the Dogon. Dogon Christians don't always tell the Fulani about Jesus because Fulani cattle sometimes ruin the Dogon crops.

The Dogon know God forgave them—and some have forgiven the Fulani. There is now even a church for the Fulani.

PERSECUTION

In 2012 and 2013, rebel Tuareg and Muslim extremists took control of the north of Mali. They tried to make people obey more strict Islamic laws. Christians in the area were attacked and sometimes killed. Around half

a million people, including most of the Christians, fled to the south or to nearby countries such as Burkina Faso. Although peace was restored, things remain tense. Many people—especially Christians—often feel unsafe.

Dogon hunter

TO HELP YOU PRAY FOR THE DOGON

YOU CAN THANK GOD FOR:

■ the translation of the Bible into one of the Dogon languages.

■ audio recordings of the New Testament for people who can't read or who prefer to listen.

■ growing numbers of Dogon people who are following Jesus.

■ Dogon Christians who are sharing the good news about Jesus with the less-reached Fulani people and with other Dogon people.

YOU CAN ASK GOD:

■ to send enough rain for crops to grow well so the Dogon have enough food for their families and to sell in the market.

■ for more training to help Dogon Christians share about Jesus with other Dogon people.

■ for Dogon women to be trained so they can teach the Bible to other Dogon women and children.

■ for Bible translations in the remaining Dogon dialects that still have no Scripture.

DRUZE
Followers of a Secret Faith

LEBANON

Mediterranean Sea

SYRIA

ISRAEL

JORDAN

A BIG SECRET

Do you find it hard to keep a secret? The Druze people have an important secret that they've kept for a thousand years!

The Druze live mainly in the mountains of Lebanon, Syria, northern Israel, and Jordan. Many are farmers who have olive groves or cherry and apple orchards on the hillsides and grow vegetables in their carefully tended gardens. There is work for everyone, but still plenty of time to visit with friends and family. The Druze are known as hardworking, trustworthy people.

What's their big secret? It's their religion, which they believe they must keep to themselves and never share with outsiders. Many people have tried to discover the secrets of the Druze religion, but the Druze often mislead them. This is a secret they're good at keeping.

No one can choose to become a Druze. To be a Druze, you have to be born into a Druze family. The Druze believe that when they die their soul immediately enters a newborn Druze baby. That's the only way someone can become a Druze. If a Druze marries someone from another faith, they are no longer considered a true Druze.

Only a few people know all the secrets of their religion. They are called the *'Uqqal*—the Informed, or Knowledgeable, Ones. Both men and women can become 'Uqqal, but they have to be at least forty years old and must have spent a long time studying the secrets of the religion. The 'Uqqal are the only ones allowed to study the Book of Wisdom—or *Kitab Al Hikma*—the Druze scriptures.

KNOWLEDGEABLE ONES

It's Thursday evening, and everyone in the Druze village is going to the meeting place, or *khilwa*. Samir's parents join the other villagers. The women wear long, dark, blue or black dresses and white veils.

"Like most Druze, my parents are 'Ignorant Ones,' or *Juhhal*," says Samir.

"Inside the room, the women sit on one side, the men on the other."

"There's my uncle. He's an 'Uqqal," Samir whispers as a tall man walks past. "His white turban is a sign of purity. He has to live by much stricter rules than our parents. He can't drink wine or smoke. At the meeting, everyone discusses village matters. Then the Juhhal leave. Uncle stays with the 'Uqqal for secret meditation and to learn more about Druze beliefs."

"The village children have to go to the meeting hall too," added Samir. "We learn how we should live, and that

 FACT FILE

NUMBERS: Around 1 million

COUNTRIES: Mostly Syria and Lebanon; smaller groups in northern Israel, Jordan, France, and the United States

LANGUAGE: Arabic

Baking taboon flatbread

DO YOU KNOW?

The Druze religion doesn't allow images of living things. Their main symbol is a colorful five-pointed star. Each of the colors—red, yellow, blue, white, and green—represents a different spiritual belief of the Druze.

Druze flag

The Druze are waiting for the day when Al-Hakim, the founder of their religion, returns to earth as their savior. But God wants the Druze to trust in Jesus, the true Savior he has sent already.

A NEW DAY

Raghida and her husband lead a group of about forty believers who gather in their home in Israel. All of them have a Druze background and call themselves "Druze followers of Christ." This group is an answer to years of prayer for the Druze.

Raghida had been living overseas and searching for the meaning of life. She started reading the Bible and encountered Jesus. When she returned home, she faced years of persecution from her family and from the Druze community. They didn't understand her new faith in Jesus. She wanted to share about the God of the Bible and the teachings of Jesus with her people. She and her family experienced many hurtful attacks but always tried to respond with love. After many years, they were accepted back because of their faithfulness to the community and their loving behavior.

it's important to be honest and truthful, particularly with other Druze. We must never tell anyone else about our Druze beliefs or believe another religion, such as Islam or Christianity. That's hard for some of us, especially if we go to Christian school." Druze children are taught to always help each other and to look after any strangers who come to their village for help.

Druze area in Israel

TO HELP YOU PRAY FOR THE DRUZE

YOU CAN THANK GOD FOR:

- Christian schools and orphanages, where Druze children learn about Jesus.

- the good teaching that Druze children are given, such as honesty and being kind to strangers.

- the small but growing number of Druze people who now trust Jesus as their Savior.

YOU CAN ASK GOD:

- that Christians will make friends with Druze people and help them understand God's love.

- that many Druze will read the Bible and discover the truth about Jesus.

- to help the few Druze Christians when they face difficulties because of their faith in Jesus.

- to form more groups where Druze believers can share fellowship with each other.

EGYPT
Land of the Pharaohs—and the Bible

Mediterranean Sea

EGYPT

Red Sea

GARBAGE COLLECTORS

"I wonder what we'll find today?"

Dirty and ragged, Fouad and Ramzi sit on top of a big pile of trash in their father's donkey-cart. Their tired, old donkey plods along a busy Cairo street. Cars, trucks, and buses honk their horns as they overtake them.

Every morning, Fouad and Ramzi go with their dad to collect trash from city streets, offices, and apartment blocks. Their family lives in a crowded slum called "Mokattam Garbage City," on the outskirts of Cairo, the capital of Egypt. When they get home, Fouad and Ramzi carefully sort through the trash. They make piles of paper, cardboard, plastic, and glass. They can make some money selling these materials for recycling. They leave the rest for the goats, dogs, and cats to paw through for food. Fouad and Ramzi are used to the dirt and smell; they've lived here all their lives.

Altogether, these garbage collectors—or *zabaleen*—recycle thousands of tons of garbage every day. It takes a lot of people, but it has to be one of the best recycling programs in the world!

HUGE CITY, HUGE COUNTRY

Egypt is a very large country. Most of it is desert. Egypt depends heavily on the Nile River, which provides most of its water. The Nile Valley and Delta—where the river empties into the sea—is home to most of its people.

The Nile Valley has been the center of Egypt's agriculture for thousands of years, since even before the days of Abraham, Isaac, Jacob, and Joseph. Today, scientists are trying to make parts of the desert capable of growing crops, too.

Close to half the people in Greater Cairo are poor, but there are also many rich people—including at least 220,000 millionaires. Nearly five million

Egyptians have gone abroad to find work, sending money home to support their families.

AN ANCIENT CHURCH

Many Bible stories took place in Egypt. Everyone knows about Moses and Pharaoh. And Joseph and Mary fled to Egypt with young Jesus. On the day of Pentecost, Egyptians were in the crowd in Jerusalem and heard the apostle Peter talk about God's love in sending Jesus. Those Egyptians brought the message of Jesus back to their own country. Soon many Egyptians had become Christians, and sent missionaries to North Africa and Europe. This early church in Egypt became known as the "Coptic" Church.

In AD 642, Arab Muslims invaded. Egypt became a Muslim country, and many Christians were forced to become Muslims. But the Coptic Church never

FACT FILE

AREA: 390,121 square miles; 96 percent of the country is desert

POPULATION: 99.4 million

CAPITAL: Cairo: the largest city in the Middle East and Africa, with 20 million people in the Greater Cairo area

MAIN LANGUAGE: Arabic

MAIN RELIGIONS: Large Muslim majority, Christian minority

MAIN EXPORTS: Oil, cotton

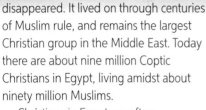
disappeared. It lived on through centuries of Muslim rule, and remains the largest Christian group in the Middle East. Today there are about nine million Coptic Christians in Egypt, living amidst about ninety million Muslims.

Christians in Egypt are often persecuted. Some Muslims want to rid the country of other religions. They frequently attack Coptic Christians and their churches. Some Egyptian Christians have left to live in safer countries in the West. However, some Muslims do respect their Christian neighbors. Sometimes they both protect each other during their worship and prayer times.

The Copts are not the only Christians in Egypt. Newer churches have also grown recently. Some of these are trying to help the poor and disabled. Most churches, new and old, are very active and their services are full of people.

WORSHIPING IN CAVES

Fouad and Ramzi are Christians, like ninety percent of the zabaleen. With their family, they go to church in a cave, in the neighborhood where they live. But this is no ordinary cave. Four thousand years ago, workers and slaves quarried out the rock to build the pyramids, which left behind a huge underground space. Christians today use the cave as a church. Imagine that—because the Pharaohs built the pyramids as tombs for when they died, Christians now have a place to worship Jesus, who rose from the dead!

There are many cave churches in the mountain just above Mokattam Garbage Village. The largest can seat twenty thousand people. It's the biggest church in the Middle East.

TO HELP YOU PRAY FOR EGYPT

YOU CAN THANK GOD FOR:

- the Coptic Church, which still survives after two thousand years.

- many good Christian books, radio and TV programs, and websites available in Arabic.

- Egypt's important role in Bible history and in Middle Eastern Christianity today.

YOU CAN ASK GOD:

- to help the *zabaleen* follow Jesus faithfully.

- to have mercy on Christians in Egypt; others sometimes treat them unfairly because of their religion.

- to reveal the love and power of Jesus to Egyptian Muslims, even those who want to attack Christians.

- to call many Egyptian Christians to share the gospel in Egypt and other countries of the Arab world.

Mosques, Cairo

ETHIOPIA
Centuries of Christianity

Seven-year-old Desta clapped his hands with joy. He'd never been to school. Now some Christians had offered him the chance to go to a school they'd started.

Desta's family used to have a farm in the highlands of Ethiopia, but they had moved to a slum in the capital, Addis Ababa. Desta's mother had told him stories about life on the farm. Growing enough food was hard, especially when there was a drought. Desta's two sisters became ill and died because their family couldn't grow enough crops even to feed themselves.

But life in the city wasn't much better. They were still very poor. For Desta, the chance to go to school offered an opportunity for a better life.

Ethiopia has high tablelands in the east and west, divided by the great East African Rift Valley. Further east are dry plains. The population is very mixed, with more than 110 different people groups. The biggest are the Amhara, Tigrinya, Oromo, Somali, and Sidama. Most people still live in rural areas.

AN ANCIENT CHURCH

The first Christians came to Ethiopia around AD 300, and Orthodox Christianity was the official religion for the next 1,700 years. During the nineteenth and twentieth centuries, many Protestant missionaries came to Ethiopia. They told people about Jesus, taught them to read and write, and cared for ill people.

Yet, even after hundreds of years of Christians living in Ethiopia, there are still people who've never heard about Jesus. And today, growing numbers are becoming Muslims.

CIVIL WAR

In 1974, a Communist government took over the country. In the years that followed, there was civil war between rival groups. The fighting, the cruelty of the Communist government, and droughts combined to create terrible

FACT FILE

AREA: 427,000 square miles

POPULATION: 108 million

CAPITAL: Addis Ababa

MAIN LANGUAGES: Amharic and English, but around 90 other languages are spoken

MAIN RELIGIONS: Christian majority; large Muslim minority

CHIEF EXPORTS: Coffee, livestock, maize, animal skins, and *khat*—leaves for chewing

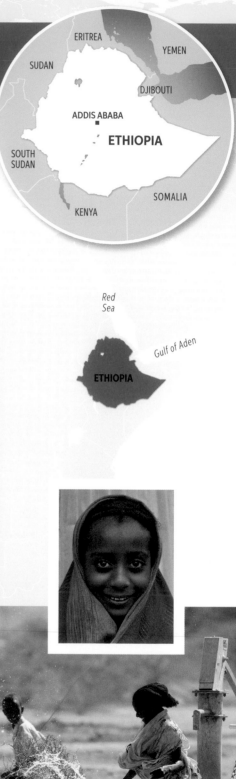

famines that caused many people to die. Millions more fled their homes, traveling to other parts of Ethiopia, or to neighboring countries.

The Communist government imprisoned Christian leaders and closed churches. Most missionaries had to leave the country. But the church grew anyway. By the time the Communist government was overthrown, hundreds of thousands of Ethiopians had come to know Jesus as their Savior.

Rock church, Lalibela

A LIVING CHURCH

Ethiopian Christians are taking the Christian gospel to people groups in their own country who have never heard of Jesus, planting new churches, and teaching the Bible. Some help missionaries with Bible translation, others teach children and work on health care projects. Some are trying to bring clean water to the villages, others help people grow food for themselves and their families. All these Christians are showing God's love in practical ways to people in need.

The Ethiopian church has grown a lot in the last twenty years. Many more people are becoming Christians, and many Muslims have started to follow Jesus. All over Ethiopia there are small Bible schools, training pastors and evangelists. They need people to teach them in their own language how to follow Jesus. Around ninety different languages are spoken in Ethiopia; more than thirty new Bible translations are under way.

Ethiopia has many needs. People are still suffering from war and drought. Ethiopia remains one of the poorest countries in the world. One third of its children don't have enough to eat. Almost five million children have lost one or both parents. Although some people are well educated and have good jobs and nice homes, other children never go to school, and their families are extremely poor. Many Christians have never read the Bible, and need good Christian teaching to help them grow.

THE LOST ARK

Ethiopia might hold the key to a great mystery! In Bible times, the ark of the covenant was the most holy object belonging to the Israelites. The ark was an ornate golden box. Inside were the stone tablets with the Ten Commandments, which God gave Moses on Mount Sinai. Many Ethiopians believe the ark of the covenant was smuggled out of Jerusalem and taken to Axum, in Ethiopia. They claim the ark is still there, closely guarded in a chapel.

African Union building, Addis Ababa

DO YOU KNOW?

The first African to win an Olympic gold medal was an Ethiopian. Abebe Bikila won the marathon in 1960, breaking the world record, all while running barefoot!

TO HELP YOU PRAY FOR ETHIOPIA

YOU CAN THANK GOD FOR:

- a church that's survived for at least 1,700 years.

- the continuing growth of the church in Ethiopia.

- Christians who bring food, medical care, education, clean water, and new ways of farming to needy people.

- many Bible schools and training programs helping Christian leaders serve their people more effectively.

YOU CAN ASK GOD:

- to help Ethiopian Christians translating the Bible into their own languages.

- to bring unity to Christians in Ethiopia, even though there are many different kinds of churches.

- to help the country find a way of growing enough food to feed everyone.

- that Christians would reach out to the many children who have lost parents or who live on the streets.

FIJI
A Nation of Islands

The beautiful islands of Fiji, with their warm, sunny beaches, are located in the South Pacific Ocean, east of Australia. Although there are more than 300 islands, only 112 have people living on them. The two main islands, Viti Levu and Vanua Levu, were formed from volcanoes. Their steep mountain slopes are covered with forests. Suva, the capital of Fiji, is the biggest city in the South Pacific region.

Fiji is a fertile country. If you look at the coat of arms on the Fijian flag, you'll find sugar cane, a coconut palm, a cocoa pod, and bananas. Two of the country's main exports are sugar and copra, or dried coconut. Coconut oil is extracted from copra and used to make many different things, including soap, shampoo, and margarine.

FIJI

South Pacific Ocean

DEEP-SEA CANOES

You can also find the dove of peace—a Christian symbol—on the Fijian flag. Christians came to Fiji almost 200 years ago to tell people about Jesus. Fijian Christians believed the good news of Jesus was too wonderful to keep to themselves. Many set out on dangerous journeys in deep-sea canoes to tell people on other Pacific islands about God's love. So, in Fiji, another symbol of Christianity is the canoe.

A missionary called Dr. George Brown wanted Christians from Fiji to go with him to Papua New Guinea to tell people there about Jesus. He thought no one would volunteer, because thousands of Fijians had recently died from measles. He was surprised when all eighty-four students at his college said they would go with him. One said, "We have given ourselves to God's work. If we live, we live. If we die, we die." They were willing to risk everything to tell others that God loved them and sent Jesus to save them.

DIVISION

In the year 1879, the British rulers of Fiji brought people from India to work on the sugar plantations. The Indians worked hard, but weren't allowed to own any land. They were mainly Hindus, Muslims, or Sikhs. Before long, there were as many Indians as iTaukei (native Fijians) in the country. A number of iTaukei worried that the Indians would soon outnumber them, and the two groups began to resent each other.

Some iTaukei set fire to mosques and temples belonging

Fijian reads the Bible

FACT FILE

AREA: 7,050 square miles

POPULATION: 912,000

CAPITAL: Suva

MAIN LANGUAGES: English (official); iTaukei (Fijian) and Fiji Hindi are also used

MAIN RELIGIONS: Christianity, Hinduism, and Islam

CHIEF EXPORTS: Cane sugar, bottled water, fish, wood, gold

iTaukei man blows conch shell

DO YOU KNOW?

The International Date Line passes between the islands of Fiji. This means Fiji is one of the first countries in the world to welcome each new day.

to the Indians. Although Christian leaders spoke out against this, the Indians felt angry and afraid. Many left Fiji.

Conflict and unrest has continued. iTaukei have often deprived Indians of rights and freedoms. This has resulted in more Indians leaving; Fijians now outnumber the Indians.

Fijian Christians have started to pray for people all over the world who haven't heard about Jesus. Some have gone as missionaries to other countries. God is reviving the Christians of Fiji—especially young people. They want to share the love of Jesus with all those in their own country. However, differences in culture, politics, and religion make it hard for Indians to accept Jesus. It is also hard for the Indians in Fiji who do accept Jesus to live openly as Christians among their own people.

Today, many people come to Fiji as tourists and workers. This gives Fijian Christians a chance to share the gospel with them. Many come from countries such as China, where it isn't always easy to hear the good news about Jesus.

TO HELP YOU PRAY FOR FIJI

YOU CAN THANK GOD FOR:

■ the many Christians in Fiji.

■ the Indians in Fiji who trust Jesus.

■ friendships between iTaukei and Indian Fijian Christians.

YOU CAN ASK GOD:

■ to help the leaders of Fiji rule wisely and fairly.

■ to help iTaukei and Indian Fijians live at peace with each other.

■ to bring Indian boys and girls in Sunday school to know and love Jesus.

■ to send people to share Jesus with the many Chinese people who work in Fiji and the many tourists who visit Fiji.

Iguana

GARIFUNA
Descendants of West Africans and Carib Indians

BELIZE

ROATÁN

Caribbean Sea

GUATEMALA

HONDURAS

EL SALVADOR

NICARAGUA

North Pacific Ocean

"LOOK WHAT I'VE GOT!"

The man checking security at a small Caribbean airport was rummaging through Roger's suitcase. He pulled out a book.

"What's this? What language is it?" the official demanded, speaking in Spanish. "This is not Spanish."

"It's a Garifuna (*gah-ree-foo-na*) Bible," Roger replied.

"Garifuna? That's my language!" the man exclaimed. "I've seen a Spanish Bible—but I've never seen a book in Garifuna. I'd love to learn to read it. Where can I get one?"

"I'm afraid that's my only copy," Roger explained.

"Please let me have it," the man pleaded.

He was so excited when Roger gave it to him. He showed the Bible to everyone.

"Look what I've got—my first book in my own language!" he exclaimed.

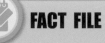

Nearly all the Garifuna speak Spanish, the language of the countries where they live. But among themselves they speak their own language. Today, more and more books are available in Garifuna. People can even read—and listen to—the New Testament in Garifuna online, for free. As the Garifuna encounter God's Word in their language, many are deciding to follow Jesus.

One Garifuna minister was so delighted with his New Testament that he said, "May we chew God's Word, swallow it, and let it enter into our veins!"

SHIPWRECKED SLAVES

The Garifuna, or Black Caribs, are descended from slaves. In the seventeenth century, British and Spanish boats brought them to the Caribbean from Africa. Sometimes the boats were shipwrecked, and the slaves escaped. Slave-owners later freed other Garifuna slaves. Many settled on Saint Vincent, in the Windward Islands, where they married Carib Indians.

Then, more than two hundred years ago, the British—who controlled the Windwards—moved them across the Caribbean Sea to the island of Roatán, near Honduras. The Garifuna eventually settled in villages along the coasts of Belize, Honduras, and Guatemala. A lot still make their living by fishing and farming.

The Garifuna religion developed as they moved around and mixed with different peoples. They kept their traditional African beliefs, but—as they married Carib Indians—they mixed in some Carib beliefs and traditions. They also added Catholic beliefs and practices.

FACT FILE

COUNTRIES: Honduras, Belize, Guatemala, and Nicaragua

NUMBERS: About 500,000

MAIN LANGUAGES: Spanish, Garifuna, and English

MAIN RELIGIONS: Christianity (mostly Catholic), animism

OCCUPATIONS: Farming, fishing

Nearly all Garifuna children are baptized into the Roman Catholic Church, but many also wear a ribbon tied around the wrist to protect them from evil spirits. They believe spirits live all around them and put a cross over the doorway of their house to protect the family from harm. They believe that dreams, crying chickens, and howling dogs all foretell the future.

JESUS IS ALIVE

Although most Garifuna knew some stories about Jesus, few understood why God sent him to earth.

Some missionaries were showing the *JESUS* film in a field just outside one village. The audience got very excited as two hundred people gathered to watch the film.

In the film, Jesus speaks to a little child in Garifuna.

"Hello. What are you doing?" he asks.

"Nothing," the child replies.

"He knows our greeting," the people murmured in surprise. "Jesus speaks Garifuna!" They watched the film eagerly, telling each other what they saw and heard.

"Who wouldn't want to follow Jesus?" said one lady. "Did you see him heal that blind man?"

"Look," some men exclaimed. "They fish like we do. We know what it's like to fish all night and catch nothing. When Jesus told them to put their nets back in the sea, they had a great catch. Amazing! And Jesus calmed a storm too. We all know people who've died in storms. Jesus must be more powerful than all the spirits of the sea if he can do that. He must be worthy of worship."

As they watched Jesus dying on the cross, many people wept. After the film, thirty-five said they wanted to follow Jesus. More people came to the film the next night, and a lot of them decided to follow him too.

With the whole Bible in their language, many Garifuna are finding out more about God's loving plan. The churches are growing, too.

A missionary among the Garifuna said, "It's great to know so many children are praying for the Garifuna." God is answering our prayers—so let's keep praying that many more Garifuna will come to know Jesus.

TO HELP YOU PRAY FOR THE GARIFUNA

YOU CAN THANK GOD FOR:

- the Garifuna Bible—both Old and New Testaments—in print and audio.

- every Garifuna who's come to know Jesus.

YOU CAN ASK GOD:

- that many Garifuna will read and listen to the Bible in their own language.

- to help the Garifuna read more—many don't read much, especially in their own language.

- to help Garifuna believers follow Jesus only, and not be confused by traditional beliefs.

- to help the Garifuna write songs and dances that praise and worship God in Garifuna styles.

- to send people to train Garifuna Christians to become pastors, evangelists, and Bible teachers.

Settlement day festival

GONDS
Forest People of Central India

"WHO CAN HELP US?"

The people of Lion village were very worried. Lots of people were ill, and several had died.

"What about the medicine man?" someone asked.

"We've been to the witch doctor," said someone else. "He prayed to the spirits, and made offerings to them—but that only made things worse."

"I don't know why the spirits are treating us like this," said another man sadly.

"Let's go talk to the Christians," someone suggested. "They say their God is more powerful than all our spirits. Maybe the Christian God can stop this cholera outbreak."

So the villagers went to the Christian missionary. He was from another part of India, and was traveling around the forest preaching about Jesus in Gond villages.

"Can you help us?" they asked.

They explained to him about the terrible situation.

"I'll pray for you, and so will all the Christians in the village," he promised. "Our God is greater than any other god or spirit. He promises to hear our prayers. He can heal this sickness."

The Christians prayed together—and within three days God had healed ten people in Lion village.

"The God of the Christians is greater than the spirits," said the villagers. "We want to follow him too!"

FOREST VILLAGE

Lion village lies deep in the forests of central India. Its people are part of the Gond tribe. Around 650 tribes have lived in India since long before other peoples migrated there from other nations and from different areas of India. The Gonds are one of the largest of these ancient tribal groups. Most of the Gonds are animists, who believe evil spirits lurk in the fields and forests, looking for ways to harm them. The Gonds make sacrifices of

INDIA

Bay of Bengal

FACT FILE

COUNTRY: India

NUMBERS: About 16 million

MAIN LANGUAGES: Hindi, Gondi (there are several Gondi languages)

MAIN RELIGIONS: Hinduism, animism

OCCUPATIONS: Farming, keeping animals, making mats; also collecting wood, bamboo, and forest products

Market in Bastar

52

DO YOU KNOW?

The Gonds believe in many gods. They think a lot of hills, rivers, trees, and large rocks have spirits that may want to harm them. They also believe in one Great God who made the earth, who is merciful and just—but he is far away from the problems of humanity.

food to these spirits, hoping this will make the spirits leave them alone.

Many of the Gonds work as farmers, and some keep goats and cattle. They also grow rice, green dal, millet, maize, and wheat. The Gonds build simple houses from bamboo and timber, with roofs of leaves. These homes usually have just one or two rooms: in one there will be a few wooden stools and a hammock or two, and in the kitchen some cooking pots.

Many older Gonds can't read or write, so people often cheat them when they sell their produce in the towns. Since Gonds are a tribal people, many people in India think they're unimportant and treat them badly. The government of India wants to help the Gonds have a better quality of life. In some places, it has set up schools where Gond children can study.

CHANGED PEOPLE

As a result of the miracle of healing, many people in Lion village became Christians. The Indian missionary visited to find out how they were getting on. He traveled to them by oxcart, making his way slowly through the forest on roads not fit for cars or buses—but great for spotting birds, and even a bear or tiger!

Everyone in Lion village was excited to see him.

"Since we started to follow Jesus," says one villager, "he's changed our lives and made us into new people. We always used to be afraid of the spirits, but now we see they have no power over us. Jesus gives us joy, peace, and authority over the spirits that want to harm us. We want to learn all we can about Jesus—and we want others to know him too."

Some Gond Christians are going to centers where they learn more about the Bible, and how to share the good news about Jesus with their people. But there are still many Gond villages where people have never heard of Jesus.

TO HELP YOU PRAY FOR THE GONDS

YOU CAN THANK GOD FOR:

- every Gond who is following Jesus.
- Gond Christians who are learning how to tell others about Jesus.

YOU CAN ASK GOD:

- that many Gond boys and girls will decide to follow Jesus.
- to show the Gonds that he's more powerful than the spirits they fear.
- to keep the Indian missionaries safe, as they travel to Gond villages.
- to help people who are translating the Bible into Gondi.
- that there will be a fellowship of Christians in every Gond village.

GREECE
Home of the First Olympic Games

LIVING HISTORY

Our world would be very different without the art, literature, theater, science, and philosophy that comes from Ancient Greece. Perhaps you've heard some of the stories of Greek gods, heroes, and monsters such as Zeus, Athena, Hercules, Pegasus, and Medusa. Many of the ideas that people in the West have today—about government, science, truth, justice, and much more—are based on what some of the great Greek thinkers wrote thousands of years ago.

Sports were important for the ancient Greeks too. The Olympic Games started as a running race, held every year in the town of Olympia, as part of a religious festival—hundreds of years before Jesus was born. In 1896, the first modern Olympic Games were hosted in Athens.

Most of Greece is quite mountainous, and the country often experiences earthquakes. In the past, some of the bigger ones caused much damage. Greece also has beautiful beaches, more than two thousand islands, and many small villages that haven't changed in centuries. Millions of tourists visit Greece every year, attracted by the sun, the sand, the sea, and by ancient Greek ruins.

A VISIT TO CHURCH

Like many other Greek boys, nine-year-old Dimitris has only been to church a few times. When his grandmother takes him, she buys him a candle, lights it, and tells him to bow to a picture of a saint. Richly decorated pictures—called "icons"—hang everywhere in the church. Dimitris makes the sign of the cross, kisses the picture, and leaves his candle beside it.

For centuries, the Orthodox Church has been the Greek national church. But today, few people go to church regularly. Christianity has become a tradition instead of a way of life. Many churches in Greece, and many Greek Christians, need the new life Jesus gives. Some ministries work among young people in Greece, with children such as Dimitris. Through Good News Clubs for kids and vacation Bible schools all over Greece, they share that Jesus is alive and wants to be a part of their life, too.

MOVING OUT, MOVING IN

Most of the population is ethnically Greek. But economic troubles in Greece meant that many ethnic Greeks had to

FACT FILE

AREA: 51,350 square miles

POPULATION: 11 million

CAPITAL: Athens

MAIN LANGUAGE: Greek

MAIN RELIGION: Christianity (mostly Greek Orthodox)

CHIEF EXPORTS: Oil, aluminum, and food—fruit, vegetables, nuts, olives and olive oil, fish

Athens

move to other countries to find jobs. Meanwhile, many people have come to Greece as refugees—from Eastern Europe, Africa, Asia, the Middle East, and especially from Syria and Afghanistan. There were more refugees than the Greek government could handle.

Christians from Greece, and from other countries, have joined together to help the refugees, who badly needed food, clothing, health care, a safe place to sleep, and kindness. Many of the refugees have experienced terrible things in the countries they have fled from, and on their journey to Greece. Christians are showing that Jesus loves them by helping them in their need.

GOOD NEWS

Groups of devoted Christians hold lively meetings in church, but also share the gospel in public. One of the main forms of outreach is sharing with the many refugees. Today there are many followers of Jesus in Greece, from lots of different countries—including refugees and Christians who have moved there for work. Thousands of people from countries that don't allow Christian missionaries are hearing about Jesus for the first time. In a city such as Athens, there may be as many foreigners meeting in their churches as Greeks going to their own churches.

MORNING STAR

In the beautiful, blue waters of the Ionian and Aegean seas that surround Greece are hundreds

The Parthenon, Athens

of islands. A group of Christians have a boat called *Morning Star* that visits these islands, telling people about Jesus. People on some islands got angry and tried to stop them. However, on other islands people welcomed them and listened to the Christian message—like on the missionary trips of the apostle Paul. When they hear the message of the Bible, some decide to follow Jesus. Some small villages only have one or two believers, and the *Morning Star* visits encourage them.

Christians are also working hard to give a copy of the New Testament to every home in Greece, in a program called "Operation Joshua." So far, volunteers have distributed more than one million New Testaments, in over 4,500 Greek villages.

Guards outside the Greek Parliament

TO HELP YOU PRAY FOR GREECE

YOU CAN THANK GOD FOR:

■ the long history of Christianity in Greece—almost two thousand years.

■ the growing number of Christians and churches among the migrants and refugees.

■ new believers, who met Jesus for the first time when they came to Greece.

■ the way Greek believers were kind and generous to migrants and refugees.

YOU CAN ASK GOD:

■ for new faith among Greek Orthodox Christians.

■ for many children to hear about Jesus through Good News clubs.

■ for the various churches, and different nationalities, of Christians in Greece to get along, working and praying together.

■ for Christians to share with migrants staying, or still arriving, in Greece.

■ for Operation Joshua—that every Greek home receives a New Testament that they will read and understand.

GREENLAND
The World's Biggest Island

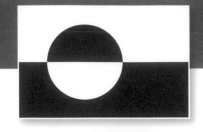

Sigssuk snuggled into bed. He was tired, but too excited to sleep. He was just eight years old, and his dad had taken him on his first ever seal-hunt. They'd caught two seals. Now he dreamed of becoming a great hunter!

Sigssuk is an Inuit. He lives with his family on the northwest coast of Greenland. Hunting is a very important part of their life. Almost as soon as Sigssuk learned to walk, his father gave him a puppy to train. His father also built him a special kayak, which he hung from a beam in the house, just a few inches off the floor. Sigssuk had fun sitting in it, learning how to balance using a little paddle.

Every summer—when it's daylight all the time—Sigssuk goes on camping trips with his family. He uses a net to catch seabirds called little auks. They cook and eat some of the birds, and put the rest in a sealskin sack to save for the winter.

During the long, dark winter months, the sun never rises in northern Greenland. During this season, Sigssuk goes to the village school and learns to read and write. School is quite exciting when some of the men also teach the children how to hunt, and how to build kayaks and sledges. In winter, it's usually too cold for Sigssuk and his friends to play outside. So they stay inside and play games, watch television, and listen to the grown-ups tell stories about hunting expeditions.

Greenland is the largest island in the world. Although it belongs to Denmark, today Greenland governs itself. Most of the country lies inside the Arctic Circle, and an enormous ice-sheet covers much of it. Some Greenlanders, like Sigssuk and his family, are Inuit. But some others are descended from Inuit who married European settlers. Nearly all of them live in small towns on the south and west coast, where they make a living from fishing and hunting.

NOT VERY GREEN

Erik the Red, a Norse Viking from Iceland, first discovered Greenland around a thousand years ago. He called the country Greenland—even though it's covered in ice—to convince

Baffin Bay

GREENLAND (KALAALLIT NUNAAT)

CANADA

Davis Strait

Nuuk

Denmark Strait

ICELAND

North Atlantic Ocean

FACT FILE

AREA: 840,020 square miles; 80 percent of the land is an ice cap

POPULATION: 56,000

CAPITAL: Nuuk

MAIN LANGUAGES: Greenlandic; Danish is also used

MAIN RELIGION: Christianity

CHIEF EXPORTS: Fish and fish products

![Do You Know icon]

DO YOU KNOW?

The ice sheet covering Greenland is on average 5,000 feet deep. If all that ice melted, the oceans of the world would rise by about 20 feet. The ice sheet is melting fast!

Soapstone carvings

his family and friends to join him there. A group of bold men, women, and children set sail across the stormy seas. They took with them horses, cows, and sheep. Erik's son, Leif the Lucky, became a Christian during a visit to Norway. When he returned to Greenland, he told everyone about Jesus, and many became Christians.

In 1721, a missionary sailed to Greenland from Denmark, hoping to find that the descendants of those first settlers were Christians. But none of them remained. They had all disappeared. More and more Christians then arrived from Denmark and Norway, and Greenland had Christians again. They built churches in almost every town and village, and the Bible was translated into Greenlandic.

THE *JESUS* FILM

Olaf and his family live in Nuuk, the capital of Greenland. Like many Greenlanders, they call themselves Christians, and by tradition always go to church at Christmas. But

when Olaf fell and broke his arm, his mother stitched a lucky charm into his coat to keep him safe, and asked the spirits of her ancestors to help him.

One day, Olaf heard that the first movie in Greenlandic, a film about Jesus, was being shown in Nuuk. As he watched the film, he realized that Jesus died on the cross for him. He decided that he wanted Jesus to give him a clean, new life. Now Olaf and his family follow Jesus for real.

But Olaf knew it would be hard to be a different kind of Christian from his friends; they all drank alcohol and took drugs when they got together. It's never easy to be different from everyone else. Even some of those who go to Bible schools and Christian training courses find it hard to keep following Jesus once they return home.

TO HELP YOU PRAY FOR GREENLAND

YOU CAN THANK GOD FOR:

- the *JESUS* film, and other ways Greenlanders hear the good news.

- camps where children and adults learn how to follow Jesus.

- the translation of the Bible in Greenlandic, completed in 2001.

YOU CAN ASK GOD:

- to show people that being a Christian means more than a tradition of going to church once a year.

- to help Christians encourage one another to keep following Jesus.

- that people who become depressed and lonely—especially in the cold, dark winters—will discover that Jesus is alive, and ready to help them when life is difficult.

GUINEA
Where Missionaries Were Banned

GUINEA

Atlantic Ocean

RICH—BUT VERY POOR

Guinea, in West Africa, is one of the poorest countries in the world. Crops such as rice, coffee, bananas, and oranges grow easily there. Iron, gold, and diamonds are found there, and Guinea is the world's second largest producer of bauxite, a mineral used to make aluminum.

Guinea used to be one of France's richest colonies. But when it became independent, the president wanted the country to be Communist. He ruled this way for twenty-six years. After him, another president controlled the country for the following twenty-four years. Many poor decisions were made during that time about how to use Guinea's wealth and resources. Foreign companies took a lot of minerals from Guinea and usually didn't pay fairly. Even with all its wealth and rich potential, Guinea remains poor.

The main rivers of West Africa—the Senegal, the Niger, and the Gambia—all start in Guinea. Despite this, one third of its people have no clean water. Most depend on crops such as rice, cassava, maize, plantains, and vegetables to survive, so water is vital.

LOOKING FOR GOD

Most of the people in Guinea are Muslims. Although missionaries worked in this country back when it was a French colony, few people became Christians during that time. Then in 1967, the Communist president forced most of the missionaries to leave.

Fishing in river

Christians around the world prayed for the millions of people in Guinea who'd never heard about the God who loves them. He answered their prayers. In 1984, when the president died, missionaries were allowed to return. Even before that, God was at work. People had become so poor, that many went to find work in other African countries. Some heard about Jesus while living abroad.

Alhaji was a Muslim. He wanted to know more about God, so he prayed, fasted, and studied the Qur'an. He went to live in Gambia, where he soon found work as a tailor for some

FACT FILE

AREA: 95,000 square miles

POPULATION: 13 million

CAPITAL: Conakry

OFFICIAL LANGUAGE: French

MAIN LANGUAGES: Pular, Malinke, Susu, and more than forty others

MAIN RELIGION: Large Muslim majority; small Christian minority

CHIEF EXPORTS: Bauxite, gold, fruit, and coffee

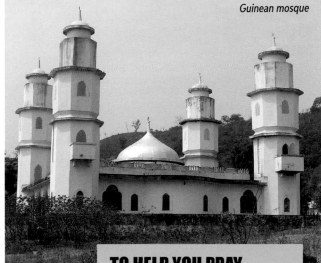
Guinean mosque

Christians. They gave him a book to read—but he couldn't understand it, because it was in English.

Alhaji learned to read English, so that he could find out what was in the book. It told him about Jesus. The Christians also gave him a Bible, which he started to read alongside his Qur'an. He prayed that God would show him the right way. One day he read in his Bible that God loved the world so much that he gave his only son, so that whoever believes in him will not perish. Instead they would have everlasting life (John 3:16). When he read this, Alhaji decided to follow Jesus.

GOD WORKS MIRACLES

When Alhaji told his wife about his decision, she was angry. She left him and returned to Guinea. Alhaji felt sad, but didn't stop following Jesus—or praying for his wife.

God answered Alhaji's prayers. His wife decided to follow Jesus, too, and came back to live with him in Gambia. They decided to return to Guinea together, to tell their people about the God who loves them.

When Alhaji and his wife got back to their village, Alhaji told the villagers about God's love. At first everyone welcomed them. Alhaji built a house, set up a little tailor's shop, and started to teach six young men to make clothes. They studied the Bible with him, and said they wanted to trust in Jesus. But, one by one, they returned to Islam.

Alhaji didn't give up. He believed God would help him explain the truth about Jesus. In time, fifteen people decided to follow Jesus. But, as a result, the community—even their own families—opposed them. Some of the villagers were angry, especially when the Christians decided to build a church. Alhaji encouraged the believers, and helped them each learn a trade as a way to make a living.

More than forty different people groups live in Guinea. Today, several Christian missions are working together, starting up new churches among many of these people groups. The New Testament is available in Pular – the most widely-spoken language. The full Bible is only available in a few languages, including Susu, one of Guinea's main languages.

THE SACRED FOREST

The people of the forest region of Guinea are animists. Some belong to the Sacred Forest cult. They claim they've been "born again" through the devil's mouth. When the leader of the cult comes into a village, everyone is supposed to hide indoors. But when the son of one village chief became a Christian, he refused to hide. His father was angry.

"I belong to Jesus," said his son. "He has set me free from the devil's power. He will keep me safe."

The chief was amazed when no harm came to his son.

"Jesus must be more powerful than all the spirits we fear!" he exclaimed.

djembe, a Guinean drum

TO HELP YOU PRAY FOR GUINEA

YOU CAN THANK GOD FOR:

- Christians in Guinea, like Alhaji, his wife, and their children.
- Christian youth centers and training projects.
- the New Testament in Pular and other languages, and the entire Bible in Susu.

YOU CAN ASK GOD:

- that Christians in Guinea will show their neighbors that Jesus loves them.
- for more Christians to share the good news about Jesus in Guinea.
- that many young people will choose to follow Jesus, even when it's difficult with their friends and family.
- that forest people will see that worshiping spirits brings fear—but following Jesus brings peace.
- to reveal to Muslims that Jesus is the Word of God.
- for the completion of the Old Testament translation into Pular.

HAITI
A Land Freed by Slaves

HAITI

PORT-AU-PRINCE

THE BAHAMAS

North Atlantic Ocean

JAMAICA

HAITI DOMINICAN REPUBLIC

Caribbean Sea

The country of Haiti occupies the western third of the Caribbean island of Hispaniola. The rest of the island is the Dominican Republic. Christopher Columbus was the first European to discover this island, in 1492—but people had been living here for hundreds of years before that. Later, the French gained control, and brought thousands of slaves from West Africa to work on the sugar cane plantations.

Eventually the slaves rebelled, and for thirteen years fought for their freedom. Finally, on January 1, 1804, the country declared itself independent from France. It was the world's first Black republic, and the only country in history to have gained independence by a slave rebellion.

FEAR, NOT FREEDOM

But after the French left, new leaders forced everyone to be either a plantation worker or a soldier. Most of the new Haitian rulers proved to be just as cruel as the French slave-owners. In revenge, France forced Haiti to pay for damages from the war. It took more than a hundred years to pay back the full amount. Other countries, such as the USA and England, were afraid that their own slaves would rebel, so they treated Haiti unfairly too. This kept the young nation from growing in a healthy way.

After two hundred years of independence, the people of Haiti have still never known real peace and prosperity. Many of their leaders have been corrupt and unjust. Since 2004, the United Nations have kept a military force in Haiti, to keep the peace.

Haiti is the poorest country in the Western world. The majority of Haitians are poor farmers, descended from African slaves. Many long for a better life, and try to make a dangerous boat journey to reach the USA, or one of the nearby Caribbean islands.

Most Haitians say they are Christians. Yet many also practice voodoo, which involves worshiping spirits and using them to control other people. When the evil spirits take control of them, people do strange and frightening things. Many who practice voodoo are sad and fearful.

WITCH DOCTOR'S SON

Gerard was the son of a wealthy witch doctor. When he was at boarding school, he liked to listen to Christian radio. His friends were surprised.

"Aren't you going to become a witch doctor?" they asked.

"Yes, just like my father," Gerard answered. "But the music the Christians

FACT FILE

AREA: 10,710 square miles

POPULATION: 11.1 million

CAPITAL: Port-au-Prince

MAIN LANGUAGES: Haitian Creole, French

MAIN RELIGIONS: Christianity, voodoo

CHIEF EXPORTS: Coffee, sugar, and tropical fruit

Haitian artwork

Farmer growing cabbage

TO HELP YOU PRAY FOR HAITI

YOU CAN THANK GOD FOR:

- Haitian Christians and missionaries in Haiti who share Jesus' love.

- the many good churches in Haiti.

- the Bible in Haitian Creole, the common language. It's available in print, audio, online—even in an app.

YOU CAN ASK GOD:

- to raise up leaders who will govern Haiti fairly and wisely.

- to help Haiti recover from the effects of destructive natural disasters.

- to help the millions of Haitians who are poor, jobless, homeless, ill, and hungry.

- to help people stop practicing voodoo, and follow Jesus instead.

- to send Christians to explain God's love and power to people in Haiti, and to offer practical help to those in need.

play is really good, and the Bible studies are OK too."

Gerard's father was furious when he discovered Gerard and his sister listening to Christian radio.

"Don't ever listen to that again!" he yelled. "If you become Christians, I'll drive you out of the house with a whip."

Soon after, Gerard became very ill. His father tried to cure him with voodoo medicine, chanting, and drumming. But it did no good.

One day, Gerard's sister heard a story about the prophet Elijah on Christian radio.

"Men who worshiped false gods shouted and danced all day, trying to get their gods to answer their prayers. But nothing happened. Then the true God answered Elijah's prayer, sending fire down on his sacrifice," she told Gerard. "Why don't you pray to the Christian God, and ask him to make you better?"

"But I don't know how to pray," Gerard said sadly.

He was still very ill, and decided to visit the radio station. When he arrived, the missionaries there gave him medicine, prayed for him, and explained how to become a Christian. Gerard was so eager to know Jesus that he no longer felt afraid of his father. He asked

Jesus to forgive his sins, and to become his friend.

More and more Haitians are discovering that Jesus will forgive them for the wrong things they've done, help them with their problems, and give them the strength to live the right way.

DISASTER!

Haiti lies over the boundary between two plates of the earth's crust. In January 2010, these plates moved, setting off a massive earthquake that killed around 316,000 people, and made more than 1.5 million people homeless. Before Haiti could rebuild after that disaster, a fierce hurricane hit the island. In some parts of Haiti, almost every building was destroyed.

Haiti was already very poor, facing the challenges of violence, corruption, drugs, and crime. These natural disasters made life still more difficult. Most people have no jobs, and up to a third of Haitians can't get clean water or enough food. When will God have mercy on this land?

"Tap-Tap," a public bus

HAZARA
Descendants of Genghis Khan's Army

AFGHANISTAN

Quetta

PAKISTAN

Persian
Gulf

Arabian Sea

GENGHIS KHAN

About eight hundred years ago, Genghis Khan,
the mighty leader of the Mongols, sent some of his men to
Central Asia. As the story goes, the ruler there seized them,
burnt their beards, and sent them back. Genghis Khan felt
insulted and very angry, so he invaded Central Asia with his fearsome
Mongol army. Some Hazara believe they are descendants of that army.
Their eyes and faces look similar to those of Mongolians. Even their
language, which is a Persian dialect, has many Mongol words.

HAZARAJAT

The Hazara mostly live in a mountainous
region called Hazarajat, in Afghanistan.
For most of the year, they live in small
village houses built of mud bricks.
Their houses have flat roofs, which are
ideal for drying the mulberries, grapes,
and peaches they grow in the hot summer
months. The Hazara store the dried fruit for
eating during the long, cold winter months.
Like many others in this region, the Hazara
people eat their food with their hands,
rather than with forks and spoons. The
Hazara also take good care of their guests,
feeding them well, and giving them the
best seats at meals.

Wealthy Hazara live in large houses that
look like walled fortresses. All the animals
belonging to the family—dogs, donkeys,
goats, sheep, hens, and even the cows—
live in the courtyard of these big houses.
But not all Hazara are wealthy; many

struggle with poverty, hunger, and disease.
They get left to do the hardest jobs in the
cities where they live.

AFGHAN GOLD

Abdul is a Hazara refugee. He lives in
the city of Quetta, in Pakistan, along with
many other Hazara. Abdul smiles sadly
when he remembers his own land.

"During the summer, we took our sheep
and goats up to the high mountain valleys.
There's plenty of grass there for them to

Bamiyan Valley, Central Afghanistan

FACT FILE

HOMELAND: Afghanistan;
others live as refugees in
Pakistan, northern Iran, the
U.A.E., and beyond

NUMBERS: About 4 million
(around 3 million live in
Afghanistan)

MAIN LANGUAGE: Hazaragi

MAIN RELIGION: Islam (Shia)

Afghan girls (Hazaras in red)

Quetta, Pakistan

DO YOU KNOW?

Most Hazara are very religious Shia Muslims, and follow strict rules. They will eat a meal with Christians or Jews, because they're both people with a holy book who believe in one God. But they don't like eating with Buddhists or atheists, because they aren't "People of the Book."

eat. We had to watch the animals very carefully. I remember driving away wolves and eagles that were trying to snatch the smaller animals. While we were in the mountains, we lived in tents called *yurts*, made from reed matting. The women and girls milked the animals. Then they churned some of the milk to make balls of hard cheese—called *crut*—to keep for winter.

"In winter, we always hoped for lots of snow, because it was our only source of water. We called it 'Afghan gold,' because—without snow—the rivers dry up, the crops die, and we starve."

A SECRET FOLLOWER

"When life became too dangerous, my father sent me here to Quetta, across the mountains. He wanted me to keep studying." Abdul looked around him, scared. "I learned English, because I knew that would help me get a good job. When I did, the people I worked with invited me to join a club, where I learned about Jesus. It's amazing that he loves the homeless and the poor. It means Jesus loves the Hazara."

"I'm a follower of Jesus," he whispered. "If some of the people around here knew, they'd make a lot of problems for me. Please pray for me."

In the 1990s, a violent Muslim group called the Taliban took over much of Afghanistan. Thousands of Hazara suffer greatly under their rule, partly because the Hazara follow a different kind of Islam from the strict version that the Taliban follow. The Hazara are Shia Muslims, while most people in Afghanistan are Sunni Muslims. The Taliban target the Hazara more than others, sometimes even attacking their mosques.

Pray that God will help Abdul and the other Hazara Christians stay faithful to Jesus, no matter what. Hazara Christians are often reluctant to meet other believers, fearing they might be spies who will report them to the Muslim authorities.

ESCAPE!

The many wars in Afghanistan, and the religious violence in nearby Pakistan, have brought suffering, poverty, and destruction to the Hazara people. Many of them, especially the men, have tried to reach countries where they might be safer, find jobs, and eventually bring their families to join them. Sometimes they go as students, sometimes as refugees, who often try to smuggle themselves into other countries. Many have traveled overland as far as northern Europe, others on boats to Australia and North America. Many Hazara have died trying to reach somewhere safe to live.

TO HELP YOU PRAY FOR THE HAZARA

YOU CAN THANK GOD FOR:

- every Hazara Christian—there aren't many yet, but more Hazara follow Jesus than any other Afghan group.

- Christian resources—including the Bible—in Dari, a language most Hazara people know.

YOU CAN ASK GOD:

- to show his love for the Hazara by sending Christians to reach them, and through dreams and visions of Jesus.

- for Christians to share Jesus' love with Hazara refugees in every country where they live.

- to give Hazara Christians the courage to tell other Hazara people about Jesus.

- that the whole Bible be translated into Hazaragi, the Hazara language. At present, they have portions of Scripture.

HUI
Descendants of Warriors and Merchants

"Come and eat dumplings with us," Kit and Lee said to their visitor, Ray. "Or, if you prefer, you can have noodles. They're both great at the Hui restaurant we're going to. Just don't ask for pork, because the Hui are Muslims."

As the three friends walked along the busy city street in north-central China, they could see the people here looked Chinese, and dressed like other Chinese. But most of the men wore little white caps, and some women had short veils made of black or dark-green cloth. These were Hui (*hway*) people.

CHINA

South China Sea

WHO ARE THE HUI?

More than a thousand years ago, hundreds of Arab and Persian merchants made the great journey along the famous Silk Road, from the Middle East all the way across Asia to China. Arab warriors also traveled to China, to help the Chinese emperors fight their enemies. Others sailed to China by sea. Many never returned to their homeland.

The Arabs were Muslims, and proud of their background. Wherever they settled in China, they built mosques, married local Chinese women, and brought up their children as Muslims. Over time, they grew in number. They became known as the Hui.

Today, Hui Muslims live in many different parts of China. In the countryside, they often work as farmers. In towns and cities, they tend to live near their mosques.

Some work in their own shops and restaurants, which have food and other products especially for Hui people. But most have jobs like everyone else. The Hui are known as particularly smart businesspeople.

In parts of China, most of the Hui seem no different from the Han, the people we usually think of as Chinese. The Hui speak Mandarin, have Chinese names, and look and dress mostly like the rest of the Chinese. But there is one big difference: they are Muslim.

There are about thirteen million Hui spread throughout all parts of China. Many live in north-central China, where

FACT FILE

NUMBERS: About 13 million

LOCATION: Mainly China; small populations in several other Asian countries

MAIN LANGUAGE: Mandarin Chinese

MAIN RELIGION: Islam (Sunni)

Muslim Quarter, Xi'an, China

the Chinese government has set up a special region for them, called the Ningxia (*Ning-shia*) Hui Autonomous Region. This region is one of only five in China specially set up for an ethnic minority group. About a third of the people living in this region are Hui. Here, they can more freely follow their own religion and culture. Although the government in China is atheist, and suspicious of all religions, they leave the Hui people to live their lives, because they are hardworking and peaceful.

ACROSS CULTURES

Although there are Han Chinese Christians in every area where the Hui live, few have tried to take the Christian good news to the Hui. The Han churches in China are young, and still learning how to take the gospel to other cultures. They are very good at sharing Jesus with other Han Chinese. But sharing the good news with other ethnic groups can be more difficult. They encounter different languages, different gods, different traditions and customs, and different ways of life. These differences affect even simple things, such as sharing a meal: one group loves to eat pork, while another considers it unclean.

But growing numbers of Han Christians realize that God loves the Hui.

They are learning how to adapt in order to be friends with Hui people. And they are learning to tell the Hui about Jesus in ways that the Hui will understand and appreciate.

LEARNING ARABIC

Liang is a young Hui. His father goes to the mosque every Friday, and has even been on the great *haj* pilgrimage to Mecca. "Sometimes I go and watch the men pray," says Liang. "But I don't want to go to the mosque with them yet, because not many other boys go. I do like to follow our other Islamic customs, though.

"My father wants me to learn to read Arabic, so I can read the holy Qur'an. We speak Mandarin Chinese at home, but we use a few Arabic words too. I've also seen Arabic words on the walls of the mosque. The writing looks beautiful, but it's going to be hard to learn. I'm still learning to write Chinese—that's difficult enough!"

Muslim traditions are very important to most Hui. However, there is now a small number of Hui Christians—possibly as many as 2,000. Millions of Hui have still never heard the gospel.

ICELAND
Land of Fire and Ice

Iceland is a large island, about 500 miles north of Scotland. It's called the land of fire and ice because it has many active volcanoes, huge glaciers, and ice-fields covering large areas. Much of the area in the center of the country is black with volcanic ash and rocks. Icelanders mostly live close to the sea where it is more green.

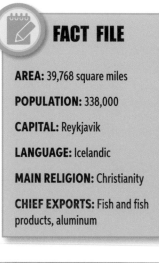

ICELAND
REYKJAVÍK
SURTSEY

ICELAND

In 1963, some fishermen out in their boats were amazed when the sea seemed to be boiling. A few weeks later, a volcano under the sea erupted, shooting steam, fire, and ash high into the air. In a very short time, the volcano became the island called Surtsey, now the southernmost point of Iceland.

Iceland is so close to the Arctic Circle that it hardly gets dark during the middle of summer; but it's dark almost all the time in winter. Then people mostly stay inside their snug, warm houses and read, play video games, and watch TV. Most of the houses in Reykjavik (*ray-kyuh-vik*), the capital city, are heated with natural hot water that is piped in from deep holes drilled down into the ground.

With all these volcanoes, hot springs, rock formations, and craggy coastlines, Iceland is very beautiful. People come from all over the world to see the

dramatic scenery. But the volcanoes can be dangerous. An eruption in 2010 led to about twenty countries in Europe canceling their flights for more than a week—the airplanes could not safely fly through the giant ash cloud.

A THOUSAND YEARS OF CHRISTIANITY

"Tell me how Iceland became a Christian country," Erik asked.

"We've been a Christian country for a thousand years," his father began. "It all started when the first settlers

FACT FILE

AREA: 39,768 square miles

POPULATION: 338,000

CAPITAL: Reykjavik

LANGUAGE: Icelandic

MAIN RELIGION: Christianity

CHIEF EXPORTS: Fish and fish products, aluminum

Icelandic tradition is to take your surname from your father's first name. If you were called Svein and your father was Jón, your name would be Svein Jónsson. Your son's surname would be Sveinsson. If you were a girl named Inga, you would be Inga Jónsdóttir.

arrived. They were great adventurers who made long, dangerous sea journeys. Around the year 1000, some came from Norway, bringing the good news of Jesus. More and more people in Iceland had decided to follow Jesus. But many people still worshiped the old Norse gods, such as Thor and Odin.

"Our ancestors wanted to decide if we should become a Christian country—or continue to follow the old gods. In the year 1000, at a great public meeting, the people decided that Iceland would be a Christian nation. So for the past millennium, Iceland has been officially a Christian country. In some homes, families still meet every day to pray and read the Bible, just as we do. But not as many as in the past."

"Hardly any of my school friends go to church, unless there's a wedding, a baptism, or a funeral," Erik said.

"Yes," said his father. "Most Icelanders call themselves Christian because it's part of our culture and tradition."

"My friends think the Christian summer camp I go to sounds fun, but they don't want to go," said Erik. "They never want to come to church with me either. They don't understand when I tell them Jesus is my friend who promises to be with me all the time. Are we still a Christian country?"

"Some of us pray that God will make the whole country excited about following Jesus," Erik's father said. "We've seen God begin to answer those prayers. We have a new translation of the Bible that is easier to understand, and some churches have programs to train Christians to share the good news about Jesus. Some Icelanders have even gone overseas to tell people about Jesus. Also, people are moving to Iceland from faraway countries, some from other religions. But some are strong Christians, which sometimes makes people in Iceland think about what *they* believe about God."

An ice cave

TO HELP YOU PRAY FOR ICELAND

YOU CAN THANK GOD FOR:

- Icelanders who are discovering that Christianity is far more than a tradition.

- the Icelandic translation of the Bible.

- those who are sharing the good news of Jesus with those who don't know him.

YOU CAN ASK GOD:

- that many children will choose to follow Jesus at Christian camps.

- that Bible school students will share the good news about Jesus wherever they go.

- for more pastors and evangelists to teach the Bible clearly.

- to help those who follow Jesus share clearly with Icelanders. Many only know Christian traditions, but don't know Jesus or what daily life with him is like.

INDIA
Land of a Million Gods

THE GREAT FESTIVAL

"Come on! Wake up!" Sanjay said, shaking his brother. "It's nearly dawn. The holy men are already on their way down to the river. It's time for us to go." All around them were the brightly colored tents of millions of people who'd also come for the *Kumbh Mela* festival.

The two brothers started their adventure a week earlier, when they left their village to walk to Allahabad, India's "city of gods." They were going to the great festival, or *mela*, at the holy place where the Ganges and Yamuna rivers meet. Sometimes a farmer gave the boys a ride on his bullock cart. Once or twice they traveled on crowded buses. But mostly they walked along hot, dusty paths and roads.

As they finally neared the river, Sanjay and his brother were caught up in a huge crowd of pilgrims. Everyone was pushing, slipping, and sliding, dodging sacred cows and wandering goats, on their way down to the riverbank. At last they reached the mighty river, and stepped into the flowing water. Sanjay faced the rising sun, and poured water over himself. He hoped it would wash away his sins.

Kumbh Mela is one of India's great religious festivals. It happens at this sacred place just once every twelve years. Hindus rich and poor, high and low caste, come from all over India, to wash away their sins in the Ganges. Most have never heard that if they call on Jesus' name he will wash away their sins forever and make their hearts clean.

A MILLION GODS

India is a highly religious country—wherever you go in India, you'll find temples and shrines. Some say there are more than 330 million gods and goddesses! Some of them are worshiped in temples all over India.

Every day, the Hindu priests wake the statues of their gods in the temple, bathe them, dress them, offer them food, and pray to them. When people worship at a Hindu temple, they bring offerings of food, or flowers, for their brightly painted gods. They ring the temple bell, to make sure the god or goddess is awake. But even after they've made their offerings and prayed, they're not sure the god will be kind to them.

MANY RELIGIONS

India is the birthplace of four world religions: Hinduism, Buddhism, Jainism, and Sikhism. Some Christians believe the Apostle Thomas came to India as a missionary. The majority of Indians are Hindus.

FACT FILE

AREA: 1.2 million square miles

POPULATION: 1.35 billion

CAPITAL: Delhi

MAIN LANGUAGES: The Indian Constitution recognizes 22 languages. Hindi, and sometimes English, are used officially. Altogether, there may be more than 800 languages and dialects spoken.

MAIN RELIGIONS: Hinduism; also Islam, Christianity, Sikhism, Buddhism

CHIEF EXPORTS: Jewelry, gems, cars, grain, textiles, machinery, electronics, medicines, and tea

Ganges River, Uttar Pradesh

Muslims are the next largest group—more Muslims live in India than in the whole Middle East. India is also home to many Christians, Sikhs, Buddhists, Jains, and animists.

With so many different religious groups living closely together, it's no surprise they struggle to get along. Sometimes there are violent clashes. In some parts of India, there are Hindu groups who believe every Indian must follow Hinduism, so they try to force people to convert away from Christianity, Islam, and Buddhism.

Today, the Christian church is thriving in India. Thousands of Indian missionaries and church members bravely talk to people about Jesus, even when threatened and attacked. Indian laws give freedom of religion, but Christians still face persecution in some places.

HOW WILL THEY HEAR?

Even with so many devoted Christians in India, more than 2,500 different people groups and cultures, speaking hundreds of different languages, haven't yet heard the good news. Some groups still have no missionaries, and no Bible in their language. Many Indians have never even met a Christian.

Indian believers are praying for more Christians to take the good news to every village, town, and city, and for churches to grow in every place. Let's pray with them!

THE NEEDIEST PLACE

India stretches from the soaring peaks of the Himalayas in the north, across broad plains where the mighty rivers flow, to the tropical south. Its population is already well over one billion. Most people expect that, before 2030, India will pass China and have the world's largest population.

Technology is rapidly changing India, with more than one billion mobile phones now in use. More people work in IT in India than in any other country, many of them developing the programs and apps we all use.

India's cities have expensive restaurants, houses, and shops. But they also have enormous slums, packed with people trying to survive. There's a huge gap between the way rich people live and the way hundreds of millions of poor people live.

Polluted water and lack of clean toilets cause illness, and sometimes even death. With so much poverty, India's people battle terrible diseases such as tuberculosis (TB) and leprosy. The majority of Indians still live in rural villages, where there are few doctors, clinics, or medicines to take care of even simple illnesses.

Christians work throughout the towns and cities of India, serving in hospitals, schools, and churches. Some help the millions of homeless people. Others travel around, giving out Christian books, showing films about Jesus, and teaching children to read.

TO HELP YOU PRAY FOR INDIA

YOU CAN THANK GOD FOR:

- every Indian Christian, the large and growing Indian church, and the many Indian missions and Bible schools.

- the thousands of Indian missionaries, in India and in nearby countries.

- the Bible, available in at least seventy of India's languages.

YOU CAN ASK GOD:

- to give strength and courage to those who follow Jesus, especially those being pressed to convert back to Hinduism.

- for more Christians to go and share the good news with every person, and every village.

- for more Bible translators, so that everyone can have the Bible in their own language.

- to help the millions of Indians who live in extreme poverty, and suffer from diseases such as leprosy, malaria, dengue fever, and blindness.

INDIA, continued

TOUCHING THE UNTOUCHABLE

As the sun set, Meira held the brown clay cup in her hands and thanked God for the cool water. She was hot, dusty, and very smelly. She had spent the whole day as she spent almost every day, cleaning the public toilets in her village. She was only eight years old, but she had to work very hard to help her family buy food. Her brother, Vinod, was even younger, and he was already working in the fields. Neither of them went to school.

Meira finished her drink and threw the cup to the ground, smashing it into pieces. She wasn't angry. She smashed it because she was a Dalit—regarded by some Indians as an "untouchable"—just like her parents and grandparents. In Meira's village, Dalits were meant to break or wash the cup when finished, so no one from an upper caste would be "polluted" by drinking from the same cup as a Dalit.

Meira heard that once Jesus took water from a woman he met at a well who was an outcast. He even drank from her cup! She wished everyone treated each other like Jesus treated people.

Some people from another village had come and shown a film about this man called Jesus. He was the Son of God and he was perfect. He was friends with poor people, and even touched people who were unclean! Meira's whole family watched with tears in their eyes when powerful, wicked men killed Jesus. But they clapped with joy when they saw death couldn't defeat him. He came back to life!

Now, Meira's family meets with other Dalits who also want to follow Jesus. The people

who showed the film told them more stories about his life and the miracles he did. Meira dreamed about going to school, and learning to read and write. They said they would help, but how could that happen if she still had to clean toilets all day? Life was hard. Yet Meira and her family had met the Son of God, who would happily share a cup with them.

LIFE IN A CHILDREN'S HOME

Kamala closed her workbook with a smile. She was done with her studies for the day. Soon she would have a meal with the other girls, then go to evening prayers with them. Kamala enjoyed eating with her friends, and the times of singing together. She loved the colors of all the flags—places she would never visit, but places she could pray for! Most of all, she loved learning at school.

Kamala knew she was blessed. She had been abandoned at birth by her family, but kind people at the children's home had taken her in. Many parents wanted baby boys, but not girls. Some days, when she thought about this, she began to feel sad and lonely, even in the crowded children's home. But she knew she was loved by the people around her, and by God!

The leaders at the children's home were Christians. They took care of many girls and some boys. They reminded every child, every day, that God had made them just as they are, and that each is a treasure in his eyes. So many other girls were never told this good news!

The leaders showed by their lives how to follow Jesus, and they taught the children how to pray. Kamala thought it was wonderful that God heard the prayers of children. They had seen for themselves that he was powerful enough to answer them, too!

Kamala's goal was to study hard, get the best marks, and go to university. Then she would study some more! Eventually, she would become a politician. She would change the laws, so that boys and girls were treated equally. She would make sure every child was able to have a safe home and an education. Kamala knew God had created her and loved her for who she was. She wanted to make India a country where every person—especially girls and orphans—knew this, too.

DO YOU KNOW?

Some of the most popular board games come from India, like Snakes & Ladders and Chess.

TO HELP YOU PRAY FOR INDIA

YOU CAN THANK GOD FOR:

- the many Dalits who find acceptance and hope in Jesus.

- the thousands of children's homes and schools that help needy children.

- Christians who help the poor, sick, disabled, and homeless—people who no one else usually wants to touch or care for.

YOU CAN ASK GOD:

- that one day Jesus will be the only God worshiped in India

- that girls and boys of all backgrounds receive care, love, and education.

- that Christians will love each other, and follow Jesus' example of loving others of all backgrounds.

- for every Indian to know they are a child of God—a treasure in his eyes.

- that leaders in the government, the courts, and police protect and serve fairly, respecting the law and the rights of all people in India.

Pottery in the Dharavi slum, Mumbai

INDONESIA
An Island Nation

SEVEN HUNDRED LANGUAGES

Indonesia consists of around 18,000 islands. If you tried to visit a different island every day, it would take nearly fifty years to see them all. The islands are spread out over an area as wide as the USA, stretching from the Indian Ocean to the Pacific Ocean. Many of these islands have volcanoes, and are covered by thick, tropical rainforests. About half of the islands are completely uninhabited.

Indonesia has the fourth largest population in the world, with more than 750 different people groups, speaking more than 700 different languages. The biggest groups are the Javanese and the Sundanese. Others include the Madurese, the Betawi, and the Bugis. Elsewhere in this book, you can find more about the Balinese (page 14), Minangkabau (page 100), and Sundanese (page 154) people groups.

For nearly 350 years, the Dutch ruled most of Indonesia, until the country became independent in 1945. Between 1950 and 1998 it was ruled by powerful presidents, first Sukarno, and then Suharto. Since that time, the country has been governed more democratically—but this can hard to do, with so many different islands, languages, and ethnic groups.

Indonesia has suffered badly from natural disasters. The greatest damage has been caused by earthquakes, volcanoes, flooding, and tsunamis. In the nineteenth century, volcanoes at Tambora and Krakatoa had two of the biggest eruptions in history. They were so big, they affected the weather of the whole world. Then in 2004, Sumatra was struck by a tsunami that killed almost a quarter of a million people. Further recent earthquakes have caused thousands more deaths.

More than half the Indonesian people work as farmers, growing rice, fruit, vegetables, tobacco, and coffee. The rainforest can produce a lot of valuable wood, but illegal logging is harming both the land and wildlife.

ONE COUNTRY?

Indonesia could be a rich country; but while some people are very wealthy, millions of others don't

FACT FILE

AREA: 735,400 square miles

POPULATION: 267 million

CAPITAL: Jakarta

MAIN LANGUAGES: Bahasa Indonesia (official); more than 700 other languages

MAIN RELIGIONS: Most are Muslim. Official religions: Islam, Protestantism, Catholicism, Hinduism, Buddhism, and Confucianism. Animist religions are not official, but are also practiced.

CHIEF EXPORTS: Oil, gas, timber, rubber, and textiles

Sumatran girls

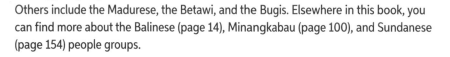

Mount Bromo, East Java

get enough to eat. One of Indonesia's biggest problems is corruption. A few dishonest, selfish, and greedy people have a lot of power. If everyone were honest and generous, Indonesia could be a much more prosperous nation.

Some of the islands that make up Indonesia—such as Java and Madura—are very crowded, while others have plenty of space. The government is trying to move people from the crowded islands to those that have more space. But people in these islands aren't happy about suddenly having to share their land with newcomers who speak different languages and sometimes follow different religions.

Although there are hundreds of different ethnic groups, the government wants all Indonesians to see themselves as one nation, with one language, and one of six approved religions. At school, everyone has to learn the same national language, Bahasa Indonesia.

Indonesia has more Muslims than any country in the world. Some just observe Muslim traditions and culture, but many practice Islam faithfully. Others mix Muslim beliefs with old magic practices. And still others want Indonesia to become a completely Muslim nation, with Islamic laws. They sometimes persecute groups who are different from them. In the past, they have burned down churches, and even killed Christians. But persecution hasn't stopped the churches from growing. In fact, in the last fifty years, the number of Christians has increased a lot.

Although Indonesia has many Christians who love Jesus, others don't learn the Bible or try to live like Jesus. For them Christianity is more like a cultural tradition.

Mosque, Central Java

SHARING ABOUT ISA

When he was six, Enjang started to read the Qur'an. As he read about hell, he got really scared. His uncle showed him where he could read about Mary's son, Isa. Enjang discovered that "Isa" is the Muslim name for Jesus. As he grew older, Enjang came to love Jesus more and more. He started to tell other Muslim children about Isa—but that made their parents angry. Enjang's brother was so angry that he made Enjang leave home. Yet, wherever he went, Enjang told people about Jesus.

Because of people like Enjang, the church in Indonesia is growing. Pray that every part of the country will hear of God's love.

Many of Indonesia's Christians are becoming more passionate about prayer and missions. They want to share the message of Jesus with every Indonesian, and with people in other countries too. Christians in Indonesia live in a Muslim country with a variety of cultures, so they quickly learn how to share the gospel with Muslims, how to suffer for Jesus, and how to live alongside many different kinds of people. God can use them as wonderful missionaries to other countries.

TO HELP YOU PRAY FOR INDONESIA

YOU CAN THANK GOD FOR:

- all Indonesians who love Jesus, especially those who have recently become Christians.

- a church that keeps growing—even while many Christians live with poverty and persecution.

- many Bible translation projects.

YOU CAN ASK GOD:

- to send Christians who will share the message of Jesus on every inhabited island in Indonesia.

- for revival in the churches, so that all Christians will really live for Jesus.

- to help Christians forgive people who want to hurt them and destroy their churches.

- for the government to be fair to all the different peoples, islands, and religions.

Traffic in Jakarta

IRAQ
Between the Tigris and Euphrates

A LAND OF THE BIBLE

Have you ever wondered where in the world the Bible story begins? Genesis chapter two talks about "Mesopotamia," the land between the Tigris and Euphrates rivers. The tower of Babel was built in this land too. From here, Abraham was called by God to go to the Promised Land.

More than one thousand years later, the Jewish people were exiled to the land of Babylon. This was where Shadrach, Meshach, and Abednego were thrown into the fiery furnace, and where Daniel served King Nebuchadnezzar.

Mesopotamia and Babylon were both in the area where Iraq is today. On the day of Pentecost, people from Mesopotamia were in the crowd that Peter preached to in Jerusalem. Some became followers of Jesus on that day, when the church was born!

Iraq is a mix of desert in the west, marshes in the south, and hills and high mountains in the north. The majority of the people living in Iraq today are Arabs, but Kurds and others live there too. Iraq has almost ten percent of the world's oil reserves, as well as fertile farmland, so it could be a prosperous country. But harsh rulers, wars, and divisions between its own people have instead brought much suffering and violence.

A TROUBLED LAND

Iraq used to be a republic controlled by powerful and dangerous men, such as President Saddam Hussein. The USA and its allies invaded Iraq in 2003 to get rid of him. But this violence created more violence. Instead of being one country under one strong leader, Iraq ended up broken into many areas, controlled by different warlords and militias. Each had different political or religious views, and they fought against each other with terrible violence.

Out of this chaos, a worse evil arose. In western Iraq and eastern Syria, a group calling itself "Islamic State" (IS) took over. They declared an "Islamic Caliphate," where everyone was to be judged

Caspian Sea

Persian Gulf

FACT FILE

AREA: 169,000 square miles

POPULATION: 39.3 million

CAPITAL: Baghdad

MAIN LANGUAGES: Arabic, Kurdish; also Assyrian

MAIN RELIGION: Islam (Shi'a majority and Sunni minority)

CHIEF EXPORT: Oil

Ziggurat of Ur from Abraham's time

Harvesting dates

by very strict Islamic laws. This group had no mercy on people of other religions, or even people from other forms of Islam. They were brutal and murderous, and fought fiercely. They were especially cruel to Christians, and to non-Arab groups such as the Yazidis and Kurds. (You can find more about Yazidis and Kurds in this book; see pages 86 and 188.) IS rapidly took over much of Iraq, and ruled it harshly. In spite of their previous differences, almost all the other groups in the region came together to fight against IS, helped by foreign allies. Eventually IS was left with hardly any territory.

All these years of fighting and unrest have left most Iraqi people very poor. Many have no electricity, clean water, or health care. Their farms have been damaged, and work is hard to find. And there is still violence—different Islamic groups still shoot and bomb each other.

FEW REMAIN

There have been Christians in this region since the first century AD. But Iraq is now almost entirely a Muslim country. Today, most Iraqi Christians belong to ancient churches that were strong in the early Christian years, such as the Chaldean Catholic Church, the Assyrian Church of the East, and the Syriac Orthodox Church.

In recent times, Iraqi Christians have been badly persecuted. Many of their churches have been attacked and destroyed, and most Christians have fled to other countries. Many may never return. Life in most parts of Iraq is extremely difficult for them. They face the same hardships as the rest of the Iraqis, but are sometimes also persecuted for being Christian. The Bible tells us that God loves the poor, the homeless, and those who are treated badly.

A DANGEROUS CHURCH

Ahmed's church in Baghdad was full to overflowing. His Sunday school class was full too. Dozens of armed guards encircled the building, protecting the congregation. Although some violent Muslims tried to blow up the church and kill its members, the number of people that came there to worship God kept growing.

Ahmed's family were Muslims, but his parents saw different Muslim groups trying to kill each other. Meanwhile, Christians from the church were trying to feed the poor and help those who were suffering. Even though the congregation does not try to convert Muslims, Ahmed's family decided to start following Jesus. They risk bombings and shootings every time they go to worship, and some Muslims want to kill them for leaving Islam. But they have never felt more at peace.

TO HELP YOU PRAY FOR IRAQ

YOU CAN THANK GOD FOR:

- the presence of Christians in Iraq since the earliest days of Christianity.
- the Bible and many Christian resources in Arabic and Kurdish languages.
- the Muslims who have decided to follow Jesus.

YOU CAN ASK GOD:

- to bring peace to this land, which has suffered so much.
- to stop the plans of wicked groups that want to hurt and kill others.
- to send Christians to care for those who are suffering, especially children and the poorest Iraqis.
- to give strength to all who follow Jesus, so they stay faithful even when it's very hard and dangerous to do so.
- to make Jesus known to every person in Iraq as the only one who can bring peace and salvation.

Great Mosque, Kufa

ISRAEL
Holy Land of Jews, Christians, and Muslims

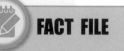

"Why do people say Israel is the homeland of the Jewish people?" Tanya asked her father. Tanya's family are "Messianic Jews"—Jewish people who follow Jesus as Messiah. Her grandparents emigrated to Israel from Russia.

"It's a story that started thousands of years ago," her father replied. "In the Torah (the first part of the Hebrew Bible), God promised this land to his people, the Hebrews, or Jews. Famous kings of the Bible, such as Saul, David, and Solomon, lived and ruled here. Jesus was born, lived, died, and rose again here—so it's very special to Christians. Muslims believe the prophet Muhammad traveled from Jerusalem to heaven on a winged horse to speak with God. So Jews, Christians, and Muslims all call it the 'Holy Land.'"

FORCED OUT

Tanya's father continued, "Two thousand years ago, this land was called Palestine. But other nations invaded, and the Jews were forced out. Over time, they settled in many different countries, but they always longed and prayed to return to their own land.

"Muslim Arabs conquered Palestine in AD 641, and settled here. Twelve centuries passed. Finally, at the end of the nineteenth century, some Jewish people arrived from Europe and set up farms. More and more settled here, in a movement known as 'Zionism.' But it still wasn't their country."

A NEW STATE

"During World War II, the Nazis tried to wipe out the Jewish people, in what we call the 'Holocaust.' After the war, the United Nations recommended dividing Palestine into separate Jewish and Arab states. On May 14, 1948, the new Jewish state of Israel was formed. Ever since,

many Jewish people have come to Israel from all around the world."

"At school, I have friends from Europe, America, Asia, and Africa," said Tanya.

"Yes, it's wonderful that Jewish people from all these different places are returning to Israel," her father said. "And people are moving here, from all over the world, who are neither Arab nor Jewish. Some are Christians."

"What about the Palestinians?" asked Tanya.

"That's a long story. Since 1948, there have been many wars and much violence between Jewish and Arab people," her father said. "Thousands of Arabs were

Mediterranean Sea

ISRAEL

Red Sea

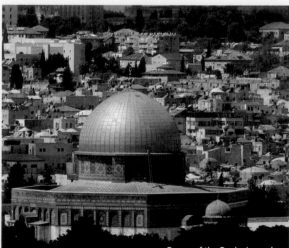

Dome of the Rock, Jerusalem

FACT FILE

AREA: 8,000 square miles.
3,000 square miles of the West Bank, Gaza, and the Golan Heights have been occupied by Israel since 1967.

POPULATION: 8.5 million

CAPITAL: Jerusalem, but the government is based in Tel Aviv

MAIN LANGUAGES: Hebrew, Arabic

MAIN RELIGIONS: Jewish majority; Muslim minority

CHIEF EXPORTS: Machinery, computer software, chemicals, textiles and clothing, cut diamonds, fruit, and vegetables

forced to leave their homes when other countries decided to give the land to the Jewish people. Naturally, they want a country of their own, too.

"Israel has built a 440-mile-long wall between Israel and the Palestinian territories. Sometimes it cuts right through Palestinian areas. Most other countries say this barrier is wrong. Suppose your home was on one side of the wall, but your job was on the other side: going to work would be like traveling to a different country."

FOLLOWING YESHUA

"Some kids at school say I can't be Jewish, because I'm a Christian," Tanya said. "Why do they say that?"

"The Old Testament tells us God promised to send a Savior," her father said. "A lot of Jewish people long for this Savior—or Messiah—to come, bringing peace to his people. We believe Jesus—*Yeshua* in Hebrew—is the Messiah God promised. But most Jews don't believe Jesus is the Messiah; they're still waiting for a Savior. That's why some think if we follow Yeshua, we can't truly be Jews."

"Don't some Palestinians follow Jesus too?" Tanya asked. "How come there are only Jewish believers in our congregation?"

"There are whole villages of Palestinian Christians—but sadly we don't often meet them," her father replied. "A friend of mine went with some people from his fellowship to visit a Palestinian church. It was a big step, because usually there isn't much friendship between Jews and Palestinians."

A SPECIAL VISIT

"What did you think, mama?" Nura asked.

Church that morning had been

Jewish father and son at Western Wall, Jerusalem

quite an experience. Some Messianic Jews visited their Palestinian congregation. At first Nura felt uncomfortable. Many Palestinians and Jews think of each other as enemies, but her pastors invited these Jewish believers to be their guests. At the end of the service, the visitors sang a blessing in Hebrew to the people in Nura's church. It sounded different, but very beautiful.

Nura's mother smiled. "It was special, don't you think? It made me remember what the Bible says in Galatians 3:28: "We are all one in Christ Jesus." If we follow Jesus, we belong to the same family—God's family. One day, we will all worship Jesus together. So why not start practicing now?"

Nura thought of the big wall at the edge of her town. That was a wall of concrete, but she imagined the wall in some people's hearts was even bigger. Nura wondered if Palestinians and Jews worshiping Jesus together could one day break down such walls.

TO HELP YOU PRAY FOR ISRAEL

YOU CAN THANK GOD FOR:

- the increasing number of people who follow Jesus—Jews, Palestinians, and others.

- the beginnings of friendship between Messianic Jews, Palestinian Arab Christians, and foreign Christians living in Israel.

YOU CAN ASK GOD:

- for peace in the land, and understanding between Palestinian and Jewish people.

- for Palestinians and Jews to know Jesus as the true Messiah, the Savior of all.

- to help Messianic Jews and Palestinian Christians trust each other, and become better friends.

- for tourists to Israel and people in other countries to pray for Israel and Palestine, and all the people who live there.

Palestinian children

IU MIEN
Children of the Dragon-Dog

HALF DRAGON, HALF DOG

A strange creature, half dragon, half dog, returned from a long journey across the seas. He had killed the enemy of the emperor of China, and had come to claim the promised reward, the emperor's beautiful daughter. They married, and had six fine sons and six lovely daughters who—the legend says—were the ancestors of the Iu Mien people.

MOUNTAIN HOME

The Iu Mien live high in the mountains of northern Thailand, Laos, Vietnam, and southern China. According to their stories and songs, the Iu Mien were once a strong, independent nation, but were defeated by the Chinese. They surrendered their right to have their own country. In exchange, the Chinese allowed them to keep their own language and culture, and to live in the mountains and hills, where they could grow crops. The Chinese name for the Iu Mien means "crossing the mountains."

In the Iu Mien villages of northern Thailand, most houses are built of wood. But poorer families live in homes with bamboo walls, grass roofs, and dirt floors. The villagers often keep pigs and chickens. In terraced fields on the hillsides, the Iu Mien grow mountain rice, maize, soybeans, and peanuts. In the past, they also grew a kind of poppy that produced the powerful and addictive opium drug. Growing opium is now illegal, but a few people still smoke it. Sadly, some Iu Mien teens give in to peer pressure at school and take drugs.

A REAL CHANGE

Fay Foo wears beautifully embroidered clothes, and a black turban with a fluffy red collar around her neck. She and her family are Christians.

"We once followed the spirits. We thought the most important things in life were money, our fields, and our feasts. When we first became Christians and stopped following the spirits, we only changed outside. But later, we realized that Jesus wanted us to change deep in our hearts. He wanted us to live in a new way."

CHINA
MYANMAR
VIETNAM
THAILAND
LAOS

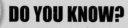

DO YOU KNOW?

The Iu Mien live in big houses: parents, children, grandchildren, aunts, uncles, and cousins all live together under one roof. When the Iu Mien build a new house, they are careful not to disturb the spirits, and have to include an altar to their ancestors.

There was a big difference between the Christians and the animists in Fay Foo's village. The animists performed magic rituals meant to heal them. But the Christians no longer asked for help from the spirits when they were ill. Instead, they prayed to God, in Jesus' name. They were always ready to help others, and to pray for them.

Many of the Christians had never been to school. But now they learned to read, so they could sing from the hymnbook and read the New Testament. In 2008, the whole Bible was published in the Iu Mien language. This Bible translation is special—it's available in four different scripts: Thai, Lao, old Roman, and new Roman. The Iu Mien live in several different countries, that use different alphabets. Now, they can read the Bible, no matter where they live.

Iu Mien Christians saved up to buy a big plot of land in northern Thailand, on which to build the Mien Outreach Center. It includes a conference center, a recording studio, Bible teaching, and a hostel for children who come from mountain villages to study at schools in town. Now Iu Mien can listen to Christian radio programs, and access Christian websites in their language. Some have become Christians and are learning more about Jesus. There are more than one million Iu Mien in southeast Asia; most have still not heard of Jesus.

WELCOME!

Welcoming visitors is important in Iu Mien culture. They have a story about being kind, even to a visitor who is unwelcome.

One day, a big snake came to visit two sisters. The older sister refused to invite the snake into the house.

But the younger sister welcomed the snake, and gave it everything it needed. During the night, she discovered the snake was actually a handsome prince in disguise. You can guess the rest of the story …

TO HELP YOU PRAY FOR THE IU MIEN

YOU CAN THANK GOD FOR:

- the whole Bible, available in all four scripts of their language.
- Iu Mien Christians who have new lives in Christ.
- the Mien Christian Outreach Center in Thailand.

YOU CAN ASK GOD:

- that many more Iu Mien will hear about Jesus and become Christians.
- that many Iu Mien people will read the Bible, listen to Christian radio, and read Christian websites in their language.
- that Iu Mien students will learn how to study the Bible and follow Jesus.
- to call Iu Mien Christians to be missionaries to other tribes in southeast Asia.

Priest's hat

JAPAN
Land of the Rising Sun

Japan consists of a chain of four large islands and nearly 7,000 smaller islands in the North Pacific Ocean. Mountains and hills cover many of the islands. Most of Japan's nearly 130 million people live crowded on narrow plains along the coasts.

Japan lies in a region where the earth's crust is very unstable. Every year it experiences more than a thousand earth tremors.

RUSSIA

HOKKAIDO

CHINA

NORTH
KOREA

Sea of Japan

JAPAN

SOUTH
KOREA

HONSHU

Kyoto

TOKYO

SHIKOKU

KYUSHU

Philippine Sea

TOO MANY CLASSES!

Toshio was angry. "I don't want to take extra classes after school," he complained. "I want to ride my bike and play computer games! Why do I have to work all night?"

"*Shhh!* Dad will hear. Only if you study hard will you get into college and find a good job."

"I don't care—and I don't see why he does either. A good job hasn't made *him* happy. He's always at work. I want to have fun with my friends."

"If you don't pass all your exams, what will our neighbors think of us?" his mother sighed. Toshio ran out of the house. He felt like crying. His mother was always worrying what other people might say.

School can be very tiring for Japanese children. They have a long day at school, compulsory school clubs afterwards, and extra classes at night to make sure they pass their exams. Some children get very little sleep.

WAY OF THE GODS

To some people, the rising sun on Japan's flag symbolizes the sun goddess. The Japanese call their country "Nippon"— "land of the sun." The Japanese have a tradition that their emperor descended from the sun goddess and was himself a god. The Japanese emperors used to be very powerful, but today they have less authority.

The traditional religion of Japan is called Shinto, "the way of the gods." Its followers worship the emperor, the sun, Mount Fuji, the fox-god, the snake-god, and spirits of water and fire. Japanese children visit Shinto shrines to learn more about their culture and beliefs.

Shintoists can't understand why Christians

FACT FILE

AREA: 145,900 square miles

POPULATION: 127 million

CAPITAL: Tokyo

MAIN LANGUAGE: Japanese

MAIN RELIGIONS: Shinto and Buddhism; there is freedom of religion

MAIN EXPORTS: Electronics, machinery, cars, ships, and chemicals

Tokyo

Shinto shrine

refuse to worship at Shinto shrines because they don't see a problem with worshiping more than one god. Many Japanese people believe that if they became Christians and worshipped only Jesus, they would be turning against their family, ancestors, and culture.

Japanese people often live to be very old. Toshio's mother takes care of his great-grandmother, who is very religious. She worships at the family shrine every day, and criticizes Toshio's mother for not

doing the same. Most younger people in Japan have no religion.

There have been Christians in Japan for five hundred years, yet most Japanese people see Christianity as a foreign religion. It is rare for a whole family to be Christian, so individuals who trust Jesus can feel quite alone. Twenty-four cities in Japan have no church at all.

LAND OF ROBOTS

The Japanese use robots more than any other country in the world. This is partly because there's more work than there are people. Japanese use robots in factories, hospitals, and laboratories, for cleaning and security, as receptionists, and even as companions for sick, lonely, and old people. There are hotels in Japan where the workers are nearly all robots. One day, there will probably be more robots than people in Japan!

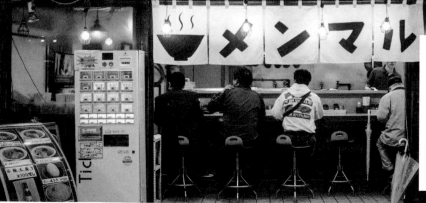

Sushi

KABYLE
God Has Done a New Thing!

Mediterranean Sea

ALGERIA

Kabylia—a large region in what is now Algeria—is the ancient homeland of the Kabyle people. They are one of North Africa's original people groups. For many centuries, the rugged mountains of Kabylia protected them from outside invaders. This allowed their languages and customs to stay the same for a long time, with little influence from outside.

Some call the Kabyle and other related groups in this region "Berbers." They call themselves Imazighen. They are different from the Arabs, who make up the majority of people in the countries where Imazighen live.

FACT FILE

NUMBERS: 6–7 million

HOMELAND: Algeria

OTHER COUNTRIES: France, Belgium, Canada, and United Kingdom

MAIN OCCUPATIONS: Farming olives, grapes, and figs; crafts such as basket-making, pottery, and weaving; herding goats; modern industry

MAIN LANGUAGES: Kabyle or Kabylian, Algerian Arabic, French

MAIN RELIGIONS: Islam; the number of Christians is increasing

Today it is possible there are people following Jesus in every city, town, and village of Kabylia. Yet just thirty years ago there were perhaps only fifty people following Jesus from among the millions of Kabyle Muslims. How did there come to be so many Imazighen disciples of Jesus in Kabylia—and even beyond?

FAITH TRIUMPHS OVER FEAR

The first Kabyle Christians decided to memorize 365 Bible verses about fear. They also began to pray and fast. This led to sick people being healed. As people saw that Jesus had such power, more began to follow him.

Around the same time, a radio station started broadcasting Christian Bible programs in the Kabyle language. One church started handing out booklets about Jesus, and showing a film about him in local cafés. The Christians were greatly encouraged by the Bible verses they memorized. They shared boldly about Jesus, even when people became angry or violent towards them.

When Christians around the world heard what God was doing among the Kabyle, they started praying for them. Kabyle families moved into areas where there were no Christians at all, so that even more people could hear about Jesus. More Kabyle people came

to Jesus, and other Imazighen—and even Arab people—did too.

THE POWERFUL ONE

"Please tell me, what does the future hold for my son-in-law?" Kahina's mother begged the fortune-teller.

"I can't see anything about his future," the woman exclaimed. "The One who is with him is more powerful than I am."

Kahina's sister and her husband had come to live with them last month. They'd been thrown out of his family's home when they were caught reading the Bible and following Jesus. Kahina was glad her parents had welcomed them in, but it meant there were now too many people in their little, three-room apartment.

Kahina's other sister, Djamila, was secretly learning about Jesus from her sister. Djamila struggled with math in school, and the big exam was coming up. Kahina's mother was worried, so they went to the fortune-teller to find out whether Djamila would pass. The

Djurdjura Mountains

woman again said, "The One with her is more powerful than I am." Kahina and her mother thought about it. Is Jesus really so powerful? And is Djamila following Jesus, too?

That night, Kahina's mother dreamed that she'd fallen into a deep well. She called to the prophet Muhammad for help, but he didn't come. She called to the prophet Jesus for help, and he rescued her from the well. Her mother shared the dream with the whole family next morning, and they decided together to follow Jesus.

HEALED!

Djamel and his cousin, Karim, were at a coffee shop one evening, when someone started to show a film about Jesus. Djamel wasn't really interested—it seemed like an old film about boring history. His entire family was Muslim, although they didn't really practice their religion. But he noticed towards the end of the film that Karim closed his eyes. He seemed to be praying.

Karim was quiet on the walk home. Finally he confessed, "Djamel, when I closed my eyes during the film, I felt God's Spirit on me. I knew that Jesus was real!" It sounded strange to Djamel, but he trusted his cousin. So maybe something real had happened?

Djamel got busy, and soon forgot all about it. Then one day a rash broke out all over his skin, and he felt very weak. The doctors tried different medicines, and

his parents tried traditional sorcery—but nothing helped. Djamel felt awful, and was angry at being stuck in bed all day: no football, and no time with friends.

Karim heard about Djamel's illness, and came to visit.

"Maybe you should pray to God, thank him, and ask him to help," he suggested. Karim had been watching Christian programs on TV, and was learning about prayer and healing. That night, Djamel prayed the way Karim told him. When he woke up the next morning, he noticed his anger was gone. *What's happening?* he thought. He looked down and saw that he was completely healed from his rash. He told his parents about his prayer. When they saw his skin was clear, they immediately prayed and thanked God.

TO HELP YOU PRAY FOR THE KABYLE

YOU CAN THANK GOD FOR:

- the growth of the church in Algeria—especially among the Kabyle people.

- Kabyle who boldly share about Jesus with their family and friends, even when badly treated.

YOU CAN ASK GOD:

- to allow all children—especially girls—to go to school.

- to bring many more Kabyle to Jesus—as well as other Imazighen and Arabs.

- for Kabyle missionaries to tell others in North Africa about Jesus.

- for the leaders of Algeria to follow God's ways, and bring security and peace to the country.

KAZAKHSTAN
Nomads and Space Rockets

Kazakhstan is a huge Central Asian country, stretching from the Caspian Sea in the west to China in the east. It's the largest landlocked country in the world. High, grassy plains called steppes stretch across the northern part of the country, while in the south are dry, sandy deserts. To the east, the Altai and Tien Shan mountains form a border with China. Astana—the new capital, in the middle of the northern steppe—rises out of the desert, sparkling like a fairy-tale city, with many futuristic buildings.

RUSSIA

ASTANA

KAZAKHSTAN

Almaty

Caspian
Sea

UZBEKISTAN

KYRGYZSTAN

TURKMENISTAN

CHINA

For centuries, the Kazakh people were nomads, traveling across the steppes with their herds of horses, sheep, cattle, and camels, looking for good pasture. About two hundred years ago, the Russian Empire began to occupy Kazakhstan. Thousands of Russians came to live here, forcing the Kazakh nomads from their land. Many nomads were made to live in villages and towns, and others fled to China with their animals. Today, the majority of people in the country are Kazakh, but as many as one in four is Russian.

The Russian settlers were mainly farmers, growing wheat on land previously used to graze animals. They also started to mine iron and lead. When Russia controlled Kazakhstan, they used the land for nuclear tests—there were as many as 470 nuclear explosions in forty years. Many people living in those areas developed serious health problems.

Kazakhstan was— and still is—used by the

Russian space program. The Baikonur Cosmodrome, in central Kazakhstan, was the world's first spaceport. In 1957, the first space rocket, Sputnik I, was launched from here, as was Vostok I in 1961, which sent the first human into outer space.

FACT FILE

AREA: Around 1 million square miles (world's ninth largest country)

POPULATION: 18.4 million

CAPITAL: Astana

MAIN LANGUAGES: Kazakh, Russian

MAIN RELIGIONS: Islam (among Kazakhs); Orthodox Christianity (among Russians)

CHIEF EXPORTS: Oil, gas, and metals

Astana

Mosque

Since 1991, Kazakhstan has been independent from Russia. It developed rapidly, because there's so much oil, coal, and gold. The country also has the world's largest chrome mine. Although some Kazakhs are still very poor, many others have the latest gadgets and smart phones. And, for the first time in their history, Kazakhs are starting to travel abroad for holidays, or to study.

There is a saying: "To be a Kazakh is to be a Muslim," although today not many Kazakhs go to the mosque. They are more likely to visit the grave of a Kazakh healer to seek a blessing or the answer to a problem. Recently, other Muslim countries have sent missionaries to Kazakhstan to spread Islam, and fasting during the Muslim month of Ramadan has become more common. Yet, at the same time, more Kazakhs have started following Jesus than ever before.

FORGIVE ME!

Aibek cried, although he was trying not to. His father had come home drunk yet again, and started to throw things at his mother. When this happened, Aibek usually hid till his father fell asleep. His mother had tried everything to stop his father drinking: she had been to the traditional healer, and carefully followed her instructions. They had all traveled twenty hours by train to visit a holy place. She had visited the mosque—and had even lit a candle in the Russian Orthodox church, just in case. But nothing seemed to work. Aibek was losing hope.

Now Aibek could hear his uncle talking to his parents. Uncle Nurlan used to drink even more than Aibek's father,

and had been to jail. But now he was different. "My cousins are so lucky!" Aibek thought. He wished his father would change too.

Uncle Nurlan was explaining that it was Jesus who had changed his life and helped him stop drinking. Would any of them like to follow Jesus, too?

There was silence.

Then Aibek rushed out of his bedroom, shouting, "Me! I want to follow Jesus. And I want a new life for dad too."

His father started to cry. It was the first time Aibek had seen him in tears.

"Yes, I want to start again with Jesus," said Aibek's father. "I know I've really messed up—not just my own life, but everyone else's too. Will you forgive me, son?"

"Let's kneel together and ask Jesus to forgive us," suggested Uncle Nurlan. "All of us have done things that hurt him, and hurt others. We can ask him to bless our family, and help us forgive one another."

They prayed. As they did so, Aibek felt peace, hope, and joy fill his heart. He was sure life would never be the same.

Kazakh eagle hunter

KURDS
A People Without a Country

PERSECUTED

There are more than thirty million Kurds in the world. They have their own culture, traditions, and languages. Most live in the heart of the Middle East, in a rugged, mountainous area often called Kurdistan, "the land of the Kurds." But Kurdistan is not a country. It spreads across parts of Turkey, Iran, Iraq, and Syria, countries that have often treated the Kurds cruelly. They want them to forget they are Kurds and see themselves only as citizens of the countries where they live. As a result, the Kurds have often been involved in long, violent struggles.

About half of all Kurds live in Turkey, mostly in the eastern part. For many, this has been their homeland for thousands of years—Kurds are even mentioned in the Bible, where they are called Medes. But some Kurds in Turkey are refugees, who have fled violence and persecution in Syria and Iraq.

HEARING THE GOOD NEWS

The Kurds are mostly Muslims, and follow different branches of Islam. But they don't usually follow as strict a version of Islam as many of the peoples around them.

For many years, it was difficult for Christians to visit areas where the Kurds live. But more recently, Christians have been able to visit some of the regions where the Kurds live, and share the good news of Jesus Christ. They have often brought food, medicine, and other aid, to help families in times of need. Groups of Kurdish believers now exist in some of these places, and want to reach out with the good news to more of their own people. This has happened especially in the area of northern Iraq where Kurds live.

Some Kurds have had dreams and visions about Jesus. Some want to learn more about him after they read God's Word in their own language.

Others hear the gospel while living abroad. Thousands of Kurds have left their homelands and settled in other countries. Although they often have to work for very low pay, they believe life there is better for their families.

TERRIBLE SCARS

Khaled clapped his hands. At last he'd passed his English exam.

A bomb hit Khaled's home in Kirkuk, Iraq, when he was younger. He has terrible scars on his face where he was burned. His parents fled to the Kurdistan Region, taking Khaled and his ten brothers and sisters. Now Khaled could start school. His father was too ill to work, so every day after school, Khaled and his brothers had to work selling cigarettes, candy, and sunflower seeds.

Because he got so tired working, and had little time to study, Khaled

Lake Darbandikhan, Iraq

DO YOU KNOW?

The Kurds are the fourth largest people group in their region after the Arabs, Persians, and Turks. Yet—unlike the other large groups—they have no country of their own.

TO HELP YOU PRAY FOR THE KURDS

YOU CAN THANK GOD FOR:

- more and more Kurdish people who are seeking the truth and encountering God.

- small groups of Kurdish believers, including entire families, who follow Jesus.

- the whole Bible in Sorani Kurdish, and the New Testament in Kurmanji, both in print and on the Internet.

YOU CAN ASK GOD:

- to give peace to the areas where Kurds live.

- for Kurds to be treated fairly by the countries where they live.

- that—wherever Kurdish refugees live—Christians will welcome them and share Jesus with them.

- that every Kurd will have a chance to hear the good news about Jesus.

- for completion of the Kurmanji Old Testament and the Behdini Kurdish New Testament.

- to help Kurdish Christians keep learning how to follow Jesus, and how to share him with other Kurds.

failed his English exam the first time. He *really* wanted to pass. A Christian family invited him to study English in their home. For two weeks, Khaled walked for an hour each day in the summer heat to their house. It was worth it, because this time he passed the exam. These Christians don't just help Khaled learn English—they pray that Khaled and his family will come to know Jesus.

"YOU DIRTY CHRISTIAN!"

Shoresh lives in a village in the mountains, with his brother, sister, and parents. Nobody in the area knew about Jesus. One day Shoresh's father found a New Testament at a friend's house. He read it from cover to cover in one sitting. His father knew this was the truth he'd been searching for all his life.

Shoresh was six years old, and loved the story of Jesus too. But today, while he was playing with the other children in the street, they started to tease him saying, "You dirty Christian!"

This made him upset, so he yelled, "I'm not a Christian!" and ran inside.

He knelt in a corner, sobbing. "Oh Jesus, I'm sorry. I didn't mean that."

OUR FATHER

Fatima lived in a Kurdish area of Turkey. One day, in her religion class, the teacher was telling all the third graders how to pray the traditional Muslim way.

"My family doesn't pray that way anymore," said Fatima.

"What?" said the teacher in surprise. "Everyone prays that way." It was the Muslim way, and everyone the teacher knew was Muslim. "How do you pray?" she asked Fatima.

"Our Father who is in heaven . . ." began Fatima. After she had recited the whole of the Lord's Prayer in the Kurmanji language, the teacher was almost in tears.

"That's a lovely prayer, and in our own language!" she said. "Let's all learn it next time."

It is not always easy for the children of Kurdish believers—but God helps them.

LESOTHO
The Switzerland of Africa

Only three countries in the world are surrounded completely by another country. Lesotho (pronounced *Le-soo-too*) is one of them—a small country entirely inside South Africa. It has no coastline, and no other neighbors. If you visited Lesotho, you would find many mountains, fast-flowing streams, and rushing rivers. Because it's usually cool and damp in Lesotho, people wrap-up in warm, colorful blankets. Traditionally, they wear cone-shaped hats, made of woven grass.

Most of the two million people living in Lesotho are Basotho and speak a language called Sesotho. Lesotho is one of the world's poorest countries. Because there aren't enough jobs in Lesotho, many of the men go to South Africa to work in mines and on farms. Over 300,000 people from Lesotho live in South Africa. Because so many of the men are away much of the farm work in Lesotho is done by the women.

MASERU
LESOTHO
SOUTH AFRICA
ZIMBABWE
NAMIBIA
BOTSWANA
MOZAMBIQUE
SWAZILAND
LESOTHO

SHEPHERD BOYS

In many countries, boys go to school while the girls stay at home to help their families. But not in Lesotho. Basotho boys from poor rural families sometimes start looking after the sheep, goats, and cattle when they're still only seven years old. Wool from the sheep and mohair made from goat's hair are two of Lesotho's main exports. The animals are very valuable.

If you were a shepherd boy in Lesotho, you would spend weeks away from home, all by yourself, looking after sheep and goats in the mountains. In summer it rains, and in winter it's very cold. You wouldn't have a warm house, a fire, or even dry clothes to wear. What would you think about during the long, dark nights? What would you do if thieves or wild animals came to steal or kill your animals? You'd be in big trouble if you didn't keep all your animals safe. Remember King David in the Bible was also a shepherd boy—you can read about his adventures in the Old Testament. May all of Lesotho's shepherd boys be as close to God as David was!

Some of the shepherd boys who can read and write teach their

FACT FILE

AREA: 11,720 square miles

POPULATION: 2.3 million

CAPITAL: Maseru

MAIN LANGUAGES: Sesotho and English

MAIN RELIGION: Christianity

CHIEF EXPORTS: Wool, diamonds, livestock, footwear, and clothing

DO YOU KNOW?

Lesotho is the only country in the world with its entire area above 3,000 feet. Its higher peaks usually have snow all year round. This is partly why Lesotho is known as "the Switzerland of Africa."

shepherd friends. If boys can read, they will get better jobs in Lesotho when they grow up. In the towns, boys and girls generally go to school. But most of Lesotho's population is rural. A Christian ministry called Scripture Union tells many Basotho children about Jesus.

TEACHERS WHO RODE ON HORSEBACK

Almost ninety percent of the people in Lesotho call themselves Christian. Churches have existed there for generations. But many people still belong to secret societies that use magic, curses, and charms. Some also worship the spirits of their ancestors. Such beliefs and practices are forbidden in the Bible—but learning what the Bible says can be difficult in Lesotho. Although there is now free schooling for children, many older Basotho can't read. And most pastors aren't able to get good Bible training. As well as pastoring, they have to do other jobs to provide for their families. Christians who live in remote mountain villages have no Bible schools nearby. In the past,

teachers or missionaries would come from the towns on horseback, by plane, or on foot to explain what the Bible says. New and better roads are being built, but more help is needed.

FLYING AMBULANCE

The Missionary Aviation Fellowship (MAF) has built forty aircraft runways throughout Lesotho. Their planes carry supplies and doctors to areas that are difficult to reach, and sometimes fly patients to hospital.

"It was lots of fun—but kind of scary—flying in the plane," recalls Mokeane, a little Basotho boy. "I broke my arm, and an MAF pilot flew me to hospital in Maseru. I loved looking out of the plane and seeing the tiny rivers and trees. It took only twenty-five minutes to get there. If we'd gone on horseback and bus, it would have taken nine or ten hours."

TO HELP YOU PRAY FOR LESOTHO

YOU CAN THANK GOD FOR:

- many people in the capital city, Maseru, who are coming to know Jesus as their friend.

- the boys and girls who are learning about Jesus through Scripture Union.

- Christians who go into mountain villages to share the good news of Jesus' love.

YOU CAN ASK GOD:

- to protect MAF pilots as they fly into remote villages with medical care.

- to keep the shepherd boys safe, and bring many of them to know Jesus. Pray that they can enjoy his creation during their long hours alone outdoors.

- to help pastors get Bible training, so they can teach others to follow his ways.

- to provide ways that Lesotho's Christians can learn the Bible and follow its teachings.

LOBI
The People Who Filed Their Teeth into Points

AN ANCIENT RITUAL

Sié watched the long line of people hurrying down the road. There were children, some not much bigger than him, women carrying cooking pots and sacks of food on their heads, and even a few men cracking whips to make everyone move quickly. Sié shivered as he heard piercing cries, chanted by the children as they marched along. These cries are heard every seven years, at the time of the *joro*. Sié was afraid. Even though he was the oldest child in his family, he was too young this time—but he knew his turn would come.

Joro means initiation. It is through this secret ceremony that a child is accepted as a true member of the Lobi. These ceremonies take place every seven years. Lobi tribal leaders in Burkina Faso and Côte d'Ivoire take children who are at least seven years old into the bush for several weeks. They undergo tests of bravery before being dedicated to a large idol. Some children's teeth are filed into points. There are also some children who sadly never return home. The families aren't allowed to ask what happened to them. It's enough to know that the spirit of the *joro* took them.

Although everyone who has been through the *joro* is forbidden to talk about it to those who haven't, Sié knew enough to be very frightened. He had heard whispered stories about the rituals. His family all had pointed teeth. As he heard the terrified cries fade into the distance, he wondered, "Do I have to go through the *joro* too? Is there no other way to become a true Lobi?"

CONTROLLED BY FEAR

Fear of the spirit world affects every part of Lobi life. Everything must be protected from evil spirits. A life-sized clay idol guards the home. Lobi homes look like mini fortresses built from clay, with very few, if any, windows.

From May to September, most Lobis work in the fields, growing millet, sorghum, maize, peanuts, and yams. The grains are

BURKINA FASO

GHANA

CÔTE D'IVOIRE

BURKINA FASO

GHANA

CÔTE D'IVOIRE

Lobi potter

90

![lightbulb icon]

DO YOU KNOW?

Many years ago, Lobi women made holes in both lips and inserted large, round pieces of wood to stretch them. To the Lobi, this made the women look beautiful. But it also made them look strange to other tribes, so slave traders wouldn't take them. Some Lobi women still wear these lip ornaments.

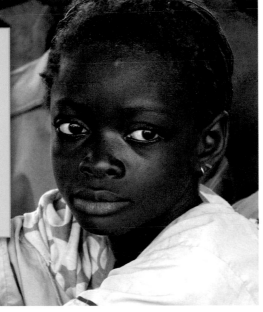

Lobi fetish or magic charm

all dried in the sun before being stored in round mud granaries with thatched roofs.

The number of Lobis who are coming to know Jesus is increasing. Every time a Lobi decides to follow Jesus, they have to break free from the power of the *joro* and the fetishes (good luck charms with spiritual power) kept by most Lobi. It is very hard for Lobi Christians to live a life free of these influences. In some areas where Lobi live, there are churches and meeting places where Christians worship. One of these churches is in Nako, one of the main places where the *joro* ceremonies take place. Groups of Christian Lobi have been trained to share the good news about Jesus with their people. They also tell other animistic and Muslim peoples in Burkina Faso about Jesus.

The New Testament has been translated into Lobi. Although today most children and young people are learning to read, very few of the older generation can read.

Perhaps Sié will not have to go to the *joro* to become a true Lobi. Every time the ceremonies are held, Christians pray that the spirits will lose their power over people. There are signs that God is answering these prayers. Please join in praying that the Lobi will become the children of God, who gives life.

Lobi granary under construction

TO HELP YOU PRAY FOR THE LOBI

YOU CAN THANK GOD FOR:

- the Lobi New Testament and good progress on the Old Testament.

- Christian Lobis training for ministry at Bible school and through other programs.

- the power of Jesus, which is stronger than the power of the *joro*.

YOU CAN ASK GOD:

- that Lobis who are learning to read will read the New Testament.

- to help the people translating the Old Testament into Lobi to find the right words.

- to free the Lobi from all fear and from the evil spirits.

- that young people will understand they need not be afraid of the *joro* if they trust in Jesus.

- that God will answer the prayers of the church in Nako. For spirits to lose their power over the people and the *joro* ceremonies to end.

MADAGASCAR
Where People Gave Their Lives for Jesus

If you look at a map of Africa, you will see a long, narrow island in the Indian Ocean, about 250 miles off the coast of southeast Africa. This is Madagascar. It's the fourth largest island in the world.

Peter is in a plane flying east across this island, bringing his friend Seth home with him for their school holidays. The western part of the island is mostly dry, with long stretches of red dirt interrupted by fields of rice, cassava, and a few grazing cattle. Soon they're over the big central plateau, where most of the people live.

"Look!" Peter says. "There's Antananarivo, the capital city. Look for the old churches and palaces."

As they pass over the central plateau, the plane flies across the forests of the eastern plain, toward the coastal sandy beaches. "These hills and valleys used to be covered with forests," he explains. "But people cut down most of the trees for firewood, and to make space for farming. With the forests gone, the heavy rains now wash away a bit more of the hillside each year. This makes it more and more difficult for people to grow crops there."

"Most people in Madagascar are very poor," Peter continues. "In some areas, there's not enough rain to farm. In others, the cyclones passing over every year destroy much of the crops. Many children can't easily get to school, either because the journey is too difficult, or their parents need them to work the fields instead. Although Madagascar is rich in resources, it's the sixth poorest country in the world."

Seth was excited to meet Peter's friends, to understand what life was like for people on the island, and to explore this new country.

Because of poverty, many people in Madagascar forget about God. They're too busy looking for ways to survive from day to day. Many get tricked by false teachers, who promise them immediate riches, while taking all their money.

FACT FILE

AREA: 226,660 square miles

POPULATION: 26.3 million

CAPITAL: Antananarivo

MAIN LANGUAGES: Malagasy, French

MAIN RELIGIONS: Most are Christian or animist; small Muslim minority

CHIEF EXPORTS: Coffee, cloves, vanilla, fish, tropical fruits, minerals, gemstones, and textiles

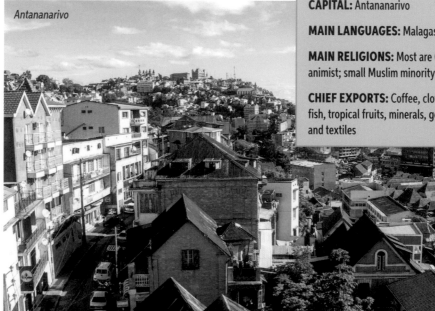
Antananarivo

Ring-tailed lemur

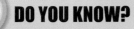
THE BOOK THAT WOULDN'T BURN

Almost two hundred years ago, two men from Wales brought the good news about Jesus to Madagascar. Only one of them, David Jones, survived more than a few months. He set up a little school, where the king's son was one of the first students. The language of Madagascar—Malagasy—had never been written down, so the children had no books.

Later, other missionaries arrived and put the language into writing. They taught both the children and their parents to read. They told them about Jesus, and translated the Bible into Malagasy. Many people asked Jesus to be their Savior.

Then a new ruler, Queen Ranavalona, decided her people should go back to their old beliefs—worshiping their ancestors and dead kings and queens. She ordered that anyone who prayed to Jesus should be put to death.

Many Christians continued to meet in secret—in houses, in caves, or on mountaintops. The queen tortured and killed thousands who wouldn't stop following Jesus. She also tried to burn all the copies of the Bible in her language. But she failed: God's words survived in Malagasy. Ranavalona reigned for thirty-three years, but when she died there were more Christians than when she became queen. God is much more powerful than any human ruler! After Ranavalona died, her son was more open to Christianity. More missionaries came and helped the church in Madagascar to grow.

MUCH TO BE DONE

Although close to half the people in Madagascar call themselves Christians, many worship the spirits of deceased members of their family, called *Razana*. They believe this helps them find favor with God. But that isn't true.

Some Christians realize this, and truly love and follow only Jesus. Christians in the villages need to learn to read and write, so they can understand what the Bible says. Some volunteers teach reading using special Bibles. Most of the population in Madagascar is younger than twenty-four, so missionaries and church members often work with children.

Some people groups in Madagascar have still never heard of Jesus because their villages are remote, and there are no roads into the mountains and rain forests where they live. Pray that they will hear about Jesus and put their trust in him.

TO HELP YOU PRAY FOR MADAGASCAR

YOU CAN THANK GOD FOR:

- missionaries, church leaders, and the work of the Malagasy Bible Society.

- the fact that people can worship God freely.

- many young people who have chosen to follow Jesus.

YOU CAN ASK GOD:

- to help Christians today to be faithful to Jesus and worship him alone.

- for many young people to know Jesus and to tell others about him.

- for more Christians to go to places where people have never heard of Jesus.

- that more Christian books and audio programs would be made available in the Malagasy language.

MALDIVES
Beautiful Ocean Islands

HOLIDAY PARADISE

Peter's father pulled an atlas from the bookshelf and opened it to show him a map of India. "Look, Peter!" he said, pointing to a chain of tiny islands in the Indian Ocean. "These are the Maldives. I thought we might go there this summer. We would fly to India, and then another 300 miles southwest." He traced the chain of islands with his finger. "We won't be able to see all the islands—they stretch right down to the equator. That's around 500 miles." He handed Peter a travel magazine. "See for yourself how beautiful they are."

"Wow!" exclaimed Peter. "Coral islands! Coconut trees! And sandy beaches! The islands look as if they're floating in the sea." Peter started to read the magazine. "I can't wait to go! We must take snorkels and do lots of swimming . . . and wind surfing . . . and scuba diving."

Every year thousands of people visit the Maldives to lie in the sun and swim in the clear blue sea. Some stay in hotels built for tourists. The government used to keep most people away from the tourists, who only ever met the Maldivians working in the hotels. But this is changing, as more travelers visit the local islands and meet people who live there.

INDIA

SRI LANKA

Indian Ocean

MALDIVES

FACT FILE

LAND AREA: 115 square miles

POPULATION: 444,000

CAPITAL: Malé

MAIN LANGUAGES: Dhivehi; some English

MAIN RELIGION: Islam

ECONOMY: Fishing and tourism

Minaret of a mosque

DO YOU KNOW?

The four Gospels were translated into Dhivehi, the language of the Maldives, more than 200 years ago. But the Christian translators all got sick and died, and the Maldivian helper went home before they could be printed. The translations were lost. To this day, only Luke and Acts have been published in Dhivehi.

MORE THAN 1,200 ISLANDS

"Dad, I've been reading more about the Maldives," Peter said a few nights later. "Did you know there are at least 1,200 little islands—but only 200 are inhabited? Most are so flat that, if the sea level rose even a little, they would disappear! And most of the beautiful coral reefs that once attracted the tropical fish are now dead. People think it's because the ocean is getting too warm. The government is very worried about the future of their country."

"I've found out a bit more too," said his father. "The people of the Maldives call themselves *Dhivehi*, which means 'islanders'. Their language is also called *Dhivehi*—and they write it from right to left! There are schools where the children learn in English. Some Maldivians later go abroad to study, but the Maldives has a national university and several colleges." "Boat building is an important business, and more than one third of the people are fishermen. Money from all the tourism is also very important."

EVIL SPIRITS

"Have you found out about their religion, dad? Do they have lots of gods and temples, like we saw in India?"

"The Maldivians are Muslims. But they're also afraid of *jinns*, or evil spirits. Many people are so frightened that they won't go out after dark. They often wear blue glass charms around their neck to protect them from the *jinns*. But we don't need to be afraid of evil spirits, because Jesus is more powerful than they are. Jesus will always protect us."

Peter shivered. "I know! But this talk about evil spirits is scary. Aren't there any Christians there?"

His father shook his head. "Very few," he said. "The government has never allowed missionaries. Christians from other countries sometimes go there to work. They can read the Bible and pray in private, but they aren't allowed to talk about Jesus to Maldivian people. Some foreign Christians have had to leave the country for talking about Jesus, and Maldivian Christians can be put in prison. It's not easy to follow Jesus there."

"But God can change things, can't he?" asked Peter. "Let's start praying that the people of the Maldives will hear the good news that Jesus saves them and protects them from evil spirits."

TO HELP YOU PRAY FOR THE MALDIVES

YOU CAN THANK GOD FOR:

- Christian material in Dhivehi—including Luke and Acts, the *JESUS* film, Christian songs, Bible stories, and Gospel messages—all available online.

- the handful of Maldivian Christians, and the Christian foreigners who live and work in the Maldives.

YOU CAN ASK GOD:

- to strengthen and encourage the Christians in the Maldives. Pray that they will fearlessly share the love of Jesus with Maldivians through their words and the lives that they live.

- for Maldivians to discover that by trusting in Jesus, they can be freed from the fear and power of evil spirits.

- to help Maldivians who study abroad meet Christians who will share God's love with them.

- that the leaders of the country will allow everyone to worship in the way they choose.

MANDINKA
The People Who Hope Charms Will Keep Them Safe

CHARMS FOR A BABY

Nene cuddled her baby boy. Outside her mud and thatch house, the village people were singing and dancing. The Muslim teacher, called a *marabout*, had come, and Nene paid him to tie ten *juju* charms around her baby's arms, neck, and waist. She hoped they would protect him from sickness and evil spirits.

But Nene was worried. The charms hadn't worked for her other three babies who had all died. She wanted to take the children to the Christian nurse at the nearby clinic, but her husband wouldn't let her. "If you do that," he told her, "they'll make you take off the *jujus* and burn them. That's against our Mandinka ways—and the children won't be protected from the evil spirits."

The *marabout* makes *jujus* by writing verses from the Qur'an on bits of paper. Then he sews them into little leather pouches and hangs them on a string. Some Mandinka believe the power of these *jujus* comes from Allah. Others say these practices are wrong and follow Islam without *jujus* or *marabouts*.

JOURNEY TO A NEW LIFE

Mandinkas make up almost half the people living in the little West African country of The Gambia. Many centuries ago, they left their homeland in Mali as traders, looking for new places to trade. Eventually they settled in The Gambia and the surrounding countries.

The Mandinkas were animists. They believed that each river, tree, and hill had a spirit. In time, almost every Mandinka became Muslim. But most have kept their traditional beliefs too.

SCARED OF THE DARK

Bakary sat near the fire and listened as the grownups told scary stories about

SENEGAL

THE GAMBIA

GUINEA-BISSAU

GUINEA

FACT FILE

LOCATION: West Africa

NUMBERS: Almost 2 million

MAIN COUNTRIES: Senegal, The Gambia, and Guinea-Bissau

MAIN LANGUAGE: Mandinka

MAIN RELIGION: Islam

OCCUPATIONS: Farming and trading

beautiful women who were really witches who sold captured children and used their power to make people sick and die. He had strange dreams and became scared of the dark.

"I'm always afraid," he told his mother one day. "I can't sleep. I wish I had a protector who would look after me, who was more powerful than the witches and spirits."

"We're Muslims," said his mother. "We believe in Allah. He will help you." So Bakary learned as much as he could from the Muslim teachers. He prayed five times a day and fasted during the month of Ramadan—but he was still afraid.

Bakary wanted to do well at school so he could get a good job and help his

Twenty-one-stringed kora

DO YOU KNOW?

Many Mandinka cannot read. People learn a lot about life and history through older people telling stories to younger people. The *griot* (*gree-oh*) is a Mandinka musician who tells ancient stories through songs— a walking history book! He usually plays a large, harp-like instrument called a *kora*.

TO HELP YOU PRAY FOR THE MANDINKA

YOU CAN THANK GOD FOR:

- the Mandinka Bible.

- medical clinics, youth centers, and other places where people can experience God's love and learn about him from Christians working there.

YOU CAN ASK GOD:

- that Mandinkas who are learning to read will read the Bible and understand it.

- to help Mandinka Christians follow Jesus faithfully, care for others, and tell them about his love.

- for Mandinka musicians who will tell Bible stories through songs using Mandinka styles and instruments.

- to show Mandinkas that he is far greater and more powerful than the spirits they fear.

- to send more missionaries to the Mandinka people to tell them about Jesus.

mother. At his Christian high school, he learned about Jesus, who the teachers called the Son of God. Bakary was confused. Islam taught that God was spirit, and could have no sons or daughters. "Which is true?" he wondered. "The religion of the Muslims or the Christians?"

Bakary started to study the Bible. He wanted to prove that Jesus wasn't really the Son of God, so he could be sure Islam was true. But while he was reading, he discovered that Jesus had power over evil spirits and could take away his fear. Now Bakary wanted to become a Christian, but was afraid his mother would be angry. He knew he'd found the truth. He could follow Jesus—or go on being afraid.

Bakary told his teacher he wanted to follow Jesus. Now he knows Jesus is with him and helps him when he's

afraid. His mother was angry at first. But when she saw the change in Bakary's life—his dreams stopped, and the dark didn't bother him—she wanted to follow Jesus too.

SHOWING GOD'S LOVE

There aren't many Mandinka Christians, but missionaries are also there to help show God's love to the Mandinka. They offer medical care, reading classes, and youth centers where young people can learn useful skills. In 2013, translators completed the Mandinka Bible. Pray that many more Mandinkas will trust Jesus, who will take away their fears.

Traditional tribal costume and mask

MEXICO
Where Gods Became Saints

TWO MARIAS

In Mexico City, two girls called Maria live just twenty feet apart. But they will never meet. Between their homes stands a high wall, dividing a poor slum from a rich neighborhood.

The first Maria goes to a private school. Her father drives her there in an expensive air-conditioned car. He works in a bank and her brother does too.

The second Maria doesn't have a father at home; her mother is raising her alone. She won't have the chance to finish school. Soon she will have to work to help her mother. Her brother belongs to a gang that sells drugs. Sometimes he visits them and tries to give them money—but they won't take it.

The first Maria occasionally goes to a Catholic church, but not very often. It has beautiful statues of many different saints. The priest there talks about God, Jesus, and Our Lady of Guadalupe (the Virgin Mary). Maria is taught to pray to Guadalupe and to some of the saints.

The second Maria goes to an evangelical church every week. The church doesn't have fancy decorations, but the singing is full of energy and the preaching full of passion. The pastor talks a lot about the power of the Holy Spirit, and how Jesus can help people with all their problems. The services overflow with people.

Both Marias love to play games and sing songs with their friends. Both Marias watch *telenovelas* (soap operas) and music shows on TV. Both Marias wonder what life is like on the other side of the wall. I wonder what would happen if the two Marias met?

RIDING "THE BEAST"

Juan edged closer to his father. He felt safer there.

"Take food and water, and may the Virgin bless you on your journey," his father told the young men. Juan was from a farming family and grew corn in their fields.

Juan's father worked all day in his fields, and on some evenings he helped the migrants who passed by the farm. When there was something to spare, Juan's mother and sister made food parcels, and his father passed them out.

"Some people don't like the migrants, Juan. They hurt them, or rob them of what little they have. They would be angry that we are helping. But the migrants are only trying to find a

FACT FILE

AREA: 762,000 square miles

POPULATION: 131 million

CAPITAL: Mexico City

MAIN LANGUAGES: Spanish, with 68 indigenous languages and 285 total languages

MAIN RELIGIONS: Christianity, mostly Roman Catholic

ECONOMY: Agriculture: mainly corn and beans; manufacturing: food, electronics, cars; oil

Traditional Mexican costume

Cathedral, Mexico City

Pre-Hispanic mask

better life in the United States. Here on the farm, we have enough to live. God would want us to be generous to them, and perhaps Our Lady of Guadalupe will bless us as we help others."

Migrants often passed by the farm because it was near the train tracks of *La Bestia* (The Beast). That's the nickname for the network of freight trains that run through Mexico to the US border. Some people call it "the train of death." Riding on it is illegal and very dangerous, but every other way to the border is dangerous too.

Juan remembered how, at first, the migrants were all from Mexico. Then they started to come from Central American countries: Guatemala, Honduras, and Nicaragua. Now, some were from as far as Africa and Asia! Sometimes there were children on their own, not much older than Juan. Juan wondered how many made it safely in to the United States.

As the group disappeared back into the cornfields, one teenager came back and kissed Juan's father's hands. "God bless you, *Señor*."

LAND OF MANY LANGUAGES AND TRIBES

Mexico has many different kinds of people—native tribes, whites, and blacks, as well as more recent immigrants from Asia and Africa. But most Mexicans are *mestizos*, a racial mix of Spanish colonists and native tribes. Mexico has more Spanish speakers than any country in the world, but there are also sixty-eight native languages.

The government has created programs to help keep these languages alive so that they are used by native cultures.

Today the biggest problem for Mexico is illegal drugs. These drugs are made in South America, but mostly used in the United States. Mexico is between these two places, so the drugs are usually shipped through Mexico. The drugs are worth a lot of money, and the gangs controlling them are rich and powerful. Even the police and the government can't stop them. Many people get killed because of this drug trade.

Most Mexicans are Roman Catholic. But Catholicism in Mexico is mixed with beliefs and traditions from local tribal religions. A lot of the saints in Mexican Catholic churches are really the local gods, just with new names.

Evangelical churches are growing fast in Mexico. They increase fastest among the poorest people and native tribes.

DO YOU KNOW?

Chocolate originally comes from Mexico. Long ago, people in Mexico made *xocoatl* to drink for strength. They added hot spices to cacao; it tasted bitter and spicy. Europeans later added sugar to make what we call chocolate.

TO HELP YOU PRAY FOR MEXICO

YOU CAN THANK GOD FOR:

■ the many people from different backgrounds who follow Jesus.

■ the growth of evangelical churches, where people can learn the Bible.

■ people who translate the Bible into native languages.

YOU CAN ASK GOD:

■ to end the evil drug trade, and change the hearts of the people involved.

■ to help the many children who are poor or fatherless.

■ to work in the hearts of Roman Catholics. They believe in him, but their native traditions get in the way of knowing Jesus personally.

■ to protect the migrants traveling through Mexico, and reveal Jesus to them.

Guanajuato

MINANGKABAU
People of the Water Buffalo

The Minangkabau people love telling a legend about a water buffalo. About six hundred years ago, the king of the nearby island of Java tried to conquer the Minang homeland of West Sumatra. The people of West Sumatra knew they weren't strong enough to win a war, but they had an idea.

"Pick your best water buffalo to fight our best buffalo," they told the king. "If your buffalo wins, we'll serve you. But if ours wins, you must never attack us again."

The king of Java agreed. He found the biggest, fiercest water buffalo in Java. He was sure he would win.

Traditional costumes

On the day of the contest, his enormous buffalo stomped onto the field. The Javanese soldiers laughed when they saw the buffalo the people of West Sumatra sent out. It was a tiny calf. How silly to think such a little creature could beat their giant!

But the Javanese didn't know their enemy had a plan. For three days, the West Sumatrans had starved the baby buffalo of its mother's milk, so it was very hungry. They also tied small, sharp knives to its little baby horns. When the calf saw the big water buffalo, he thought it was his mother, and rushed toward it. He pushed his head under the Javanese buffalo's belly searching for milk. As he did so, the knives on his horns cut into the big animal. Bellowing with pain, the huge buffalo ran away and lost the fight.

"*Minang kabau!*" ("Our buffalo is the winner!") the West Sumatrans shouted. So the people of West Sumatra began to call themselves the Minangkabau, because they were proud of how clever they were. Even today, the Minangkabau make horn-shaped corners on the roofs of their houses, and for special ceremonies the women wear fancy headdresses shaped like the horns of the water

buffalo. The Minang people are proud of their commitment to good education, keeping up the tradition of being smart, clever people.

MOTHER'S NAME

In most parts of the world, a person's surname comes from their father. But the Minangkabau use their mother's name instead. Other customs are unusual, too. The men are leaders in the clan; but the women own the rice fields and houses. Because they don't own land, the men often leave their home village to find work

DO YOU KNOW?

All Minangkabau children learn at least two languages. They speak Minangkabau at home, but at school they speak Indonesian, the national language.

in bigger towns, only returning to help at harvest time.

Some never go back to their home village, so there are now Minangkabau men in every part of Indonesia. Many of them open restaurants, where they serve a well-known hot, spicy food called *Nasi Padang*. They are known as good politicians, religious leaders, and skilled artists.

SCATTERED PEOPLE

Altogether, there are close to nine million Minangkabau. Around half of them live in the mountainous region of West Sumatra. The rest are scattered elsewhere on Sumatra and throughout the Indonesian islands.

Sumatra suffers badly from natural disasters. In 2004, a tsunami killed thousands of people. Just five years later, a major earthquake caused more damage in West Sumatra, the homeland of the Minangkabau.

Most of the Minangkabau are Muslim. They have a saying, "To be Minangkabau is to be Muslim." Along with their Islamic beliefs, they also hold onto some of the traditions from the religion they followed before Islam came to Indonesia. They try to use magic to protect themselves from the spirits that live in the forests and mountains and cause sickness or trouble.

Minangkabau who become Christians know they'll probably lose their jobs, and their families may throw them out of the house. They may even be taken to the religious courts and be put in jail.

There are only a few thousand Minangkabau Christians. How will the rest of the Minang hear the good news? Many are well-educated, successful people, who travel widely. Some hear about Jesus as they listen to the radio, watch TV, or browse the internet.

On a business trip to the United States, a Minangkabau man named Pak Iman found a Bible in his hotel room. He started to read it and took it home with him. For six years, Pak Iman read the Bible. He also watched the Christians where he worked, to see how they lived. Finally, he decided to follow Jesus—but he was afraid to tell his wife and children. How surprised he was when he discovered his wife had been reading the Bible! Pak Iman found out that she and their children wanted to become Christians too.

TO HELP YOU PRAY FOR THE MINANGKABAU

YOU CAN THANK GOD FOR:

- the few thousand Minangkabau who know Jesus.

- the whole Bible, in print, audio, and digital formats, in the Minangkabau language.

YOU CAN ASK GOD:

- for more Christians, especially Minang believers, to talk about Jesus with the Minangkabau who haven't heard the good news.

- that Minangkabau families will decide to follow Jesus together.

- that Minangkabau people won't let their traditions and fears get in the way of following Jesus.

- to show them that they can be Christians and still be Minangkabau.

Nasi Padang

101

MONGOLIA
Burning Hot—or Bitterly Cold

MOUNTAINS AND DESERTS

Mongolia is a huge country between Russia and China. It is about the size of the whole of Western Europe. In the north are windswept mountains, plains, forests, and lakes. The Gobi Desert, in the south, is a vast wilderness of sand and gravel. Winter in Mongolia is long and bitterly cold; but summer is extremely hot in some places.

Today most Mongolians live in cities. Air pollution in the winter is one of the worst problems for city dwellers. Smoke from the coal used for cooking and heating, together with car pollution, engulfs the city for several months.

RUSSIA

KAZAKHSTAN

Erdenet

ULAANBAATAR

MONGOLIA

CHINA

During the same cold winter months, the country dwellers are busy taking their herds of sheep, goats, camels, yaks, and horses to pastures up in the mountains. They hope for a little snow so that the animals can drink, but not too much, or the animals cannot find the grass beneath the snow. Many Mongolians learn to ride a horse almost as soon as they learn to walk. There are around sixty million herd animals in Mongolia—that's almost twenty animals for every person! During the summer months, they all move back down to the grassy plains, and graze along streams and rivers or lakes, so the grass in the hills can regrow. The herding people live in felt-covered tents called *gers* (rhymes with pears), which they take with them. The gers protect them from both heat and cold.

Finding jobs can be very hard in Mongolia, and poverty is common. Most Mongolian kids go to school; but in the countryside, many kids stay at school all week and only go home on weekends. Schools are far away, and roads are not good enough to travel back and forth every day.

GENGHIS KHAN

Eight hundred years ago, the famous warrior Genghis Khan built Mongolia into the largest land empire ever known. There were a few Christians among the Mongolian tribes at the time he arrived.

Then for many centuries, Mongolia became a Buddhist country. Most families sent their eldest sons to become Buddhist monks. Few people were allowed to talk about Jesus, and few wanted to hear about him.

In 1924, Mongolia became a Communist country, under Russian rule. For the next sixty-five years, Mongolia was completely closed off to the outside world. The government destroyed many Buddhist monasteries, and banned all religion. In 1990, the Communists lost power, and people became free to choose which religion they wanted to follow. Some people returned to Buddhism,

FACT FILE

AREA: 604,250 square miles

POPULATION: 3.1 million

CAPITAL: Ulaanbaatar (around half of Mongolia's population lives here)

MAIN LANGUAGES: Khalkha Mongol, Russian

MAIN RELIGIONS: Tibetan Buddhism, large nonreligious minority

CHIEF EXPORTS: Minerals, meat, wool, and clothing

102

Ger in winter

while some turned to traditional Mongolian shamanism and consulted spirits when they needed advice. But praise God—today more and more Mongolians are becoming Christians!

GROWING UP

Udval grew up in Ulaanbaatar, Mongolia's capital. "It's the only big city in our country," she told her new Korean friend, Elaine, who was learning about Mongolia at the university. "Some city people live in apartments, but many still prefer to live in a ger. In the city, you often see tall buildings and gers standing next to each other. Gers in the city have electricity, but no running water and no inside toilets, only outhouses."

"There are some people living on the streets in Ulaanbaatar. In winter, they have to go underground into the tunnels—where pipes carry hot water to heat the buildings—because it's icy cold on the street."

"What was life like when you were a child?" asked Elaine.

"My parents both had jobs. So, with my brothers and sisters, I carried water, chopped wood, shopped, cooked, and cleaned," said Udval. "When I was at school, Buddhism was never mentioned. The Communists were in power, and they allowed just one Buddhist monastery to stay open. My father still doesn't believe in God."

"When I was little, I sometimes wondered who made the world. A man came from abroad and asked me to help translate the New Testament because I had learned to speak English in school. At first, I thought it was a children's book because of the exciting stories. Then gradually I realized it was a special book about God and his son Jesus. Now I believe what the Bible says."

NEW CHRISTIANS

In 1989, there were possibly only four Christians in Mongolia. But now tens of thousands of Mongolians are following Jesus, worshiping in hundreds of churches and groups all over the country. Already Mongolia is sending its own missionaries to places that haven't heard about Jesus. They are also making their own Mongolian-style worship music.

Christians are a large group now and recently they were given their own time for public worship in the central square of Ulaanbaatar. More than 3,000 gathered to sing and pray, and they ended by praying the Lord's Prayer together. What a change God has brought to this country in just twenty-five years!

ONE LANGUAGE, TWO SCRIPTS

Since 2000, there have been several new Mongolian translations of the Bible. One reason for this is that Mongolians speak the same language, but use two different ways of writing it. One uses the Russian alphabet, which was imposed during the Communist era and is still used today. The older Mongolian style uses a completely different alphabet, and is written vertically. It is mostly used by the Mongolians living in Inner Mongolia, a nearby province of China.

NAVAJO
Craftspeople of the American West

SKILLED WORKERS

The Navajo are the biggest group of Native Americans in the United States. They live in the western states of Arizona, New Mexico, and Utah. Although most now live in modern houses, nearly every family still has at least one *hogan*. The *hogan* is a traditional one-room home, made of wood and mud or stone. A Navajo storyteller explains the *hogan* like this:

"Long, long ago, our holy people told us that the door of the *hogan* must face east toward the rising sun. Inside, there's a special place for everyone and everything. The area for the mother and her little children is on the north side, the father and older boys use the south side for their things, and any special guests are honored with a place on the west. We hang our belongings from nails in the walls, and tuck them into crevices in the walls or up in the domed ceiling."

The Navajo are very artistic. They color wool with dyes made from desert plants, and then use it to weave beautiful rugs on handmade looms. They also make beautiful silver and turquoise jewelry. The Navajo medicine men use an amazing mixture of pollen, corn meal, crushed flowers, charcoal, and ground minerals to make sand paintings for their ceremonies. Today, the Navajo also sell framed sand paintings to art collectors and tourists.

CEREMONIES AND CELEBRATIONS

As part of their traditional religion, Navajo memorize and recite songs and chants. Some ceremonies last for nine days, and they mustn't make any mistakes. The Navajo who perform these ceremonies are often called "singers," and the ceremony is often called a "sing" or "chant."

When a baby laughs out loud for the first time, there's a special celebration for the whole family—and the person who makes the child laugh pays for the party! No wonder visitors are careful to ask if a baby has laughed out loud

FACT FILE

LOCATION: USA
Navajo Nation covers territory in Arizona, New Mexico, and Utah

NUMBERS: More than 300,000

MAIN LANGUAGES: English and Navajo

Rocks known as "Navajo Twins," in Utah

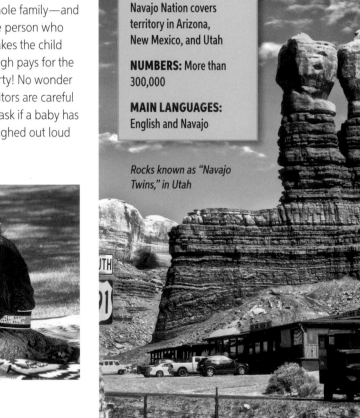

Monument Valley, Utah

Petroglyphs

yet before playing with it. Grandparents, uncles, aunts, and cousins are all included in the celebration. During the party, all the guests walk past the mother and baby, and the baby gives each of them a piece of rock salt. Salt has always been a prized item for the Navajo. By giving it away, the mother is teaching her child to be generous and share with others. This is important to the Navajo: to be stingy is to be a bad Navajo.

Many Navajo are afraid of evil spirits and witches. They take care not to do wrong things, as these make the spirits angry. They have special ceremonies to keep them from the power of evil, such as "sings" to protect them from harm, and other rituals to ask spirits to bless them.

Navajo Christians love to sing praises to the one true God, who doesn't mind if they make mistakes when they sing.

A DIFFICULT LANGUAGE

Because the Navajo language is one of the most difficult languages to learn, few people outside the tribe know how to speak it. The Americans knew this: during World War II, Navajo soldiers played an important role for the United States, sending radio messages in the Navajo language. Only the people who were meant to receive them understood them.

Only a handful of North American tribes have the whole Bible in their own language, and the Navajo are one of them. It took forty years to translate the Navajo Bible, which was first published in 1986. One of the translators was a blind Navajo, Geronimo Martin. He knew English and learned to read Braille. As he read an English Braille Bible with his fingers, he translated it aloud into Navajo, and his wife recorded his words. A blind man was able to help his own people see Jesus—by giving them the Bible.

Most of the younger generation of Navajo speak English as their first language. But many older Navajo speak only their own language. The Navajo like listening to stories, so Geronimo's wife and some other Navajo Christians have been recorded reading the Navajo Bible.

FINDING FAMILY

White settlers— including Christians—treated Navajo people poorly in the past. Today some white Christians are learning how to say sorry, and Navajo Christians are learning how to forgive. But more must join in. Other Christian groups in the United States can learn a lot from the Navajo about God and about following Jesus in a world where we all need forgiveness sometimes. We are all part of God's family, after all, and we should all serve him together!

TO HELP YOU PRAY FOR THE NAVAJO

YOU CAN THANK GOD FOR:

■ the Navajo Bible, one of the only complete Bibles in a Native American language.

■ every Navajo believer, pastor, missionary, and church leader.

YOU CAN ASK GOD:

■ that the Navajo will discover the beauty of the Bible in their own language.

■ that the Navajo will not see Christianity as the "white people's religion," but see that Jesus—a person from the Middle East—is for the Navajo as much as anyone.

■ that Navajo Christians will share Jesus' love among their families, friends, and communities.

■ that Christian leaders in the Navajo Nation will be wise and serve their people well.

■ to change the hearts of Christians who treat people from other ethnic groups badly. Pray for all God's people in the United States to work together in unity.

NEPAL
The Roof of the World

The mighty Himalayas run along the northern border of Nepal. These snow-covered peaks are among the highest in the world, with Mount Everest the highest of all. Surrounded by mountains, the fertile Kathmandu Valley is home to the capital city, many towns and villages, rivers, green fields, and ancient Hindu and Buddhist temples. The tropical Terai lowlands along the southern border have forests, tall grasslands, and wetlands—and now the majority of Nepal's people.

At least a hundred different people groups live in Nepal, speaking more than a hundred languages. A lot of these groups live in remote villages, in deep river valleys, or on the side of mountains. These areas have few roads—only rough, narrow trails. If people need food, medicine, or anything else, usually men or donkeys have to carry it in.

A FAST-GROWING CHURCH

Nepal was once the only Hindu kingdom in the world. Hindus here have often mixed their Hindu practices with Buddhism and animism. For more than a hundred years, Nepal shut itself off from the rest of the world. Christians on India's border with Nepal talked about Jesus with Nepalis they met. They prayed for the day when they could enter Nepal themselves.

At last, after a short revolution in 1951, Christians were among the first to enter, to help the new king and his country. But Nepalis who became Christians were often put in prison. After democracy was introduced in 1991, Christians had greater freedom to worship God.

The Hindu kingdom came to an end when Nepal became a republic in 2008. Today there are more than 850,000 Christians in Nepal, and the church there is one of the fastest growing in the world. All the seventy-five districts of Nepal have at least one church. But there are still many villages all over Nepal where the people have not heard about God's love.

MANY DIFFERENT GODS

Maya picked up a brass water-pot and joined the other girls going to the water tank. Talking and laughing, they passed temples where people were worshiping and making offerings to the gods. At the tank, Maya washed herself, then filled the pot.

As she went back into her house, Maya looked up at the figure of Ganesh, the Hindu elephant-god. Maya knew that her people, the Newars, were supposed to be Buddhists and worship Buddha. But they worshiped other gods too, so she wasn't sure if they were also Hindus.

"Why do we have so many gods?" Maya asked her mother.

They were mixing red vermilion powder, rice, and flower petals, to make

FACT FILE

AREA: 56,827 square miles

POPULATION: 29.6 million

CAPITAL: Kathmandu

MAIN LANGUAGE: Nepali

MAIN RELIGIONS: Large Hindu majority; Buddhist minority

ECONOMY: Foreign aid and tourism. Most people are farmers. Large numbers of Nepalis, especially young people, work abroad and send money back home to Nepal.

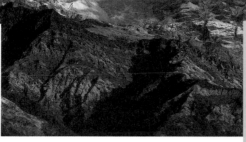

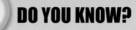

DO YOU KNOW?

The flag of Nepal is the only national flag that isn't a square or rectangle. It's in the shape of two triangles to look like the Himalaya Mountains.

Hindu holy man

offerings for the Buddha and the other gods in their house.

"We have gods for every part of our lives," her mother told her. "There's a different god for each of our needs."

THE GOD WHO HEALS

Down the road, Neela's family was finishing their daily prayers. For the last few months, they'd been praying to Jesus every day. Neela knew that Jesus was powerful—more powerful than even Buddha or Ganesh. When her mother was very ill, they had looked for help from local religious men, but nothing worked.

Some Christians from a nearby church had heard about her family. A few women came to help Neela with her chores. Two men from the church talked to her father. "May we have your permission to pray

for your wife in Jesus' name?" they asked. "Jesus is the living God we follow. He has power over every evil spirit."

They said Jesus had already healed people in their church.

Neela's father knew his wife might die soon, and he was afraid. He was willing to do anything to save her. They prayed for a long time. Neela didn't understand all the words they said, but she noticed this kind of praying was different. But nothing happened. The Christians came back the next day and prayed again. Neela was getting bored.

Suddenly, Neela's mother sat up! She smiled a big smile and called Neela over to hug her. Soon Neela was working alongside her mother again, doing daily chores. Jesus had healed her! Perhaps her family should worship him instead of Buddha or Ganesh. They asked the Christians to come back and tell them more about Jesus and how to follow him.

TO HELP YOU PRAY FOR NEPAL

YOU CAN THANK GOD FOR:

- every person in Nepal who loves and follows Jesus.

- Christians in Nepal who care for the poor, the sick, and the disabled—many pray with people who others will not touch or talk to.

- Christian books available in several of Nepal's languages.

YOU CAN ASK GOD:

- that many Nepali children will hear about Jesus and know that he is the only true and living God, more powerful than all the others.

- for Christians to keep showing God's love to Hindu and Buddhist families around them.

- for the gospel to reach every town and village in Nepal, especially those most difficult to get to.

NEW ZEALAND

Aotearoa: Land of the Long White Cloud

KIWIS

New Zealand has two main islands, which are called *Te Ika a Maui* (North Island) and *Te Wai Pounamu* (South Island). It's a beautiful country with long, sandy beaches, rolling hills, steep mountains, volcanoes, giant trees, and hot, bubbling pools and springs. Some plants, animals, and birds that live in New Zealand are found nowhere else in the world. One of them is the Kiwi, a large bird that can't fly and looks like a hen. "Kiwi" is also a nickname for New Zealanders. People in New Zealand love sports. The "All Blacks," the national rugby team, are known all over the world.

NEW ZEALAND

NORTH ISLAND

Auckland

WELLINGTON

Christchurch

SOUTH ISLAND

AUSTRALIA

South Pacific Ocean

Tasman Sea

NEW ZEALAND

MAORI

The Maori name for New Zealand is "Aotearoa," which means "land of the long white cloud." In most parts of New Zealand, it's usually neither too hot nor too cold, and there's plenty of rain—so it's an ideal place for sheep farming. Four and a half million people live there along with more than 29 million sheep. That's more than six sheep for every person!

Most of the people living in New Zealand are descended from British and European settlers, but over 5 percent are Maoris. Twelve or more centuries ago, the Maori traveled vast distances from the Pacific islands of Polynesia. They came in sixty-foot-long canoes, each carved from a single log. They gained control of the land and made it their home. They built beautiful meeting places where Maori

FACT FILE

AREA: 103,500 square miles

POPULATION: 4.8 million

CAPITAL: Wellington

MAIN LANGUAGE: English

MAIN RELIGIONS: Christianity and "no religion" are the largest groups

CHIEF EXPORTS: Meat, dairy products, wool, fruit, and chemicals

Maori dancers, New Plymouth

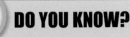
In the North Island there are four active volcanoes. It's a common sight to see geysers and clouds of steam rising from hot bubbling springs that well up from volcanic rocks in the same area.

tribes still meet. On special occasions they cook food in leaves buried between hot stones in the ground. Sweet potatoes, cabbage, beef, lamb, and pork all taste delicious cooked this way.

When the settlers arrived from Europe in the nineteenth century, they fought the Maori people fiercely for land. At that time, many Maori people lost the land where their people had lived for hundreds of years. In school, Maori children were often punished for speaking their own language rather than English, until their leaders demanded their rights. "We've been here more than a thousand years, so why shouldn't we speak our own language?" they asked. Today Maori artists, painters, craftspeople, and

film producers are reviving old customs and traditions. Children often learn their history in action songs. Some Maoris have become strong Christians, and some study at Bible schools.

MANY COUNTRIES, MANY FAITHS

Although around half the people in New Zealand say they are Christians, few Kiwis really follow Jesus. People of different faiths from many other countries have come to live in New Zealand. Some are refugees, and others have come to look for work, but they have all brought their own religions with them. Among them are Buddhists and Muslims from Southeast Asia, Hindus from India, and atheists from China. In fact, many people in New Zealand have no religion at all.

New Zealand Kiwi Bird

TO HELP YOU PRAY FOR NEW ZEALAND

YOU CAN THANK GOD FOR:

- the many Christians in New Zealand who know Jesus and want to tell others that Jesus loves them.

- missionaries from New Zealand who go and share Jesus with people in other countries.

- every Christian who volunteers to teach Bible in school classes and to run camps, after-school clubs, and other activities so that children will learn to follow Jesus.

YOU CAN ASK GOD:

- to help Christians talk about Jesus in a loving, caring way to people who worship other gods or don't believe in God at all.

- that as Maori bring back some of their old customs and traditions, Maori Christians will stay faithful, following Jesus.

- to bring many people, both Kiwis and immigrants, to follow Jesus.

- for all Christians in New Zealand to love and care for each other because they all belong to God's family.

NORTH CAUCASUS
Between Two Seas

RUSSIA

Caspian Sea

STAVROPOL KRAI

KARACHAY-CHERKESSIA

KABARDINO-BALKARIA

CHECHNYA

INGUSHETIA

NORTH OSSETIA

DAGESTAN

Black Sea

GEORGIA

AZERBAIJAN

Between the Black Sea and Caspian Sea are the Caucasus Mountains, the gateway between Europe and Asia. To pass from north to south, you have to climb over mountains, and trek down valleys and through forests. In some places there are no roads.

Over the centuries, the Persians, Mongols, Ottomans, and Russians have all fought to control this area. Today, many tribes with different languages, cultures, and religions call this region home.

The North Caucasus Federal District consists of seven republics controlled by Russia. These republics include Ossetia, Chechnya, and Dagestan. Some of the people groups living here have few Christians or churches, no Bible in their language, and no way of hearing about Jesus. This area is the part of Europe least reached by the good news about Jesus.

FACT FILE

NUMBERS: 9–10 million

NUMBER OF PEOPLE GROUPS: 50–60

MAIN LANGUAGES: Russian (official); each group speaks its own language

MAIN RELIGIONS: Islam; some Orthodox Christianity, some pagan

EXPORTS: Minerals such as gold, copper, and iron ore; energy such as oil and natural gas

OSSETIA—DESCENDANTS OF KINGS

Viktoria stared at the map of the Caucasus in her schoolbook. "Why are we so different from the other people in these mountains?" she asked.

"We Ossetians are descended from the Alans, who had a large kingdom in the north, centuries ago," said her mother. "But Mongol armies invaded our land and forced our ancestors to flee for safety to these mountains. Our language, our culture, and our blood are all different from the other peoples in this region."

She pointed out the window to the church. Viktoria could see its high spires, with crosses atop each of them.

"When our people moved into these mountains, our new neighbors—the Georgian people—introduced us to Christianity. The Alans worshiped a creator god but also many lesser gods— as well as their own ancestors. Today we know Jesus is the only way to the one true God. Most Ossetians are Christian, but some are trying to return to the old ways, worshiping many gods," her mother said.

CHECHNYA—MOUNTAIN LAND OF WARRIORS

"Khasan, watch out!" his father shouted. Khasan caught his footing on the edge of the cliff. "If you want to hunt for mountain goats with us, then act like a Chechen man, not a boy."

Khasan followed the men carefully down the narrow path to the empty village. Their group had stopped for water and flat bread in the abandoned *aul* (a fortified village). The stone buildings were built into the steep rock-face.

"For centuries we've withstood foreign armies in auls like this," said old Sulim. "First the Mongols, then the Russians. We were almost destroyed, but Allah preserved us, and we fight on. We will never surrender our land, our religion, or our culture."

Khasan remembered Sulim's story. During World War II, Russian Communists forced all the Chechen people to go and live in a distant

country. Up to half of them died. Those who survived were only allowed to return years later.

Chechen men are famous as fierce fighters, resisting all invaders, especially the Russians. They are strongly loyal to their Muslim faith, their family, and *nokhchallah*, their traditional code of honor.

Cemetery in North Ossetia

DAGESTAN—MANY TRIBES, ONE REPUBLIC

Magomed was confused. He thought that only Russians were Christians. But his Korean schoolmate, Hyun, was also a Christian. Hyun was the only Korean he knew, and Magomed knew a lot of tribes.

Here in the capital city of Makhachkala, school classes were in Russian, but most families spoke their tribal language at home. Magomed was an Avar, but his school also had Dargins, Kumyks, Lezgians, Laks, and others. They were all living together in the same city, so they had to work at keeping the peace.

It wasn't easy, Magomed thought to himself. At school today, the Avar boys were fighting boys from other tribes. Religion was sometimes a problem too. Almost everyone he knew was a Muslim. But there were different kinds of Muslims. For some, religion was only important on special occasions. Others were Sufi Muslims—the traditional Dagestani way. But now, some Muslims were Wahhabis. Their men grew long beards. Their women veiled themselves completely. They wanted everyone to live like them, and talked about fighting the "infidels." This kind of fighting—usually against

the Russians, sometimes against other Muslims—made Magomed sad. *Why so much fighting?* he thought.

It was hard to be friends with people from a different tribe or religious group. But Hyun was different. His father was a doctor who was happy to help anyone. When Magomed's grandfather was ill, Hyun's father had helped him for free. Hyun didn't fight other boys. He said he followed Jesus, and that Jesus was kind to everyone—even his enemies. When Jesus' enemies wanted to kill him, Jesus didn't fight them—he prayed that God would forgive them. What kind of man loves and forgives his enemies? Imagine if all the people in Dagestan did that? Magomed decided that tomorrow he would ask Hyun to tell him more about Jesus.

Mosque, Grozny, Chechnya

TO HELP YOU PRAY FOR THE NORTH CAUCASUS

YOU CAN THANK GOD FOR:

- the churches and Christians in the Caucasus.

- more and more Christians who are praying for the peoples of the Caucasus.

YOU CAN ASK GOD:

- to stop the fighting between different tribes and religious groups.

- for every Christian living in the Caucasus to have a stronger relationship with God.

- for more missionaries to go to the North Caucasus so that the people there can hear about Jesus.

NORTH KOREA
From God-King to Great Leader

CHINA

RUSSIA

NORTH KOREA •Hamhung

PYONGYANG ■

Sea of Japan

SOUTH KOREA

GOD-KING

According to a Korean legend, Hwanung, son of the Great Creator, one day decided to come down from heaven and become king of all he could see. As he looked around his beautiful country, he heard a bear praying.

"Turn me into a human being," it asked. "I'm tired of being a bear!"

Hwanung felt sorry for the bear. He told it to eat twenty pieces of garlic and a bitter plant called mugwort, and then stay in a cave for one hundred days. The bear did as it was told—and turned into a woman. This woman gave birth to a son named Tangun. According to the legend, Tangun was the first king of Korea. He reigned for more than a thousand years and was worshiped by his people.

NORTH KOREA

Sea of Japan

Yellow Sea

GREAT LEADER

The official name for North Korea is the Democratic People's Republic of Korea.

More than three-quarters of the country is made up of mountains and high plateaus, while in the southwest is a lowland area where most people live. Here agriculture is possible: important crops include rice, corn, and potatoes.

In 1948, after World War II, Korea was divided into two separate countries: North Korea and South Korea. Kim Il-sung, the "Great Leader," ruled North Korea. At one time there were so many Christians in North Korea that some people called the capital city, Pyongyang, the "Jerusalem of the East." But Kim Il-sung insisted everyone worship him. He made all the people wear a badge with his picture, and his face was on posters all over the city. He built a 330-foot statue of himself, high on a hill, smiling down on Pyongyang.

Kim Il-sung was a Communist. He wanted to get rid of every trace of religion, and replace it with *juche* (a complete devotion to the country and its great

leader). He had every church building destroyed. He also had millions of people killed, including thousands of Christians. Two million people fled to South Korea, but in 1950 Kim Il-sung invaded South Korea. That war is still not officially over, although North and South Korea are not actively fighting today.

A national celebration

FACT FILE

AREA: 46,540 square miles, a bit smaller than England

POPULATION: 25.6 million

CAPITAL: Pyongyang

MAIN LANGUAGE: Korean

MAIN RELIGIONS: Officially atheism; many follow *Juche* as a religion.

CHIEF EXPORTS: Coal, metals, and seafood

LITTLE BLACK BOOK

The Communists provided good schooling for every child. However, at school, children were taught to worship Kim Il-sung.

"He is our Great Leader," they sang. "We keep his image in our hearts."

Teachers showed children a little black book.

"Are there any books like this at home?" they asked. "Search for them—even in your parents' bedroom. Then come and tell us."

Some children found the book and told their teachers. Their parents were taken away to prison. The "little black book" was the Bible.

Some brave people continued to follow Jesus, meeting secretly to worship God.

A NEW ERA

Kim Jong-un—the grandson of the Great Leader—is the leader of North Korea today. The world hoped he might make good changes to his country. But millions of people have starved since the time of the Great Leader. Most of Korea's money is spent on building a better army. Although it's a small country, North Korea has the fourth largest army in the world.

Today, Kim Jong-un spends some money to improve the life of the people. But he is also developing nuclear weapons and long-range missiles that he threatens to use against the United States, South Korea, and Japan.

THE TRUE GOD

It's very dangerous to be a Christian in North Korea. Even saying the name "Jesus" can be punished by death. Christianity is seen as the religion of North Korea's enemies, and Christians as spies. Tens of thousands of Christians are kept in prison and work camps. There are some secret churches, but we don't know much about them. There are four official churches in Pyongyang, but they are mainly there to pretend to the world that North Korea has religious freedom.

No missionaries are allowed in North Korea, but there are foreign Christians working there. Christian organizations run farms, schools, factories, medical clinics, and even a university. They go there to help the suffering North Korean people and to show God's love in practical ways, even though they're not allowed to speak about Jesus. These Christians pray that North Koreans will realize that God loves them when they see the kind and good things the Christians do.

Christians believe that one day God will open North Korea to the good news. Millions of hearts are hungry for God's love. But when will that day come? When will Jesus' name be freely spoken in North Korea again?

People bow before statues of Kim Il-sung and Kim Jong-il, Pyongyang

TO HELP YOU PRAY FOR NORTH KOREA

YOU CAN THANK GOD FOR:

- secret believers in North Korea.

- the patient work and prayer of Christians who prepare for the day when North Korea is open.

YOU CAN ASK GOD:

- to protect those who follow Jesus and allow them to grow closer to God.

- to bring a peaceful reunification of North and South Korea.

- to prepare the hearts of North Koreans to hear the good news.

- to open North Korea to the gospel so that many can be saved.

OMAN
Oil—Not Frankincense

David's Uncle Jack had worked in many interesting places. For the last year he'd been in Oman.

"What's it like there?" asked David.

"Oman is in the Middle East, on the east side of the Arabian Peninsula," said his uncle. "Its coastline stretches along the Arabian Sea and the Gulf of Oman, and it shares borders with Saudi Arabia, Yemen, and the United Arab Emirates. I think you'd really enjoy hiking in the mountains and into the hidden oases in the desert, David."

"Part of Oman is called the Musandam Peninsula, which is completely separated from the rest of the country by the United Arab Emirates. This peninsula is made up of a line of razor-sharp peaks, some as a much as a mile high," he said.

"Musandam overlooks the Strait of Hormuz, a narrow stretch of water between the Persian Gulf and the Gulf of Oman. From there, Oman protects the 33,000 cargo and passenger ships that pass through the strait every year—many of them oil tankers from the Persian Gulf."

PAST AND PRESENT

"On the coast there's the capital city, Muscat, where many of the Omani people live. It has beautiful buildings, but no skyscrapers, so it feels like a very large town even though it is a busy city. Oman is around twice the size of New York state. But fewer than five million people live in Oman; New York has twenty million," his uncle explained.

"What are the people like?" David asked.

Uncle Jack continued, "A bit more than half of the population is Omani. They are Arabs and almost all follow Islam. The other half are foreign workers—like me. A lot come from India, Pakistan, and Bangladesh and work in low-paid jobs. Others are experts in their professions, who come to train Omanis."

"In Oman, there's an amazing network of underground and surface irrigation channels, called *aflaj*. Some are more than nine miles long and 150 feet deep. They were built around 1,500 years ago. Some are still in use today. But modern farmers are running short of water for their crops and animals," he said.

A NEW DAY

"Today, Oman's wealth comes mostly from oil. But, for a long time, Omanis grew wealthy by selling a natural perfume called frankincense. Frankincense was one of the gifts the wise men gave baby Jesus. By the 1950s, Oman had become one of the poorest Arab countries," explained David's uncle. "Even when oil was discovered in the 1960s, the ruler didn't use the money earned to modernize his country. He even told people they weren't allowed to ride bicycles or wear sunglasses—because they were too modern. Many Omanis went abroad to find work at that time, and those left behind were very unhappy. In 1970, Sultan Qaboos took over. He told his people, 'Yesterday it was complete darkness and, with the

FACT FILE

POPULATION: 4.8 million

CAPITAL: Muscat

MAIN LANGUAGES: Arabic; English, Baluchi, Urdu, Hindi, and other languages are also used

MAIN RELIGION: Islam

CHIEF EXPORTS: Oil and gas, fertilizer, copper, fish, dates, and textiles

Muscat

help of God, tomorrow will be a new dawn on Muscat, Oman, and its people," he said.

"At that time, there were only three schools and one hospital in Oman. Today, there are many modern hospitals, hundreds of schools, and several universities. The government has built good roads, new harbors, and modern airports. Many people now own expensive cars, mobile phones, and televisions. People live much longer, and are better educated."

FREEDOM?

"If Omanis are mostly Muslims, does that mean there aren't any Christians? Where did you go to church?" David asked, full of questions.

"There are a few Christians," Uncle Jack replied. "Missionaries built the first hospital, clinics, and schools in Oman, so people respect them. But most of the Christians in Oman are foreign workers. They're allowed to meet to worship God as long as they don't include Omanis.

"Unlike many other Arab countries, Oman is gradually becoming more open and free. People of all religions living in Oman can worship in government-approved places of worship—mosques, churches, and temples. There are at least four centers where Christians are allowed to hold services in several different languages. Just in the capital alone, more than fifty different groups of Christians meet. And Omanis can find lots of Christian material in Arabic on the internet and on satellite TV," he said.

"But only a few hundred Omanis have ever become Christians. Those who want to follow Jesus know their families, their friends, and the authorities will try to prevent them. There will be lots of pressure to leave their Christian faith. It is illegal to try to convert Muslims to faith in Jesus. Life today is much more comfortable for Omanis, but they still don't know the love of Jesus."

Great Mosque

DO YOU KNOW?

The Gulf of Oman is home to the spinner dolphin, which twists its body as it leaps out of the water for air.

PAKISTAN
Land of Extremes

PAKISTAN

In the north of Pakistan is the world's second highest mountain, K2, which is always covered in snow. In the south is the scorching desert of the Sindh and a very hot coastline on the Arabian Sea. Between north and south, the great Indus River flows through lush, green valleys. Pakistan has huge, crowded cities—such as Karachi and Lahore—but also thousands of tiny villages.

There are Christians in Pakistan, and the church is growing. Many of the Christians come from Hindu backgrounds. However, Pakistanis are mostly Muslims. Hundreds of Pakistan's Muslim people groups still have no churches, no Christians, and no missionaries living among them.

CHRISTIANS IN A MUSLIM LAND

"You should be thankful," said Ibrahim's father, as he drank his *chai* (a spiced milk tea) in their two-room home. "Hot days like today make me wish I were a schoolboy. I wouldn't have to be so careful about Ramadan." Ibrahim's father drove an auto-rickshaw all day, carrying customers through the crowded, polluted streets of Lahore. It was really hot and dusty out there.

"You're lucky to be at school," his father continued. "Many Christian children don't have that privilege." As his family settled down to the evening meal, Ibrahim thought about his father's words. The children at his school were young enough to still avoid the Ramadan fast.

(Ramadan is the month where Muslims must not eat or drink between sunrise and sunset.) School wasn't easy, but at least Ibrahim could eat lunch and drink water there.

Ibrahim and his friend Razzaq were the only Christians at school. He knew other Christian children, like his cousins, who couldn't go to school because they had to work all day. There were also a few Hindus in their large class. But most of the students were Muslim, like the school and the lessons. It was hard being a Christian in Lahore. The older boys were usually mean to the younger ones, especially to non-Muslim children. They called them bad names, but never got into trouble for it. It just wasn't fair!

FACT FILE

AREA: 307,400 square miles

POPULATION: 200.8 million

CAPITAL: Islamabad

OTHER MAJOR CITIES: Karachi, Lahore

MAIN LANGUAGES: Urdu, English

MAIN RELIGION: Islam

CHIEF EXPORTS: Clothing, fabric, cotton, leather, sports clothing and equipment, and medical instruments

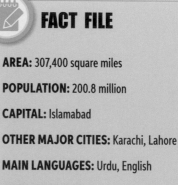

DO YOU KNOW?

Most Pakistani Christians have the family name "Masih." This is the Urdu word for *Messiah*.

Badshahi Mosque, Lahore

Ibrahim was one of the school's best cricket players. Cricket was the most popular game at school—and in the whole of Pakistan. Ibrahim would have played every day if he could. On the cricket pitch, he didn't have to worry about being a Christian, about getting bullied, or about how to get better grades. He could just enjoy the game. Everyone wanted to be on Ibrahim's team because he was such a good batsman. Even the cricket coach said he was good. But the coach also said, "If you want to go a long way in cricket, you need to become a Muslim. Then you will be selected for the best coaching and programs. As a Christian, you will get passed over."

Ibrahim complained to his father. After a moment, his father's strong, gentle hands were on Ibrahim's shoulders. "Son, you're right. It's not fair. We're Christians and we live in Pakistan. It will never be fair for us. We suffer unjustly. But Jesus suffered for us. Can we not do the same for him? He won salvation for us. Should we run away to another land? Can we abandon the God who loves us so much? No, we will stay, and love our enemies, even when they mistreat us. This is a hard way, but it's the right way," he said.

Even if his father couldn't fix the problem, Ibrahim was glad that he understood. His father was kind, and not every boy was so blessed.

PERSECUTION AND POVERTY

Tonight Ibrahim was thinking of his cousins. Across the city, an angry crowd had burned down their home, along with many other homes owned by Christians. Now they would have to live in a *katchi abadi*—a slum for people who've lost everything. The crowd had got angry when they heard a rumor that a Christian had said something bad about the Muslim prophet, Muhammad. That was against the law. Sometimes people used this law to get people into trouble and to take revenge on someone they didn't like. Christians had to be really careful what they said about religion. And not just Christians—Hindus, and sometimes other Muslims, suffered the same kind of attacks. Sometimes there were attacks with grenades—and even bombs. Ibrahim wished there could be peace in his country, no matter what religion people were from.

TO HELP YOU PRAY FOR PAKISTAN

YOU CAN THANK GOD FOR:

- Christians who are faithful, even when they face persecution and violence—the church is growing!

- all the people in Pakistan and around the world who pray for this spiritually needy country.

- the Bible and other helpful Christian books in Urdu.

YOU CAN ASK GOD:

- to bring peace to Pakistan.

- to help Christian young people go to school and university, and get good jobs.

- for Christians to learn more about what the Bible teaches.

- for Muslims in Pakistan to have open hearts so they can hear about Jesus.

- that God will give wisdom to the pastors who teach and take care of the poorest Christians. Many pastors also have another job to pay the bills, and usually don't have much training.

PAPUA NEW GUINEA
A Wild Place

Papua New Guinea (PNG for short) occupies half of the world's second largest island (Papua, part of Indonesia, is on the other half). If you wanted to visit someone in another part of PNG, you might have to climb steep mountains, cross fast-flowing rivers, and trek through tropical jungle. You wouldn't need a car, because there aren't many roads outside the towns and cities.

There are about 1,000 different people groups in PNG, speaking more than 800 languages! Even people living in neighboring valleys often don't speak the same language. It's good that almost everyone also speaks Tok Pisin, a kind of "pidgin", or simplified English. The Bible has been translated into Tok Pisin.

Sometimes in PNG, everyone in a village became a Christian at the same time! Although this seems wonderful, not everyone really changed to become more like Jesus at first—or even over time. Instead, some carried on with their traditional witchcraft, and continued fighting with each other and with other tribes. But those who truly follow Jesus are trying to teach people what God says so the people of PNG may live at peace with one another.

TO THE CITY!

Most of PNG's history has been in rural villages, but today its cities are growing quickly—so quickly that the city planners cannot keep up, and people struggle with finding housing, water, trash collection, and other basics. Away from their home cultures, more people turn to crime or

FACT FILE

AREA: 178,700 square miles

POPULATION: 8.4 million

CAPITAL: Port Moresby

OFFICIAL LANGUAGES: English, Tok Pisin, and Motu

MAIN RELIGION: Christianity

CHIEF EXPORTS: Gold, coffee, cocoa, timber, copper, and oil

other bad habits. The churches grow in the cities too, but they have a big job to care for the people struggling to make a new life in the city.

FEAR OF SPIRITS

When John was having a haircut one day, some of his hair fell on the ground. "Don't leave your hair there!" his friend Aiyako warned. "A witch doctor could use it to put a curse on you."

Another day Aiyako and John were eating with some people from a different tribe. "Don't leave any food on your plate!" whispered Aiyako. "Someone might use it to attack us through the spirits."

Although John didn't believe superstitions, he knew Aiyako was really scared. "Aiyako, the Bible tells us that if we trust in God, we don't need to be afraid," John said. "God is bigger and stronger than anything that might hurt us." Many people in PNG have fears like Aiyako's.

BABIES IN BAGS

Most people in PNG carry their belongings in net bags. One of the people groups in PNG, the Nabak, call such a bag an *ele*. They hang these bags from the walls, and use them like drawers or shelves. Nabak boys carry everything in an ele slung over the shoulder, while their sisters' ele hangs down their back from a strap around the head. Mothers even carry their baby in an ele on their back.

Nabak women sometimes make these bags from tree bark, but more often from strands of the yucca plant. First they pull the yucca plant through a slit in a big piece of bamboo, to scrape off its green surface. Then they spread out the strands and leave them to parch in the sun. When the strands are dry enough, the women make them into a coarse thread. They rub cold ashes from the fire on their thigh, then roll the strands back and forth across the thigh until they form a thread. When they have enough thread, the women start crocheting the bag, using needles made from the wingbones of bats and flying foxes. It takes several weeks to make just one bag in this traditional way.

GOD'S *ELE*

Christians inside and outside the country have prayed for PNG, and God is changing the country. Pastors teach the people what God says in the Bible, so they can learn to serve God in everything they do. Christians from PNG journey all over the world, telling others about Jesus. God is using these people as his *ele*, to carry the good news of Jesus around the globe!

PERSIANS
Children of a Great Empire

A LONG HISTORY

For thousands of years, the Persians have lived in the region we now call Iran. The Bible contains stories about them. King Cyrus of Persia set the Jews free from exile, and ordered them to rebuild Jerusalem and God's temple there. Daniel was an advisor to King Cyrus. Esther became a queen when she married the Persian King Xerxes.

During those times, the Persian Empire was the largest in the world. Persians had their own religion, called Zoroastrianism. Persians are very proud of their ancient culture, and its world-famous art and poetry. Later, Muslims conquered the area, and most Persians converted to Islam. Like Christianity, Islam has different branches with different traditions, rules, and leaders. Most Persians today follow Shi'a Islam. In 1979, a Shi'a religious leader called Ayatollah Khomeini became supreme leader of Iran, and made the religious laws in Iran very strict.

Christians in Iran suffer badly. Many have fled the country. But the more cruel the ayatollah and his laws became, the more people wanted freedom and peace. Iranians in the country, and around the world, are turning to Jesus to find true peace and freedom. This started with small numbers, but those numbers are growing fast.

ARE CHRISTIANS UNCLEAN?

Maryam stood in the line of students, listening to the teacher. This was the hardest part of her day. The teacher was lecturing them about all the wrong things they could possibly do, and how God would punish them for each sin.

"You must never accept food from a Christian," said the teacher. "They're unclean people!" The list of sins went on and on.

But Maryam knew some Christian girls. They weren't dirty. They were Armenians—a different people group from Persians—and they were kind. Even when they were treated badly, they forgave the people who wronged them. Why were her teachers so angry with Christians, when the ones she knew were peaceful, honest, and even happy? Maryam decided to find out for herself.

SECRET BELIEVERS

"I don't want to go, Maman!" Shahnaz cried at the apartment door. "It's too hard to be a Christian at my school."

Her mother gave Shahnaz a big hug.

"I'm sorry, my love. I don't know what else we can do.

DO YOU KNOW?

The longest poem by a single author was written by a Persian. The *Shahnameh* ("Book of Kings"), by Ferdowsi, tells the history of Persia. It took thirty-three years to write, and has more than 100,000 lines!

You must be strong. We'll pray for you, and God will make a way for us to get through this."

Shahnaz and her family in Tehran were Christians—but few people knew. They'd been Muslims until a year ago. When her father had started to follow Jesus, everything changed. Before that, he was always yelling and fighting with Shahnaz's mother. Her brother Adel was always the favorite, and Shahnaz had felt neglected. But now her mother and father had stopped quarreling. The love in their family had become strong, and was shared between all of them. They watched Christian programs online, read the Farsi Bible, and met secretly in their home with a few other Christians, to sing and pray together.

Shahnaz was very happy her family had found Jesus. But in Iran, it was dangerous to become a Christian. It was hard to keep the best news of her life secret from her school friends. At school, Shahnaz still had to pray the Muslim way, and learn from the Qur'an about the Muslim religion. She longed for the day when she would be free to follow Jesus openly.

WHAT IS FREEDOM?

Nariman's family fled Iran to find freedom in Europe. The strict rules in Iran were no fun. Here in the West, people seemed to eat and drink what they wanted, dress how they wished, and go where they pleased—all things the ayatollahs preached against. But people in the West didn't seem any happier than people in Iran. In fact, people here seemed … empty. "Come, Nariman, it's time!" His parents stood at the door. "Did you forget we're going to the Christian meeting?"

Suddenly he remembered. Their Persian neighbors had also fled Iran, and became Christians here in Europe. Last week they brought over *ranginak* (Iranian date and walnut cake), to welcome Nariman's family. They shared with great excitement how they now had a relationship with God based on love, rather than a religion based on fear. They talked about "freedom in Christ."

They had been inviting Nariman's family to go to a church meeting, until finally his father agreed. Nariman was full of curiosity about this Christian meeting.

TO HELP YOU PRAY FOR THE PERSIANS

YOU CAN THANK GOD FOR:

- Persians who are hungry for spiritual truth.

- the Persian church, which is growing quickly around the world—even in Iran, where it's dangerous to openly follow Jesus.

- Christians who make books, videos, and TV shows in Farsi.

YOU CAN ASK GOD:

- for millions more Persians to hear about Jesus—in Iran it is hard to hear the gospel.

- for Persian Christians to get access to Bibles and good Christian teaching in their language.

- for Christians in Iran to keep strong in their faith, even when they are persecuted.

- for Persian Christians outside Iran to keep their passion for Jesus.

Tehran

PYGMIES
Children of the Forests of Central Africa

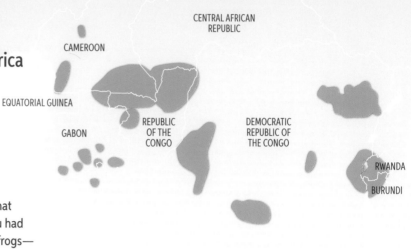

CENTRAL AFRICAN REPUBLIC

CAMEROON

EQUATORIAL GUINEA

GABON

REPUBLIC OF THE CONGO

DEMOCRATIC REPUBLIC OF THE CONGO

RWANDA

BURUNDI

HUNTING

"You'll be ready to come hunting with us soon," said Mateke's father. Mateke tried to hide his excitement. He couldn't wait to go hunting with the men instead of looking after his baby brother and gathering fruit, nuts, leaves, and grubs. He was very proud that every arrow he'd shot at the tree stump that morning had hit the target. He and his friend Matedu had spent a lot of time shooting at big spiders, rats, and frogs—and their practice had paid off.

Mateke watched as the men got ready to go hunting. They dipped their sharpened arrows into poison from the bark of the *anga* tree. Then they dried the arrows over the fire.

When they were all ready to go, two women walked first into the forest. The men followed silently. The giant trees were so tall that they shut out the sunlight. Huge vines hung from their branches. On the ground, great twisted roots and young trees tangled around each other.

The women carried beaters made from the strong stems and leaves of the *mangunga* plant. They beat the ground, calling out to frighten the animals and make them run towards the hunters. What would the men catch today? Monkeys? Birds? Perhaps even a deer? Mateke's mouth watered as he thought of the delicious stew his mother would make.

MOVING ON

Mateke looked around at his village. There were nine little huts. He had heard the men say they would have to move again soon, because there weren't many animals left in this part of the forest.

Every time they move, the Pygmies collect their few belongings—bows and arrows, knives, and cooking pots—and travel into the forest. When they find a good place to settle for a bit, the men

clear the trees. Then the women build new huts, by bending long, thin tree branches to make a small dome. They

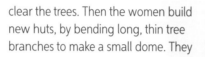

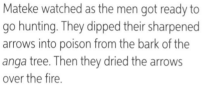

FACT FILE

NUMBERS: Around 900,000

LOCATION: The tropical rain forests of Burundi, Cameroon, Central African Republic, Democratic Republic of the Congo, Gabon, Republic of the Congo, and Rwanda

MAIN LANGUAGES: Each pygmy tribe has its own language or dialect, or speaks the local language of the region where they live

MAIN RELIGIONS: Animism and Christianity

OCCUPATION: Semi-nomadic hunter-gatherers

cover the dome with big *mangunga* leaves, leaving a small opening for the door. The only furniture is a mattress made of *mangunga* leaves.

Drinking from branch of liana vine

GOD'S BOOK

"Do you think the preacher will find us again when we move?" Mateke asked Matedu. "I do hope so," said Matedu. "I love listening to his stories about the God who made us. Do you remember how we all hid in the forest the first time the preacher came? I can't believe we were so frightened of him!"

"I remember," Matedu said. "He knew we needed salt, so he brought us some. He asked my father if he ever prayed to God."

"Yes," Mateke remembered. "Your father said he did. He told the preacher the forest is our God, that it is our father and mother. It gives us all we need— houses, food, and clothing—and when a big storm comes, it protects us."

"Then the preacher showed my father God's book, which says there's only one God," said Mateke. "I was amazed when the preacher told us God made the trees, the animals, and even us. He told us how this God wants us to walk with him in his ways, but that we chose to disobey and walk in our own ways. He said God sent his son Jesus to show us how we can walk in his ways. Jesus even suffered and died so that our disobedience could be forgiven— but then he defeated death and came back to life again! The preacher said that because of Jesus, we can walk

with God again! My father says his heart tells him this news is true."

WHO ARE THE PYGMIES?

Mateke and Matedu are Pygmies. Mateke's tribe lives in the great Ituri Rainforest of northeast Congo. There are about seventeen different Pygmy groups living in the forests of west and central Africa. They are nomadic hunters who gather food from the forest. They also trade meat and honey with neighboring peoples for things they need, such as salt, clothing, tools, and vegetables.

The Pygmies are different from the other tribes around them, and have often been treated badly, and persecuted by neighboring peoples. During civil wars in Rwanda and Congo, thousands of Pygmies were killed.

Although most Pygmies live in forests far away from anyone else, many have heard the good news about Jesus, and have learned to follow him. Some Pygmies live in towns and go to schools. A number who studied at Bible schools now serve their own people as pastors of Pygmy churches, or as evangelists who share the good news with others.

TO HELP YOU PRAY FOR THE PYGMIES

YOU CAN THANK GOD FOR:

- many Pygmies—from many different Pygmy groups—who now follow Jesus.

- Pygmy pastors and evangelists who serve their own people.

- friendship between Christian Pygmies and the Christians from other groups in their countries.

YOU CAN ASK GOD:

- for more Christians to live and travel in the forests with the Pygmies.

- to help pastors and evangelists explain how much Jesus loves us, in ways and in languages that the many Pygmy groups will understand.

- that Pygmies will figure out a way to follow God's ways that is suitable for their wandering lives in the great forests of Africa—a moving church!

- that lots of Pygmy boys and girls will hear about Jesus, follow him, and help others to know him.

QATAR
The Thumb of the Arabian Gulf

BAHRAIN

QATAR

DOHA

SAUDI
ARABIA

Six-year-old Ahmed felt very important. At last he was old enough to help his father entertain their guests in the special room for men visitors, called the *majlis*. Dressed in his ankle-length shirt, or *thawb*, and embroidered cap, he served coffee for his dad's guests. He spoke only when he was spoken to. His father had a special guest today—an American called Jim who'd just started working in his father's company.

A WEALTHY COUNTRY

Qatar, Ahmed's country, sticks out like a thumb into the Persian Gulf. It's a small desert country with a population of nearly three million. Ahmed was used to seeing foreigners, since most people in his country are workers from abroad. There are nine foreign workers in the country for every one Qatari. They come from all over the world, but the largest number come from Nepal, Bangladesh, India, the Philippines, Egypt, and Sri Lanka.

Soon the men started talking about business.

"Life is so different since they found so much natural gas offshore," said Ahmed's dad. "Our country is now so rich that we have free school, free university, free medical care, and even help with housing—for

Qataris. We can thank our emir. He doesn't answer to anyone, but he's generous and takes good care of his people."

"What work did people do before they discovered oil and gas?" Jim asked.

"Most Qataris tried to make a living from fishing, camel herding, or pearl diving. But that was a lifetime ago. Now, everything is about oil and gas. So keep driving your big American cars and trucks! We need to sell you more oil," one of the men said as he laughed.

"I guess life has changed a lot for young people since the country became rich," Jim said.

But Ahmed's father didn't answer. One of Ahmed's older brothers liked racing around the desert in fast cars, and he was secretly into drinking. Ahmed knew his brother was afraid of being punished by Allah, or by their parents, for his bad habits and for not keeping Islamic laws.

QATAR   *Persian Gulf*

Inside a Bedouin tent

FACT FILE

AREA: 4,400 square miles

POPULATION: 2.7 million

CAPITAL: Doha

MAIN LANGUAGES: Arabic (official), English widely spoken

MAIN RELIGION: Islam; foreign workers are also mostly Muslim, but some are Christian, Hindu, or Buddhist

CHIEF EXPORTS: Natural gas, petroleum, fertilizers, and steel

Doha

His father didn't want to tell all this to a foreigner.

FIRST QATARI BELIEVER

One day in 1985, some young Christians in England met a man from Qatar and told him about Jesus. He became the first known Qatari believer.

But this man suffered when he gave up Islam and decided to follow Jesus. His wife divorced him, his children were taken away, and he wasn't allowed to return to Qatar. Since then, other Qataris living abroad have come to know Jesus. They too suffer for their faith, but they believe it's worth it for the hope they have in Jesus.

Almost every Qatari is Muslim. But the government of Qatar allows Christians to meet on a piece of land at the edge of the capital. Here, dozens of congregations from foreign Christian groups can worship freely. The Christians come from many countries around the world but the largest number are from India, the Philippines, and Egypt. Churches have an important ministry encouraging these Christians, teaching them God's Word, and helping them to be strong. Living far from home and family is hard for foreign workers.

FAR FROM HOME

Kiran slumped onto his thin mattress. He was exhausted from a long day of work.

At least I'm still alive! he thought. He'd just heard about another Nepali worker who had been killed in an accident.

Kiran—and thousands of other Nepalis— came to Qatar to build soccer stadiums for the World Cup to be played in 2022. Not long after he arrived, Kiran regretted it. He wasn't allowed to return home until his contract was finished—in two years' time. The money wasn't bad, but the work was

dangerous and tiring. He and his friends had to live in dorms that weren't much more than concrete boxes. Because the Nepalis were Hindus and didn't believe in only one god, they weren't always treated as well as the Muslims or Christians.

Kiran reached into his pocket for the photo of his younger brothers and sisters. He was doing this for them: he wanted to take care of them now that their parents had died. But his hand found something else. Someone had given him a booklet in his Nepali language, "The Gospel of Luke." It was about a man called Jesus. Kiran had heard a bit about this man—he had been sent from God and did miracles. Kiran felt he could use a miracle in his life. He opened the booklet and started reading.

TO HELP YOU PRAY FOR QATAR

YOU CAN THANK GOD FOR:

- the freedom for Christians who live in Qatar to go to church openly.
- the few Qataris who follow Jesus.

YOU CAN ASK GOD:

- that Qataris living abroad will meet Christians who show them Jesus' love.
- to help Qatari believers when their families reject them.
- that many foreign workers—Muslims, Hindus, and Buddhists—meet Jesus while in Qatar.
- that Christian workers in Qatar have the wisdom and courage to share Jesus in powerful ways.
- to help churches encourage and bless foreign workers while they are in Qatar.

Arab dhow in harbor

QUECHUA
People of the Andes

MOUNTAIN VILLAGE

"Hey, Tupac! How much further do we have to climb to get to your house?" Juan asked as he panted. "I'm out of breath."

"Not much further," Tupac said, grinning. "Only about an hour!" Tupac is a Quechua (*kech-wah*) boy. His family lives high in the Andes Mountains of Peru. Wearing warm ponchos and *chullos* (caps), the two boys went on climbing the steep path. Tupac pointed out little terraced fields of maize and potatoes. As they got higher, they passed sheep, llamas, and alpacas—bred for their soft fleece.

"Ever seen an Andean condor?" Tupac asked as he pointed to the world's largest flying bird passing overhead.

"You'll be surprised when you see my house," he told his new friend. "It's got just one room and a dirt floor. We don't have electricity or running water. But you'll be very welcome. My mom's a great cook."

At last they reached Tupac's home. "Here we are," he said, stopping at a lone thatched hut built of adobe bricks. "Come in!"

Soon they were eating a hearty stew made of maize, potatoes, and beans that Tupac's mother had cooked over a fire in a corner of the hut.

"A lot of Quechua are poor," Tupac said. "But we have some sheep, a few llamas, and a bit of land. Some people don't have any land, so they go down to the cities. Even if they learn Spanish and find jobs, they don't earn much. Sometimes you can find Quechua communities in rough areas on the edge of towns."

LEGACY OF THE INCAS

Some Quechua are descended from the Incas, who ruled this region hundreds of years ago. The Incas built huge terraces, great palaces and temples, and an amazing network of roads and cities. By the sixteenth century, the Inca Empire spread all the way from Colombia to Chile and made Quechua its official language. Even today— almost five hundred years later—it's still the most widely spoken native language in the Americas.

In 1532, the Spanish came to Peru looking for new lands and gold. They found two Inca leaders fighting over who should be the next emperor. While the Incas were fighting among themselves, the Spanish quickly defeated them and took over their land, their gold and silver mines, and their people.

HOLDING ON TO HISTORY

Spanish soon became the main language spoken across the region, but the Quechua peoples managed to keep their own language alive these five hundred years. The Quechua are among the poorest people

Machu Picchu

FACT FILE

COUNTRIES: Peru, possibly 3-4.5 million; Bolivia, around 2 million; Ecuador, around 1 million; also Argentina; Colombia; and Chile

NUMBERS: Between 10 and 12 million

MAIN LANGUAGES: Quechua, with at least 45 different dialects—some very different from one another; many people also speak Spanish

COLOMBIA

ECUADOR

PERU

BOLIVIA

South Pacific Ocean

CHILE

ARGENTINA

DO YOU KNOW?

The music of the Andes Mountains is famous all over the world. Can you recognize the mysterious sound of the panpipe when you hear it?

in the countries where they live, and they struggle to keep ownership of their traditional lands. Governments and other groups often mistreated them in the past. Quechua groups have more rights and protections now, but still find life difficult.

Most jobs, schools, universities, and governments use the Spanish language, so Quechua families get left behind. Things may change as the Quechua language gets used in higher profile settings. The first Quechua television news program has started in Peru, and Microsoft and Google offer Quechua as a language option.

The Quechua began to follow the Catholic Christianity they learned from their Spanish conquerors. But many continued to follow the traditional animist religions as well, including worship of spirits and nature. Quechua may make offerings or perform rituals to try to avoid bad things happening, such as natural disasters or illness. Often the religions get blended, mixing Catholic saints with Andean gods or spirits of nature.

A GOOD SHEPHERD

When he was a little boy, Romulo Sauñe looked after his family's sheep. After he started to follow Jesus, his favorite Bible verses were about Jesus, the Good Shepherd. Romulo became a Christian leader and spent his life helping his Quechua people. He loved to tell them about the Good Shepherd. He knew how important it was for his people to have the Bible in their own language, so he worked with others to translate it into Quechua dialects.

Romulo often visited Christians in remote mountain villages to tell them more about Jesus. One day, as he returned from a visit, Romulo was murdered by a rebel group that opposed his Christian work. He was a good shepherd who gave his life for his sheep, the Quechua.

Romulo's family and friends have carried on his work so that Quechua believers can read the Bible for themselves. High up in the Andes Mountains, whole Quechua villages like Tupac's are coming to know Jesus and learning to follow him. Quechua Christians enjoy their own worship music, their own Bible translations, and even their own style of church.

But there are still Quechua villages throughout the Andes that have not heard the gospel. Pray for missionaries who want to share the gospel with Quechua throughout the Andes Mountains region.

TO HELP YOU PRAY FOR THE QUECHUA

YOU CAN THANK GOD FOR:

■ Quechua people who are learning to follow Jesus, the Good Shepherd.

■ the Bible in some Quechua dialects and in audio forms that people can listen to while weaving or working in the fields.

■ Christian radio programs in local languages that can reach communities high in the mountains.

YOU CAN ASK GOD:

■ that each Quechua will come to know Jesus and follow him faithfully.

■ that every Quechua will have access to the Bible in their own language. Pray for translators to complete the Bible projects.

■ for governments and people who live alongside the Quechua to treat them fairly.

■ to help Quechua people who are poor and those who are sick without medicine or a doctor.

REFUGEES
In Search of Safety

HOMELESS

"Run! Run—as fast as you can!" screamed Chantale. "We have to get away from here."

She ran into the forest, her baby brother clutched in her arms and her frightened sisters following. They'd arrived home to find that rebels had burned down their village and were hunting down villagers.

For seven days, Chantale led her brother and sisters through the forests of eastern Congo. At last they reached safety at a refugee settlement in the nearby country of Uganda.

With so many villagers coming into the settlement food was scarce, and they had to take shelter under a bit of plastic sheeting for now. Hopefully more supplies would soon arrive so she could build a shelter for them.

In Uganda, refugees can at least move freely and work for others. Sometimes Chantale earned a little money to buy food for her brother and sisters. Her sisters went to a school near the settlement, run by volunteers, but she was so busy looking after them that she couldn't attend herself. She was only thirteen, but with their parents gone, she had to look after her family.

OVER THE MOUNTAINS

"Don't make a sound!" Sherzad's father warned his children as he woke them. "Put on your warmest clothes—then come quickly."

Silently, the children followed their parents out into the night to start the long, cold journey through the rugged mountains from their home in Afghanistan to neighboring Pakistan. They wanted to get away from the constant fighting in their part of Afghanistan.

When they finally arrived, Sherzad and his family had to live in a tent in an area where other refugees were camped. Most were trying to travel west through Pakistan, Iran, and Turkey into Europe. Would they have to walk the whole way? They were already terribly tired and cold.

THE MISSING GIRLS

Hawa wept as she lay on the bed. It was a month since Boko Haram terrorists had swept into her town in northern Nigeria.

They attacked without warning, and many people had died in the violent raid. Hawa had been late for school that day. As she arrived, she'd seen the fighters loading her classmates from the Christian school onto a truck. They took them all.

Hawa had turned and run home. Her family were all alive—praise God! But Hawa cried because she didn't know what had happened to her classmates. Would they return home? Would she ever see them again?

Zaatari Camp, Jordan

128

CIVIL WAR

In 2011, a terrible war began in Syria. As it continued, nearly half the population had to leave their homes. Six million Syrians fled to other parts of the country, and five million went abroad to escape the violence and destruction. Most ended up in refugee camps in neighboring countries such as Turkey, Lebanon, and Jordan. Others made the long, dangerous journey to Europe trying to find safety in countries such as Germany and Sweden. What would it be like if half the people of your country had to leave their homes and flee to safety?

66 MILLION

There are about sixty-six million refugees in the world—and at least half of them are children. That's more than the entire population of the United Kingdom.

There are many reasons why refugees are too scared to stay in their own country. Sometimes they fear racial hatred, sometimes religious persecution, and sometimes war. Refugees often have to leave everything behind and try to start a new life elsewhere. They are looking for somewhere safe where they can find food, shelter, care for their family—and hope for the future.

REFUGEES IN THE BIBLE

There have always been refugees—history is full of them. In the book of Exodus in the Bible, there's the story of how the Israelites escaped from slavery in Egypt to find safety in a land of their own. Years later, Joseph and Mary fled with baby Jesus to Egypt to escape from cruel King Herod.

The Bible says we should care for the poor, the suffering, and refugees. Jesus says that people who feed the hungry, give water to the thirsty, and clothes to those who have none, and people who look after the ill and visit prisoners, are doing all this for *him*. Check this out in Matthew 25:34–40.

Pray for all refugees around the world today. And think of practical ways to obey Jesus' call to help people who are looking for safety in your country.

TO HELP YOU PRAY FOR REFUGEES

YOU CAN THANK GOD FOR:

- organizations that help refugees, such as the United Nations High Commission for Refugees (UNHCR).

- churches and Christian organizations that help refugees settle in new countries.

- millions of refugees who hear about Jesus for the first time in the camps, on the journey, or in the countries where they settle.

YOU CAN ASK GOD:

- that Christians will show God's love to the millions of refugees in practical ways.

- that Christians will share the good news about Jesus with refugees from other countries.

- for people to comfort and look after refugee children who are lost or whose parents have died.

- that governments will welcome refugees and be kind to them.

- to bring peace to troubled countries so that refugees can return home.

ROHINGYA
People Without a Country

The Rohingya are a group of between two and three million people who live on the west coast of Myanmar. They think of this area as their homeland, which it has been for generations.

But the government of Myanmar says the Rohingya came from Bangladesh and should go back there. They won't allow the Rohingya to become citizens of Myanmar. So it is hard for Rohingya to get permission to work, travel, go to school, own land, get married, see a doctor, or most of the things people normally need to do. How can the Rohingya look after their families without a job, schooling, or help from the doctor? Many live in extreme poverty without enough food, water, or medicine to survive. Many Rohingya can't read. And without travel documents, how can they go anyplace else?

INDIA

BANGLADESH

MYANMAR

Bay of Bengal

CAUGHT IN THE CAMPS

The Rohingya also have problems with their neighbors. Most people in Myanmar are Buddhist, but the Rohingya are Muslim. Sometimes their conflict turns violent. Buddhists have attacked and burned Rohingya villages. Many Rohingya have died or been injured, and hundreds of thousands have been forced into camps.

The camps set up for the Rohingya in Myanmar are horrible places. Some have police and army checkpoints, and the Rohingya aren't allowed to leave. There isn't enough food and water in the camps, and there's no medicine. Often the government doesn't even allow foreign organizations to bring aid to the people. Many Rohingya die of starvation and disease.

SEARCHING FOR A HOME

When things get violent, the survivors flee their villages and find another place to stay. Myanmar wants to send the Rohingya to Bangladesh, but Bangladesh cannot take them all. Bangladesh receives large numbers of Rohingya into their better camps, but others must try to find new homes to the south—in Thailand, Malaysia, and Indonesia. Malaysians are mostly Muslim, like the Rohingya, and some try to help by offering schooling for children or small jobs for adults. But it's hard for Rohingyas to find real work and earn enough money to live.

Thailand doesn't want the Rohingya, either. They worry that, if they let Rohingya in, many more will follow. The Thais are mostly Buddhist, so they don't want to accept thousands of Muslim Rohingya. When boats full of Rohingya arrive in Thailand trying to escape the violence in Myanmar, the Thai navy sometimes stops them and sends them back. Then Myanmar officials stop the boats and send them back out to sea again. Many "boat people" die in these crowded vessels, stranded at sea, with nowhere to land.

FACT FILE

NUMBERS: More than 2 million

COUNTRIES WHERE THEY LIVE: Bangladesh, Myanmar, Saudi Arabia, Pakistan, Malaysia, Thailand, and a few other countries

MAIN LANGUAGE: Rohingya—similar to a Bengali dialect called Chittagonian

MAIN RELIGION: Islam

What can the Rohingya do? There seems to be nowhere for them to go. No country welcomes them. Will the government of Myanmar grant them the rights other citizens have? Can they live in peace alongside their Buddhist neighbors? It seems impossible—but not for God. He loves the Rohingya and wants to welcome them as his people. He has a purpose for them on earth and offers them a true home—with him—in heaven.

OUTCASTS OF THE OUTCASTS

Some Rohingya have escaped to other countries such as Saudi Arabia, Pakistan, and India. Small communities also exist in the United States, Australia, and other Western countries. So many have fled persecution in Myanmar that more Rohingya now live outside Myanmar than inside. They try to exist quietly, often as illegal immigrants. A few are officially recognized as refugees and become citizens. They try hard to stay in touch with their families in Myanmar and scattered throughout the world, and to tell the world how their people are suffering.

Almost every Rohingya is a Muslim, but a few are Christian. The Christians try to meet together as a church to worship. Those who decide to follow Jesus often face persecution from their neighbors. The Rohingya are outcasts of the world, but Rohingya Christians are also excluded by their own people.

TO HELP YOU PRAY FOR THE ROHINGYA

YOU CAN THANK GOD FOR:

■ Rohingya who have found Jesus and now follow him.

■ countries that allow Rohingya to enter as refugees.

■ people in Malaysia, the United States, and other countries who want to help the Rohingya.

YOU CAN ASK GOD:

■ to end the persecution of the Rohingya so they don't lose their homes, families, and lives.

■ to provide a peaceful place for the Rohingya to live and a solution to their current problems.

■ for many Rohingya people to meet Jesus, and for churches in Rohingya communities around the world.

■ to help people translate the Bible into the Rohingya language.

■ to help the few Rohingya Christians stay strong in their faith and talk boldly about Jesus with families and friends.

ROMANI
Gossiping the Gospel

Who are the Romani, and where do they come from? About 1,200 years ago, large groups of people began moving out of an area in northwest India and northeast Pakistan called the Punjab. As they traveled they often earned their living as musicians and entertainers, horse-traders, blacksmiths, and craftspeople. Today, millions of their descendants—too many to accurately count—live all over the world in more than sixty countries and on every continent. These groups are often known as Romani, or sometimes Roma. Perhaps you have heard them called Gypsies. Some use this name for themselves, but many Romani don't like it. In different countries they are known by different names, such as Sinti, Manuch, Kalderash, Nawar, and Gitanos.

Although most Romani speak the language of the country where they live, many also speak one of several Romani languages. The different Romani groups around the world have dozens of slightly different dialects and even different lifestyles.

DWELLING BUT NOT ALWAYS BELONGING

Some Romani still live as nomads, moving from place to place. But more Romani communities have settled and found jobs where they live. Some are politicians, business leaders, and respected academics. A few are well-known musicians, writers, actors, and athletes.

The Romani have kept their own way of life and are rarely fully accepted by the society where they have settled—even after many years. Because they are different, the Romani are often misunderstood and even despised, disliked, and neglected. In many places, this makes finding jobs or going to school difficult for the Romani. Some Romani communities are very poor. Children don't always get enough schooling to learn to read and write.

Romani parents bring up their children to respect older people in their families and community. Showing hospitality to others is the way of life for the Romani. Traveling Romani traditionally live in a caravan, which the children help to keep tidy.

Romani customs differ from place to place. Muslim Romani eat chicken, but not pork. But in Finland, Romani don't eat chicken. Some Romani eat hedgehogs—others think hedgehogs are unclean.

The Roma usually adopt the main religion of the country where they settle—often Roman Catholicism, Orthodox Christianity, or Islam. They don't always follow those religions closely and often mix in some of their own folk beliefs.

But over the last fifty years, millions of Romani have left their old ways to passionately follow Jesus.

CLARA'S DISCOVERY

Clara was twenty years old. She lived with her parents in their caravan. Sometimes, as a child, she had gone to school, but she had never learned to read. One night she was very upset after an argument with her parents.

Although she had heard about God's love for her, she didn't know much about him. That night she asked God to help her read the Bible so she could find the right way to live. She was disappointed because nothing seemed to happen.

The next morning as she helped her mother clean the caravan, Clara found an old Bible and opened it. She was amazed to discover she could read it! She told her mother, who couldn't believe it until Clara read from it to her.

Over the next few weeks, Clara began to understand what Jesus had done for her, and she put her trust in him. Since then, she's been telling people about God's special gift to her: his gift of forgiveness and her new life in Jesus.

A HUGE TENT

Danny stared, speechless. He'd never seen such a big tent! Thousands of people were gathered under its roof. Around the tent was a giant Romani campsite: modern trailers and traditional wagons, horses, campfires, and a constant bustle of activity. For one week—all day and well into the night—Romani worshiped Jesus with singing, preaching, and prayer.

Danny heard that similar gatherings happened in other Romani communities too. In France, Spain, Romania, and all over Europe, Romani people were coming to Jesus.

Danny's parents used to drink alcohol every night and argue so loudly he couldn't get to sleep. But after they started going to a Pentecostal church, their lives changed. There was no more alcohol, much less fighting and a much happier atmosphere at home. Danny's parents started praying with him each night before bed.

Danny didn't understand everything the preacher said, and he couldn't read well enough yet to follow in his Bible. But when the guitars, fiddles, and accordions started playing, and people started clapping, Danny sang his heart out! He knew Jesus loved him and had changed his family.

Life is often a challenge for Romani. But they are spreading the hope and peace God that has given them to other Romani. Christian Romani often send money to help their people in poorer countries. Some have gone abroad as missionaries to tell other Romani about God's love. As one evangelist said, "We Romani are a nation of evangelists, we can't help gossiping the gospel."

TO HELP YOU PRAY FOR THE ROMANI

YOU CAN THANK GOD FOR:

- the growing churches among Romani people around the world.

- the passion Romani Christians have for sharing about Jesus.

- gatherings for teaching, fellowship, and worship that encourage Romani Christians.

YOU CAN ASK GOD:

- to help Christians who are translating the Bible into the different Romani languages.

- that more Romani Christians and non-Romani Christians will form friendships and encourage one another.

- to help Romani Christians learn how to "gossip the gospel" to non-Romani people.

RUSSIA
A Thousand Years of Christianity

FAITH LIVES ON

Olga and her grandmother left the church, with its onion-shaped, golden domes. She was glad her *baba* took her to church. Her parents just weren't interested. Her grandmother's stories about the old days were both sad and exciting.

"What was it like when the churches were closed?" asked Olga. "Was it *really* against the law for children to hear Bible stories?"

They sat on a park bench and Olga's grandmother told her a story.

CHOOSING A RELIGION

"It all started more than a thousand years ago, when Prince Vladimir ruled our country," she said. "A legend says he saw a light shining over the city of Kiev. He thought it came from Jesus, and decided the nation should follow him—so Russia became a Christian country. Poor peasants, rich nobles, and even the king worshiped God the same way we worshiped this morning. The Russian Orthodox Church has hardly changed in a thousand years.

"Some Russians were rich, but most have always been poor. Eventually, many of the workers felt they were treated unfairly. In 1917, they mounted a revolution that drove out the ruler, Czar Nicholas II. A Communist group called the Bolsheviks took control of the government, the farms, and the factories. The whole of Russia became Communist. Most Russians thought no one would be poor and oppressed any longer. But in the end, the Communist government became even worse oppressors than the ones they threw out.

"They are the ones who banned religion, Olga," her grandmother continued. "Few people had Bibles, and most churches were closed. Our

FACT FILE

AREA: 6.6 million square miles

POPULATION: 144 million

CAPITAL: Moscow

MAIN LANGUAGE: Russian; 109 other languages

MAIN RELIGIONS: Christianity (mostly Russian Orthodox, but some other churches); also Islam

CHIEF EXPORTS: Oil, natural gas, coal, and aluminum

beautiful church was turned into a cowshed. I was sad—then I remembered that Jesus was born in a stable." Baba smiled.

"The government allowed just a few churches to stay open, but the secret police watched them carefully. People were afraid," Baba said. "Some churches met in secret. When the police

discovered them, they took away the pastors, tortured them, put them in prison, or sent them to Siberia—far away in the east of Russia. The Communists made life very hard for Christians. But they couldn't destroy our faith!"

Olga shuddered. It sounded awful. "I'm glad it's different now," she said. "What changed things?"

NEW FREEDOM

"Russia started to open up and religion wasn't banned any longer. In 1988,

St Basil's Cathedral

DO YOU KNOW?

Russia stretches so far that it crosses eleven time zones. When it's morning in western Russia, it's already night in eastern Russia.

Christian leaders from around the world came to Russia to celebrate one thousand years of Christianity here. Since then, we've been more free to worship God," Baba said.

"But as the country opened up, false teaching about Jesus came in from other countries along with good teaching. We didn't know the Bible anymore, so many people were deceived and led astray. Many young people started to chase money, power, pleasure, and thrills. Some refused to believe anything—like your mom and dad."

"But we have the good teaching, right Baba?" Olga asked.

"Yes, my dear, as long as we follow Christ, he will lead us into all truth," her grandmother replied.

A LONG JOURNEY

Russia is the biggest country in the world, spanning two continents. It takes seven days to travel by the Trans-Siberian Railway from Vladivostok in the east to Moscow in the west—the longest train journey in the world. And the world's largest country has just about everything: mountains, forests, plains, rivers, and marshes. Most people who live there are

ethnically Russian. But Russia also has more than 170 other ethnic groups, speaking more than one hundred different languages. You can read about some of them in this book: the Caucasus region on page 110, and the Buryats on page 30.

A NEW CHALLENGE

Today, Russia calls itself a democracy. But the president holds all the political power. And a handful of rich, influential men—called oligarchs—control most of the country's huge wealth and resources. Poverty is still common. For millions of people, life is as bad as ever. They have nothing to put their hope in. Many turn to alcohol to escape the pain of life.

After Communism ended, Christians had greater freedom to spread the good news, start churches, and translate the Bible into minority languages. Many people started to follow Jesus again—others for the first time.

But in recent years, the government has favored the Russian Orthodox Church. It tries to control or limit what all the other churches and Christian organizations can do. The laws have changed. It's now a lot harder for missionaries from abroad to work in Russia. Russian Christians need to do a lot of the work that missionaries used to do.

TO HELP YOU PRAY FOR RUSSIA

YOU CAN THANK GOD FOR:

- Russians who followed Jesus, even when they were put in prison.

- churches and Christians increasing in number.

- the many Bible translations completed, and the translations in progress, into the many languages of Russia.

YOU CAN ASK GOD:

- for people in Russia who feel hopeless to discover a new hope in Jesus.

- to give faith to Christians when the future seems so uncertain.

- for young people to follow Jesus instead of chasing false teachings, money, or pleasures.

- for good Russian pastors and Christian leaders for the churches and ministries in Russia.

Moscow

135

SAMOANS
Whose Homes Had No Walls

TOKELAU

AMERICAN
SAMOA
SAMOA

VANUATU

FIJI

South
Pacific
Ocean

NEW ZEALAND

DAILY PRAYERS

At the end of Ben and Mary's first day on Samoa, they heard church bells ringing. It sounded as if they were ringing all over the island.

"We have to be quiet now," their host, Tili, whispered. "It's the time for prayer. Each day at dusk, when the church bells ring, everyone in Samoa stops what they're doing to pray, read the Bible, and sing together. Let's go back to my house—you can join my family for prayers."

THE SAMOAN WAY

Wherever you find Samoans, you will find lively communities who enjoy being together to eat, dance, relax, and enjoy good music. You will also find *fa'asamoa* ("the Samoan Way"), which guides Samoans in how they act toward others. Samoans respect and care for one another—especially their elders—in a special way.

The Samoan homelands are a group of islands in the South Pacific Ocean. Ten islands make up the country of Samoa. Only four of them are inhabited year-round. A smaller group of islands make up American Samoa, a territory governed by the United States.

Today more Samoans live abroad than in the Samoan islands in countries such as New Zealand, the United States, and Australia. Some Samoans have never experienced island life. Their parents and grandparents tell them stories about the beautiful beaches and mountains, sweet mangoes, and breadfruit—which grows on trees but tastes like potatoes.

The family, or *aiga*, is the most important part of Samoan culture. It's bigger than the immediate family, and is a wider web of related community.

Turtle

Each *aiga* has a leader who cares for all the people and helps find solutions to any problems they might face.

On the islands, Samoans live in close families and villages. They do many things together. They only pull down the walls of their traditional island homes, or *fales*, in bad weather. The children are involved in day-to-day activities of village life alongside adults and elders.

Even when Samoans move abroad, they usually stay close to other Samoans to care for one other. The *aiga* remains an important part of life, and elders pass on to young people their traditions, dances, and stories—how to follow the Samoan Way.

FACT FILE

HOMELAND: Samoa and American Samoa. Around half of all Samoans—250,000—live on the islands. The rest live abroad in countries such as the United States, New Zealand, Australia, and Fiji

MAIN OCCUPATIONS: On the islands: traditionally fishing, but now tourism. Samoans abroad have various jobs and send money to the islands to support their families

MAIN LANGUAGES: Samoan, English

MAIN RELIGION: Christianity

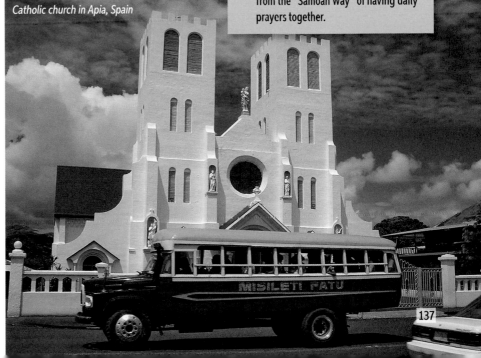

DO YOU KNOW?

The word *tattoo* comes from the Samoan word *tatau*. Tattooing has been part of Samoan culture for centuries. Men and women have different styles of tattoo and symbols with a special meaning for their family. Getting these large tattoos hurts so much that the specialized Samoan tattoo artist can only paint a bit at a time, over several weeks. Sometimes older family members get a tattoo at the same time as younger ones to share in this significant event together.

A LAND FOUNDED ON GOD

"Are all Samoans Christian?" Mary asked Tili later. "Is that why everyone stops to pray and read the Bible every day?"

"Most Samoans would say they're Christians," Tili replied. "But not everyone really follows Jesus. Being a Christian and going to church is just a part of normal life. We had another religion a long time ago—before we learned Christianity. Some people still follow that too.

"Samoa has a motto that says, 'The nation is founded on God.' I wish that were true for every Samoan—then maybe all the different churches would work together better. People would probably also be happier," Tili said.

THE GOSPEL OF PEACE

Two centuries ago, missionaries from Britain came to Samoa, along with Christians from nearby islands, to tell people about Jesus. Some Samoans who traveled on ships to other islands had heard Christian teachings, but there were not yet any churches in Samoa.

In those days, Samoans had been fighting one another fiercely. The missionaries shared how the gospel of Jesus brings peace. One chief chose to become a Christian. Soon his family followed him. Today there is at least one church in every town and village. Christianity became an important part of Samoan life and culture.

Less than ten years after Christianity came to Samoa, Samoan missionaries sailed off to nearby Pacific islands to share about God's love with other people. Samoans still send missionaries to other parts of the world.

A TALENT FOR SPORT

Samoans may be few in number, but several have become famous, especially in hip-hop music, dance, and sports.

Samoans are especially good at rugby, so watch for them on rugby teams around the world. You can also find Samoans on professional American football teams and in boxing and wrestling.

TO HELP YOU PRAY FOR THE SAMOANS

YOU CAN THANK GOD FOR:

- Samoans who tell other people in the South Pacific about Jesus.

- the time Samoans have each day to pray, sing, and read the Bible together.

- the humility, respect for elders, and care for children that Samoans practice as part of their culture and families.

YOU CAN ASK GOD:

- to help Samoan churches around the world teach families to follow Jesus.

- to help young people find true happiness in knowing Jesus.

- to help Samoan Christians from different churches work together.

- for families around the world to learn from the "Samoan Way" of having daily prayers together.

Catholic church in Apia, Spain

SAN
Hunter-Gatherers of the Kalahari Desert

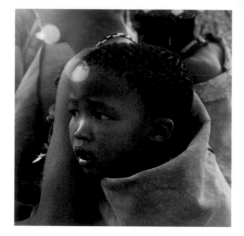

ANGOLA

BOTSWANA

NAMIBIA

SOUTH AFRICA

DESERT RESCUE

More than one hundred years ago, a Scottish missionary named Frederick Arnot was traveling through the Kalahari Desert. He and his African helpers were fainting from thirst. They struggled toward a water hole and knelt by its side. It was completely dry! They lost hope. Some collapsed, unconscious, on the sand. Without water, they could not go on. They knew they might die.

From the distance, a group of San saw them. They ran up and began digging furiously, scooping up handfuls of sand. Their leader took some lengths of reed and carefully joined them together. Then he slid the long reed pipe into the hole. After sucking and blowing for some time, he smiled. Water!

The man sucked steadily on the reed. As the water rose up the stem, he spat it into a tortoise shell. In ten minutes, the shell was full. He gently poured the precious water on to Arnot's tongue and down his throat. Finally, Arnot could swallow again. For six hours, the sweating men worked without stopping, getting water for the whole group. Then—without waiting to be thanked—they left as silently as they had arrived.

Although at that time the San were cruelly treated by others, they saved the lives of these strangers. After seeing how God took care of Arnot's group, his chief guide, named Tinka, became a Christian.

POISONED ARROWS

It hardly ever rains in the Kalahari Desert. Not much other than thorn bushes and coarse grass can grow there. Wild animals such as giraffes, lions, impala, and wildebeest roam the desert. In the past, the San moved around the desert gathering roots and berries, and hunting animals with poisoned arrows. They could go without food or water for long periods, which helped if they had to track animals for a long distance before they could kill them.

The San used to roam freely over much of southern and eastern Africa. They left beautiful rock paintings that tell us about the animals they hunted, their way of life, and their beliefs. The San still believe

FACT FILE

NUMBERS: Less than 100,000

MAIN COUNTRIES: Botswana, Namibia, South Africa, and Angola

MAIN LANGUAGES: Several Khoisan languages and dialects. Most have no writing, and few remain who speak the language.

MAIN RELIGIONS: Animism, Christianity

OCCUPATIONS: Very few still live as nomadic hunter-gatherers. Most now work as laborers on farms or in towns.

DO YOU KNOW?

The San love eating sweet honeycomb, which gives them energy. When they see a bees' nest in a tree, they climb up and smoke out the bees. The San reckon bee grubs are the tastiest part of the comb and keep them for their elders to eat.

strongly in the power of the spirit world. But their painful history and kind ways help them understand the forgiveness and love of Jesus, who gave himself to save others.

Eventually, other African tribes—and later European settlers—moved into San areas. The San are a peaceful people, but others hunted and killed them as if they were wild animals. Those who survived were forced into empty land—places with little water or vegetation.

These days, most of the San have had to give up their nomadic lifestyle and live on farms or in towns. The government of Botswana is trying to assist the San with this huge change in their lives. It gives them land rights, water, and schooling, and helps them adjust to new ways of living. But the San remain famous for being able to survive in harsh, desert conditions, where no other people could.

CLICK SOUNDS

The San have two main language groups, with about thirty different spoken dialects and languages. Many of their words contain click sounds, usually made by the

tongue against the teeth or the roof of the mouth. The San have more click sounds as part of their language than the sounds most of us can make with our mouths!

Most San people can't read. They love telling stories out loud, from memory. The San need Bible stories to be told in their language. Some San have heard about Jesus and decided to follow him.

THE MOUTHS OF LIONS

"What a great story!" Xiri said to his friend Puso.

The Bible teacher was sharing some newly translated stories with San children. They gathered in a shady spot under one of the few trees to hear stories about the Christian God.

"Can you imagine a God who can keep the lions from eating you, even when you're in their den?" Xiri asked.

The San have a tradition about a god who is good—but far away and uncaring.

"Yes!" Puso replied. "Think of the surprise those wicked men got when they discovered Daniel wasn't hurt—even after a whole night with the lions."

The San know just how dangerous lions can be.

Rock painting

TO HELP YOU PRAY FOR THE SAN

YOU CAN THANK GOD FOR:

■ San people who follow Jesus.

■ Bible stories in Khoisan languages, which are being told and recorded for the San people.

YOU CAN ASK GOD:

■ to show the San that he can free them from fear of the spirit world.

■ to send missionaries who will understand and love San people, and will learn their difficult language and culture.

■ that more San people will follow Jesus, especially respected tribal elders who can help their people live godly lives.

■ to help the San people adjust to their new lives in towns and on farms, and to protect them from disease and troubles.

■ for many more Bible stories in San languages to help the San understand the gospel.

SAUDI ARABIA
Where Islam Was Born

PILGRIMAGE

"It's nearly time for the *haj*," Hassan told his son Abdul. "You're twelve years old, so this year you can come with me on pilgrimage to Mecca."

Abdul was excited about traveling hundreds of miles to Mecca from their home in Riyadh. While Riyadh is the largest city in Saudi Arabia, Mecca is the birthplace of Muhammad, the prophet of Islam.

Abdul had been studying Islam for years. He knew the *haj* was one of the five duties or "pillars" of their religion. Every Muslim should, if possible, make this pilgrimage at least once in his or her lifetime.

"I can't wait!" Abdul told his dad. "Tell me what it will be like."

"Up to three million Muslim pilgrims from all over the world go to Mecca every year for the *haj*. There are five or six days of ceremonies. Everyone wears a white robe to show we're all equal in the sight of Allah," Hassan explained. "After ritual washing and prayer, we go to the Kaaba and walk around it seven times. We have to touch and—if possible—kiss the black stone set into the Kaaba's side."

"The Kaaba's very old, isn't it?" Abdul asked. "I read in the Qur'an that Abraham built it at the place where Allah provided water for Hagar and her son Ishmael in the desert." (You can read about God speaking to Hagar in the Bible in Genesis chapter 21.)

"That's right." said Hassan. "Allah told Muhammad that Muslims must turn toward Mecca when they worship him. After we've walked seven times around the Kaaba, we have to run between two special pillars seven times, praying as we go. The next day, we will go to the Plain of Arafat, about ten miles outside Mecca, to listen to a sermon. After that, we collect pebbles and throw them at three stone pillars to get rid of the evil inside us. Although it's not part of the *haj*, on our way home we'll visit Muhammad's tomb in the city of Medina."

RELIGIOUS POLICE

Islam is the only religion allowed in Saudi Arabia. The government sees itself as the keeper and protector of Islam and makes sure everyone keeps the Islamic laws. Five times each day, when the call for prayer sounds from towers attached to mosques all over the country, all the shops close.

FACT FILE

AREA: 830,000 square miles

POPULATION: 34 million

CAPITAL: Riyadh

OTHER MAJOR CITIES: Jeddah, Mecca, and Medina

OFFICIAL LANGUAGE: Arabic

MAIN RELIGION: Islam

CHIEF EXPORT: Oil; Saudi Arabia has the world's second largest oil deposits.

The Kaaba and Great Mosque, Mecca

Women have a lot less freedom than men. In public, most women cover themselves completely, from head to toe, in loose black robes. Woman mustn't even talk to men who aren't related to them. Most buildings have separate entrances for men and women, and buses, parks, and beaches are divided into men's and women's sections so they don't mix.

Perhaps one day Abdul will meet Christians who can explain that keeping strict laws and following religious traditions can't take away our sins. Only Jesus can do that. Abdul would be amazed to hear that he can come to Jesus any time and know God will hear and answer his prayers.

OIL RICH

Saudi Arabia is a hot, dry, desert country. In 1932, Ibn Saud, a strong Arab leader, brought together the nomadic tribes who lived there and created the new Islamic kingdom of Saudi Arabia. The king's word is law, and the extended royal family controls everything.

When oil was discovered, Saudi Arabia became wealthy and powerful as countries around the world bought their oil. Money from oil was used to build better houses for people, set up free schools, universities, and hospitals, make roads across the desert, and develop industries. A lot of money has also been spent to create a strong army.

The Saudi Arabia government sends a lot of money to Muslim organizations abroad to help them publish Muslim literature, train Muslim missionaries, and build mosques.

SECRET WORSHIP

Nine million people from other countries work in Saudi Arabia. Some work for oil companies; while others work as laborers, housemaids, and nurses. Some are Christians, but they have to meet in secret to worship. While they're working in Saudi Arabia, other foreigners often learn about Jesus from these Christians. Some decide to follow Jesus, becoming Christians in the birthplace of Islam! If the authorities find out that a Saudi came to know Jesus, he or she could be put in prison. Sometimes, a new Christian's own family tries to kill them if they don't return to Islam. Despite this, there is a small—but growing—number of Saudi Christians.

People in Saudi Arabia, especially the young, love technology and gadgets—almost everyone has a smartphone. So, some Christians have developed smartphone apps and websites to share about Jesus with Saudis. There are even TV shows from overseas for Saudi people who want to learn about Jesus.

TO HELP YOU PRAY FOR SAUDI ARABIA

YOU CAN THANK GOD FOR:

- Christian websites, satellite TV shows, and apps that share the gospel with Saudis and help them grow as believers.

- Saudis who bravely follow Jesus.

- Christian guest workers in Saudi Arabia.

YOU CAN ASK GOD:

- that Saudis who go abroad to study will meet Christians who tell them about Jesus.

- to help Christian guest workers share their faith with other guest workers.

- that many Saudis will use Christian TV programs and websites to read the Bible and learn about the good news.

- that the millions of Muslims who go on pilgrimage to Mecca will meet God on their journey.

SOMALIS
A Little-Reached People

A HOSTILE LAND

Much of Somalia has a dry climate. The land suffers from drought and sometimes famine because it's difficult to grow crops. So Somalis keep livestock—especially camels—as a source of wealth, milk, and meat.

Somalia has had a civil war for close to thirty years. Sometimes there has been no effective government. At present, the government is fighting rebels called Al Shabaab, who want to rule the country with strict Islamic laws.

Among Somalis, your family and your clan (a large group of related families) are very important. Most people in Somalia are poor, and many can't read. Yet Somalis are sometimes called a "nation of poets." Some living abroad have become well-known as singers and rappers. Most Somalis live in Somalia or nearby countries, but some have gone to live farther away.

Almost all Somalis are Muslims. They're among the hardest people in the world to reach with the good news about Jesus. In Somalia, it's against the law to ask someone to become a Christian. Anyone who becomes a Christian is in danger, so people who follow Jesus usually keep it secret.

NO GOING BACK

"I never want to go back," Sulekha told her mother. "Please don't let them make us leave!" Sulekha lived with her mother and sisters in Dadaab, a refugee camp for Somalis in the neighboring country of Kenya. Everyone lived in plastic tents in a camp the size of a city. Food and water were scarce, but the camp had hospitals, a bus station, and—most important for Sulekha—schools.

Everyone in Dadaab was very poor. But here they were safe from the war between the Somali government and the Al Shabaab fighters. Sulekha could go to school for free and learn such interesting things. In her home village, Sulekha would

FACT FILE

MAIN COUNTRIES: Somalia, Ethiopia, Kenya, Yemen, and Djibouti; smaller communities elsewhere

NUMBERS: 20 million, including about 8 million outside of Somalia

MAIN LANGUAGE: Somali

MAIN RELIGION: Sunni Islam

MAIN OCCUPATIONS: Herding camels, goats, sheep, and cows; farming; fishing

FAR FROM HOME

Mohammed hugged himself tightly as he hurried through the falling snow. *I come from near the equator, but I'm stuck in this freezing country!* he thought. His family had left Somalia shortly after he was born, and he'd lived his entire life in Toronto, Canada. His father had been a powerful member of an important clan in Somalia, but in Toronto he was just another shopkeeper. When he grew up, Mohammed would probably be stuck running the same little corner shop.

Mohammed's family lived in a mainly Somali neighborhood. Many of the shops and restaurants were Somali, and most of the kids at his school were Somali too. He didn't want to get to know other kids. They weren't Muslims, so they were "unclean." They ate pork, didn't wash the Muslim way, and didn't live in submission to Allah.

As Mohammed walked home, he passed a little church. A sign outside said, "Jesus loves you." For Somali Muslims, Jesus was revered as a prophet. *Why would the prophet Jesus love everyone?* wondered Mohammed.

probably not have been allowed to go to school because she was a girl. Even if she could go, the lessons would mostly be memorizing things about Islam. She would probably be put to work or married off to an older man before she turned sixteen. Sulekha didn't think there was anything in Somalia she wanted to go back to.

PROUD TO BE A SLAVE

Cabdullaahi was proud to be Somali, proud to be from a good clan, and proud to be a son in a family that owned lots of camels. His name means "Allah's slave," and he was proud of it. He wanted to serve Allah well.

The sun beat down mercilessly, and he was almost out of water. But his family trusted him with the livestock, so he had to look after them. The army had taken his older brother to be a soldier, and his younger brother went to work each day at a shop in town.

Cabdullaahi's family had many camels, which meant they were well off. But these days, there wasn't enough food for camels or for people. Cabdullaahi's family wasn't poor, but sometimes they had to miss meals. There just wasn't enough to eat, even for people who had the money to buy food.

Somali huts

TO HELP YOU PRAY FOR THE SOMALI

YOU CAN THANK GOD FOR:

- the Bible in the Somali language.

- Christian websites, YouTube channels, and social media that talk about Jesus in Somali.

- the few thousand Somalis who follow Jesus—in Somalia and in other countries.

YOU CAN ASK GOD:

- to end the famine and war in Somalia.

- to soften the hearts of Somali people toward Jesus.

- to help many more Somali people hear about Jesus.

- for Christians to pray for and share the good news with Somalis living abroad.

- to keep Somali Christians safe and to grow them in their faith.

SOUTH AFRICA
The Rainbow Nation

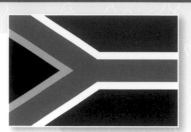

SOUTH
AFRICA

South Africa's forests, savannah, mountains, beaches, and rocky coasts are home to elephants, lions, giraffes, hippos, and even penguins and sharks! South Africa is also home to many different peoples: the many Bantu tribes, the ancient Khoisan (koy-sahn) tribes, the Coloureds, and the Cape Malay. Immigrants from Europe and Asia now also call South Africa home, and millions of Africans have come here to escape war or poverty in their own countries. There is a variety of languages, foods, songs, and dances!

Most South Africans say they are Christian. Not all of them follow Jesus faithfully, but those who go to church worship God in many different ways. They come from almost all of South Africa's tribes.

South Africa also has Muslim and Hindu communities, people who follow African traditional religions, and some who don't follow any religion at all. You can see why South Africa is called the "rainbow nation." Even its eye-catching flag brings many different colors and histories together.

PRAYING KIDS AND FUTURE LEADERS

Sipho and Lerato raced down the dusty path toward the big tent in the center of the township. "I will beat you again!" Lerato laughed. It was the same every day, Sipho thought. But he didn't mind losing because they had so much fun at Royal Kids.

Every weekday after school was out, dozens of children came to the program at the prayer tent. First, the leaders would make sure all the children had a healthy meal. Sometimes this was their only meal of the day, as most of the children were poor. Sipho was one of the few who had

both parents at home, although they had little money for food. Lerato's parents had both died. His oldest sister—still a teenager—was taking care of him and his younger brother.

After the meal came English lessons. Each child spoke his or her own tribal language. As the children learned English, they could start to speak together. Next they learned some new dances and songs, and how to talk to other people about Jesus.

FACT FILE

AREA: 470,700 square miles

POPULATION: 57 million

THREE CAPITALS: Cape Town, Pretoria, and Bloemfontein

MAIN LANGUAGES: 11 official languages

MAIN RELIGIONS: Christianity; some follow African traditional religions or none at all; smaller numbers are Muslim or Hindu

ECONOMY: One of Africa's richest countries, but many people remain poor; farming, mining, and tourism

DO YOU KNOW?

South Africans are really good at getting together to pray. The Global Day of Prayer started in South Africa and spread to every country in the world. In 2017, more than one million Christians gathered in a field to pray for the country's future.

Maybe Lerato could run faster, thought Sipho, but I'm the better dancer!

Royal Kids often shared about Jesus with different townships through group dances and songs.

After practice, it was time for prayer and teaching. Every day they prayed the Lord's Prayer together. Then the leader, Uncle Peter, taught them. He always said God was their Abba Father who loved to listen to every child who prayed. Imagine that! When Sipho prayed, God Almighty would listen, and even answer. Uncle Peter told the kids they were the leaders of tomorrow. Even if they came from a poor township, God could use them to bring peace, hope, and joy to South Africa.

As the sun went down, Sipho and Lerato walked back to the metal shacks that were their homes. They promised each other they would go on following Jesus and become leaders who would change their country. It was great to have a friend like Lerato. Tomorrow morning they would walk back to school

together. But tomorrow afternoon, Sipho would win the race to Royal Kids!

WATERING THE SEEDS OF FORGIVENESS

Madiba was glad he had an old straw hat to keep the sun off his face. This rooftop garden was not much, but it brought him some happiness. Madiba—also known as Nelson Mandela—had been a prisoner for a long time. This garden gave him a place to plant seeds and to tend the plants as they grew. He shared the food he harvested with the prison kitchen to cook for his fellow prisoners, and even with the prison guards.

A court had found Madiba guilty of trying to overthrow the government. For many years, South Africa had an unfair system called *apartheid* that gave power to the white government to rule the other races and forced the races to live separately from each other. People who resisted this unjust system were often put in jail.

After twenty-seven years, Nelson Mandela was released from prison. Apartheid ended, and he was elected president by the entire country—black, white, Coloured, and Indian. He showed the many angry people of South Africa how to forgive those who hurt them, and taught them to build a better future by working together as equals.

Nelson Mandela statue

TO HELP YOU PRAY FOR SOUTH AFRICA

YOU CAN THANK GOD FOR:

- South Africans who gather to pray and inspire Christians around the world to pray together.

- Christian camps, tent meetings, school groups, and churches where South Africans learn how to live for God.

YOU CAN ASK GOD:

- to help people of all races in South Africa to love, respect, and forgive one another.

- for Christian leaders to teach—and live—the message of the Bible clearly.

- to help the many poor people who can't find jobs.

- to protect and care for children living without parents.

- for leaders who will govern in ways that honor God.

SOUTH SUDAN
The World's Newest Country

This new nation was born in 2011 and its people celebrated with happiness and hope!

Sudan was once the largest country in Africa. Sadly, the north (mostly Arab, Muslim people) and the south (mostly black African, Christian people) fought each other for many years. An agreement in 2005 made it possible for South Sudan to separate and become an independent country. This felt like freedom for the people of South Sudan. Freedom from violence. Freedom from the strict control of the north. Freedom to be Christian!

Starting a new country hasn't been as easy as everyone hoped. Just two years after the nation was born, another war broke out. The fighters from the different tribes used to have a common enemy to fight: the Sudanese forces of the north. Now they are fighting each other. Proud leaders from different tribes didn't want to work together for peace in the new nation. This new war has caused much suffering for the people, just as the old war did.

The government leaders met to talk about peace, which can only come when people are truly sorry, ask forgiveness, and forgive one another. A new country isn't the only answer—new hearts are needed. At a National Day of Prayer, the president confessed his sins and asked forgiveness from God and from the people for things he had done wrong.

PEOPLE ON THE MOVE

Elisabeth was helping her mother prepare lunch. Suddenly a neighbor ran through the village warning everyone of an attack. They gathered a few things and ran into the trees as fast as they could. Hiding in some bushes, Elisabeth was terrified. She held her mom tightly.

"Where are father and Godwin?" she said, crying softly. Her father and

brother hadn't been in the village when the attackers came.

"I don't know, my child," said her mother. "But God knows. We must pray and then look for them when we start moving again."

They waited silently for ages until the gunmen left. Then Elizabeth and her mom started walking.

Godwin's school in a nearby village was also warned about the attack, and the students had run for cover. They kept running all night toward a refugee camp.

FACT FILE

AREA: 240,000 square miles

POPULATION: 12.9 million

CAPITAL: Juba

MAIN LANGUAGES: Official: English and Arabic; also, Juba Arabic, Dinka

MAIN RELIGIONS: Christianity, traditional religions

CHIEF EXPORT: Oil

Traditional dance

After two days on the move, Elisabeth was really tired from walking. She worried about her brother and her dad.

"Elisabeth!" She recognized the familiar voice. "Papa!" She almost fell over in her excitement and relief. Other travelers had joined their group as they walked, and her father must have been among them. She hugged him close and he carried her for a while.

"Where's Godwin, Papa?" she asked. "I don't know, child. But God knows. We must pray and keep searching for him," he said.

Millions of people have fled to nearby countries—such as Uganda or Sudan—or to camps inside South Sudan.

LIFE IN THE CAMPS

Elisabeth sat outside the crowded, dirty tent feeling bored. This had been their home for the last two months. Every time new people arrived at the camp, her parents asked for news about Godwin. Yesterday they found out that Godwin and his schoolmates had run to a camp on the border.

"He's alive! Praise God!" they said. Their hearts ached to be with him.

DO YOU KNOW?

Many schools have closed or have been damaged in the fighting, and few camps have schools. Many teachers have run away too. In South Sudan more children are missing out on primary school than in any other country.

"Come inside and get ready for church," Elisabeth heard her mother say. She liked going to church. They didn't have a building, but Christians in the camp met together to sing, pray, and hear stories from God's Word. Last week, the preacher told them that Jesus and his family once had to leave home and run away to Egypt because they were in danger. She wondered if Jesus got bored in his camp and missed his village too. Elisabeth was thankful to God—her parents and brother were alive. She had heard talk in the camp about thousands of children who lived on their own on the streets of the cities such as Juba.

Refugee camps offer some safety, but there isn't enough food and water for everyone. More than two million people have fled their homes. Many South Sudanese can't do their usual work of farming or raising animals, which means there's no food. Life is very difficult for the South Sudanese. For much of the

TO HELP YOU PRAY FOR SOUTH SUDAN

YOU CAN THANK GOD FOR:

- freedom from the long, harsh rule by the north, and hope for a new future for South Sudan.
- South Sudanese Christians who choose to rejoice and thank God, even when they're hungry, ill, or sad.

YOU CAN ASK GOD:

- to change the hearts of the leaders so that fighting will end and peace and fairness will win.
- for Christians to learn more about Jesus, the Bible, and how to live as a Christian.
- for pastors and leaders who care for the many hurting people around them, even though they themselves suffer.
- to keep safe the many children separated from their parents, and to help them stay out of trouble.
- to help the millions of people in camps or villages who need food and water.

country, the famine is as great a danger as the fighters with their guns. What happened to the joy of freedom and the dream of peace?

SPAIN
Miracles and Missionaries

A BIG PROBLEM

"Come on, Carlos!" José said impatiently as they passed the bustling cafés at the station entrance. They pushed to the front of the crowd that was listening to some young people playing guitars and singing. The boys didn't want to miss the story.

"I hope it'll be about one of the people Jesus healed—just like he healed your brother Juan," Carlos said excitedly.

José and Carlos live in Madrid, the capital of Spain. Many people have moved to the city thinking it will be easy to find work. But there aren't enough jobs for everyone.

When José's family came to Madrid, they stopped going to church. They said they no longer believed in God. They had no jobs and no faith. José's brothers started stealing to get money for drugs. More than two million Spaniards take drugs—many of them young people. "There's nothing else to do," his brothers complained.

One of José's brothers died, and the other—Juan—became very sick. Their parents didn't know what to do. In this busy, lonely city, no one seemed to care what happened to them.

One night, they stopped at an outdoor Christian meeting. A man saw the parents' sad faces and asked if he could help. When they told him about their sons, he said, "We could take Juan to a center where they help people who've been taking drugs."

At this Christian center, God worked a miracle in Juan's life. As he got better, he started to help other young people. Juan learned that Jesus is alive, and that he has the power to heal. Jesus forgave him for all the bad things he'd done and gave him the strength to stop taking drugs. Juan had a new life, following Jesus!

FACT FILE

AREA: 195,000 square miles

POPULATION: 46.4 million

CAPITAL: Madrid

MAIN LANGUAGES: Castilian (Spanish); Catalan, Galician, and Basque languages used in their regions

MAIN RELIGION: Christianity, mostly Roman Catholic

CHIEF EXPORTS: Cars, computers, oil, fruit, nuts, and vegetables

North Atlantic Ocean

CANARY ISLANDS

FRANCE
ANDORRA
Barcelona
PORTUGAL
MADRID
SPAIN
Valencia
BALEARIC ISLANDS
Seville
GIBRALTAR
CEUTA
MELILLA
ALGERIA
MOROCCO

Paella

A FEAST DAY

It's not just drug addicts who need Jesus. Most Spaniards have stopped going to the Catholic churches, or go only on special occasions such as Easter. At one time in history, Spanish Catholic missionaries took Christianity around the world to people who didn't know about Jesus. That day is long past, but Spaniards still celebrate the feast days of Catholic saints.

In Lidia's village, everyone worked hard

Madrid

DO YOU KNOW?

In Catalonia—a region with its own language and culture—there's an old tradition of building human towers or "castles." The highest castle (*castell*) built so far reached to ten levels of people!

cleaning the street and preparing for the feast day of their village saint. When the church bells rang, Lidia and her family went to church for mass. As Lidia looked at the statue of Jesus on the cross, she remembered her cousin Marta telling her that she had come to know Jesus as her friend at a Christian club for kids. Marta told her that Jesus is alive. *When I visit Marta,* she thought, *maybe I can find out how to know Jesus like that too.*

Soon the service was over. Outside, the band started to play, and everyone joined the parade. Young men carried a painted statue of their saint and statues of Jesus and the Virgin Mary. Lidia forgot about her cousin for a while as she and her friends joined the feasting and dancing.

A NEW HOME

Spain is a country that loves to party! *Fiestas* (festivals) are a big part of Spanish life. Some are religious, and some are just historical, but every city, town, and village has them. People celebrate in the streets with their neighbors late into the night. This sunny country lies in the southwest corner of Europe. With its castles, cathedrals, beautiful beaches, and delicious foods, it's little wonder many people think of holidays when they think of Spain.

A lot of migrants have come to Spain, especially from Latin America, Eastern Europe, and North Africa. Muslims, Catholics, and other kinds of Christians bring their cultures and religions with them. Spain is now much more diverse as a result.

Santiago's family had just moved to Spain from Colombia. His parents work for a mission organization based in Spain. His family was talking about the church they'd just visited.

Santiago's sister was excited. "At Sunday school, I met another Colombian girl, a Brazilian, a Romanian, an American, and a German. Oh—and a Chinese boy," she said.

"The pastor said more than fifty countries are represented at the church," his mom added.

"But how many of them speak Spanish?" his dad asked. "Let's pray for Spain every day while we live here, each morning at breakfast. We'll pray that God will use these Christians from all over the world to help bring Spanish people back to God."

TO HELP YOU PRAY FOR SPAIN

YOU CAN THANK GOD FOR:

- freedom to preach the good news about Jesus in Spain.

- Christian centers that care for drug addicts and share Jesus' love.

- the many Christian immigrants in Spain who help grow the churches there.

YOU CAN ASK GOD:

- that people will realize God is real, and that Jesus is alive and able to help them.

- for Spanish followers of Jesus to have courage to tell the people of Spain about Jesus.

- that lots of children will learn about Jesus.

- that soon there will be followers of Jesus in every village, town, and neighborhood.

Image of Virgin Mary

SRI LANKA
The Tear-Shaped Island

SRI LANKA

COLOMBO ■

GOLDEN BEACHES

Sri Lanka—a beautiful, sunny island just south of India—has golden beaches lined with palm trees. There are plenty of fish in the sea, and all around the coast are villages where fishermen live. It's a fertile country, and many crops grow here: tea, rubber, rice, spices, coconuts, and tropical fruits. No wonder farming is an important job! Others work in factories, making clothes that are sold all around the world.

Yet it's still difficult for everyone to find work. More than a million Sri Lankans have gone overseas to find jobs to support their families. Colombo, the capital, is a busy city, and its streets are often jammed with bicycles, small three-wheeled taxis, cars, and buses.

More than twenty million people live in Sri Lanka. The large majority are Sinhalese who are mostly Buddhist. The next largest group is the Tamils who originally came from India. Tamils are mainly Hindu, but some are Muslim or even Christian. There are also Muslim Moors who are descended from Arab traders. There are also more than thirty smaller groups, with different backgrounds and beliefs.

MANY BATTLES

Between 1980 and 2009 there was a terrible civil war in Sri Lanka. The fighting was mainly between Sri Lankan Tamil rebels, sometimes called the "Tamil Tigers," and government forces controlled by the Sinhalese. The Tamil rebels wanted to create their own, independent Tamil country on part of the island. In the end the Sri Lankan army defeated the Tamil Tigers.

During the war, tens of thousands of innocent people were killed by both sides.

FACT FILE

AREA: 25,330 square miles

POPULATION: 21 million

CAPITAL: Colombo

MAIN LANGUAGES: Sinhala, Tamil, and English

MAJOR RELIGIONS: Buddhism; also Hinduism, Islam, and Christianity

CHIEF EXPORTS: Tea, rubber, textiles, gems, and clothing

BANGLADESH

INDIA

Bay of Bengal

SRI LANKA

Tea plantation

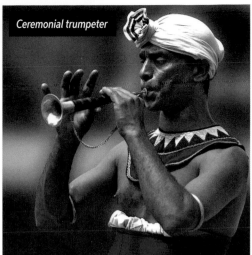

Ceremonial trumpeter

Many children lost one or both parents in the fighting.

There was also another battle. Some Buddhists got angry when Christians shared the gospel with others. They were so angry that they burned down churches to try to make them stop sharing the good news about Jesus. But the Christians haven't stopped sharing. Some Buddhists have even started to follow Jesus as a result.

Sri Lanka is sometimes called the "Pearl of the Indian Ocean" because of its shape and beauty. But it is also called the "teardrop of India." This is because of its shape, but also because of all the suffering Sri Lanka has endured throughout its history. Besides the civil war, a huge tsunami hit the island in December 2004 and wrecked many towns and villages on the coast. 31,000 people lost their lives.

Even so, Christians believe that Jesus can wipe away all the tears of the people of Sri Lanka.

A CHURCH IN THE COUNTRY

As we drove along the narrow dirt road in our van, Pastor Mahes told us his story. "When I first came here," he said, "Buddhist monks told people they must not listen when I told them about God's love for them. I tried to help people; they burned down my house. But I kept telling them that God wants to help them. One day, a man whose son was very ill came to see me. The doctor couldn't make him better. Monks at the temple couldn't help either. I prayed for the boy, and he got well. Soon the boy's whole family was following Jesus."

The van stopped beside a simple stone house. A crowd of men and women, boys and girls was waiting outside. "This is the church," Mahes said, "and also my home!"

Everyone went into the church to worship. At the end of the service, a little girl took my hand and gave me a shy smile. "Please pray for me!" she said. "My name is Kumari. I'm nine years old, and I live with my aunt because my mother and father have gone away to work. Sometimes I think they've forgotten me. But I'm glad I can come to church. Here they treat me as part of the family."

TO HELP YOU PRAY FOR SRI LANKA

YOU CAN THANK GOD FOR:

- the end of the civil war and all the killing that went with it.

- Sinhalese and Tamils who are finding a new way of life with Jesus.

- Christians who bravely share God's love in villages where people have never heard about Jesus.

- Christians who give care and compassion to those who are suffering with physical problems and emotional pain.

YOU CAN ASK GOD:

- to help people of all races and beliefs in Sri Lanka learn to live together peacefully.

- for Christians from the different ethnic groups to be examples of forgiveness, love, and living together in peace.

- to help Christians in Sri Lanka be bold and loving as they share Jesus with Buddhists, Hindus, and Muslims—even if they are persecuted.

- to help Christians in Sri Lanka to love and help children who are hurt, lonely, or abused.

STREET CHILDREN
Unseen Millions

RUSSIA

"Go!" Anton's mother screamed. "And don't come back till you've got some money."

Anton raced out of the house before she could beat him. He was hungry, cold, and had been coughing for months. His parents had no work, and they spent the little money they had on alcohol. Anton ran out the door and straight to the attic of the abandoned house where he and his friends often slept. Like him, most of them spent their days scrounging for food or money. Anton was frightened that one day they'd get caught by the police.

Many children like Anton live on the streets of St. Petersburg and other cities in Russia—maybe more than a million. A group called Russia Without Orphans brings together churches and organizations to help needy children find a permanent home where they are loved. Some run shelters where children can get food, a shower, and clothing, and where they can see a doctor if they're ill. Some help children get into school or learn a trade such as carpentry or computing. Some visit boys and girls who are in prison.

These loving workers can't help everyone, but they want to make sure every child they meet knows that God loves them and has not forgotten them.

INDIA

"Rupee! Rupee! Give me!" Little Ram stuck out a dirty, empty hand. His huge, brown eyes pleaded for one of the hundreds of passengers to give him a coin so he could buy a *chapati*. He'd eaten nothing all day and felt really hungry. Ram's parents were both dead, and he had no one else to look after him. At night, he huddled on the railway platform with lots of other homeless boys.

India has millions of children who live on the streets, often on railway platforms. Some—like Ram—are orphans. Others have run away from home or come from homeless families. Some are lost after jumping on a train and getting carried away on India's huge railway system. Many are controlled by gangs who take most of the money the children get from begging.

COLOMBIA

A businessman in Bogotá noticed a little girl climbing down into a sewer. He was shocked! He went home, put on a wetsuit, and climbed down. He was horrified to discover so many homeless children living in the city's sewers.

Out of his compassion for the children, this man started going down the sewers regularly to take the children food and get them into school or find work for them.

But not all children come off the street easily. With nobody else to care for them, the gangs they belong to become a sort of family to them. Even though life on

the streets is dangerous and dirty, fear of being alone again can feel worse.

SOUTH AFRICA

Bafana couldn't remember a time when he hadn't felt miserable. His mom and dad were forever drinking and fighting. They beat him cruelly. He thought they didn't want him, so he ran away from home to live on the streets of Johannesburg. When he managed to steal a bit of money for food, older kids or adults often stole it from him. Some other kids got him into sniffing glue—a cheap way to escape the pain of living. Once he was addicted, he had to steal even more money for glue.

That was five years ago. Today, Bafana says with a smile, "I never knew there were such kind people who want to help children like me. Now I go to school. And I've decided to follow Jesus, who loves all children. I thank God for protecting me."

Someone had found Bafana on the street and invited him to a Christian shelter for street children. He decided to go, and it changed his life for good.

LIFE ON THE STREETS

In almost every country, and in nearly every major city, children are living on the streets. We may walk right by them without noticing. Today, there may be as many as one hundred million street children. Some are orphans. Others have parents, but their whole family is homeless. Some have homes they visit from time to time, but they come into the streets to find little jobs or beg for money or food. Many children live on the streets to escape violence or abuse at home. Others run away from home for a life where they can do whatever they want. Natural disasters and wars can also separate families, leaving children alone as refugees.

City streets are dangerous places for any child to live. Drug use, violence, and abuse happen a lot. Many children sleep on cardboard boxes in train stations and doorways, under bridges, and even in sewers. They have to quickly learn to steal or fight in order to survive. In some countries, the police beat them—even shoot them.

Some children find friends on the streets—other kids or adults, some are eventually reunited with their family, and others are helped by churches or charities that care for children in need. Every child needs a place of safety, where people will take care of them and love them. Many of these street children are your age—or even younger.

SUNDANESE
"Land of the Gods" (*Parahyangan*)

Java Sea

INDONESIA

JAVA

Indian Ocean

CAN THE GODS HELP?

Why do I always forget everything I've learned? Paru wondered. *I can never remember the passages from the holy Qur'an that I'm supposed to memorize. I feel so stupid. Even my little brother can learn them.*

Paru was walking home, up a path between steeply terraced rice fields. Every time he walked this way he was amazed by the high volcanic mountains, which everyone called the "home of the gods."

The gods must have been happy with the offerings we made this year before we planted our fields, because the rice, corn, tea, and hot peppers are all growing well, Paru thought.

FACT FILE

HOMELAND: West Java, Indonesia

NUMBERS: Close to 40 million

MAIN LANGUAGE: Sunda

NUMBER OF CHRISTIANS: About 190,000

MAIN RELIGION: Islam

OCCUPATION: Farming: rice, fruit, and tea

Java, the home of the Sundanese people, is the most important island of Indonesia. Jakarta, the capital of Indonesia, is on Java's northwest coast. About forty million Sundanese live in beautiful West Java, and millions of them have never heard the truth about Jesus.

Most Sundanese are Muslims. But long before they became Muslims, the Sundanese worshiped their own gods. When people from India brought Hinduism and Buddhism to Java 1,500 years ago, the Sundanese began to worship the gods of those religions too. Even though they're now Muslims, many continue to worship the spirits they believe live in nature. And even though Islam forbids it, the Sundanese still use a lot of magic—especially for healing and trying to tell the future.

CHRISTIAN VILLAGES

In the nineteenth century, Dutch people made Java a colony of the Netherlands. Some missionaries wanted to help the Sundanese by setting up clinics, schools, and churches, and trying to tell them of God's love. But the Dutch government didn't want missionaries there. And the

Sundanese didn't want to hear about Christianity. To them Christianity was the religion of the Dutch people who had taken their land and were now telling them how they should live.

The few Sundanese who did become Christians at that time were often persecuted by their community. So missionaries built special villages for new Christians.

Rice barns

154

DO YOU KNOW?

Sundanese food is popular throughout Indonesia. It is known for having fresh, clean, and simple flavors. Some of the most popular dishes are soups—tamarind soup (tamarind is a sweet-and-sour fruit), beef and *daikon* (an Asian radish) soup, and noodle soup with beef and cartilage. In many Sundanese restaurants customers sit on woven mats on the floor. The food is served on banana leaves that are placed on low tables or on the bamboo mats on the floor.

Some of these villages still exist but are no longer entirely Christian. Many of the villagers say they're Christian because their parents and grandparents were Christian, but they're not yet following or worshiping Jesus themselves.

MUSIC AND DRAMA

Some Sundanese Christians are trying to show that their faith is not just a religion for Western people like the Dutch. They use Sundanese styles of drama and music to tell Bible stories so people can understand that God loves them too.

One evening, two young people stopped Sita and her friends as they were walking along a busy street in Jakarta. "Come and watch this play!" they said. "It's about why God in heaven sent Jesus to earth."

After the show Sita said, "What an amazing story! Anyone

could understand it because it's like our Sundanese plays. I'm so glad God brought Jesus back to life again after he died. I'd like to know more about Jesus."

A few months later, Sita decided to follow Jesus. But her family was angry. "What do you mean, you've become a Christian?" shouted her brother. "You can't be a Christian! We're Sundanese—and that means we're Muslims." Sita felt sad because her family was so angry, but she knew she had to follow Jesus.

Pray for the Sundanese. Like Sita, more and more are becoming Christians. Sometimes they are persecuted and their church buildings get destroyed. But even though they have the entire Bible in their language, many Sundanese, like Paru, still have not heard the good news about Jesus.

TO HELP YOU PRAY FOR THE SUNDANESE

YOU CAN THANK GOD FOR:

■ the whole Bible in the Sundanese language.

■ Indonesian Christians who are telling the Sundanese about Jesus.

■ the growing numbers of Sundanese Christians like Sita who follow Jesus even when it's very difficult.

YOU CAN ASK GOD:

■ to send more Christians to Sundanese communities to show children like Paru that Jesus is more powerful than the spirits that live in nature.

■ to use Christian drama and music to show the Sundanese that they can know and follow Jesus.

■ to help Sundanese who become Christians to stay faithful to Jesus, even when they are persecuted, and to be good witnesses to family and friends.

■ to bring true faith to those who say they are Christian only because their parents or grandparents were, but who haven't yet believed in Jesus for themselves.

■ to help the Sundanese people do well in their farming so their families can be healthy.

SYRIA
Divided and Hurting

TURKEY
Aleppo
SYRIA
LEBANON
DAMASCUS
ISRAEL
JORDAN
IRAQ

WHAT IS A CHRISTIAN?

"What do you mean you've become a Christian?" Yana asked her brother Ibrahim. "You've always been a Christian. It's been our family tradition for hundreds of years. We belong to a church, don't we? We Christians have lived here in Damascus since New Testament times."

"That's true, Yana," said Ibrahim. "It was on the road to Damascus that Saul met with Jesus. Later he became the apostle Paul here. But this is different. I've met Christians who are really *excited* about their faith. They told me I could know Jesus as a friend and have a relationship with God. They showed me how to read the Bible properly. It's a great book!"

Mediterranean
Sea

SYRIA

AN ANCIENT LAND

Damascus, the capital of modern Syria, may be the world's oldest city. It's mentioned in the book of Genesis. The Bible also mentions the Euphrates River, which flows through Syria. The Arameans appear as enemies of Israel in the Old Testament books of Judges, Samuel, and Kings. The land called "Aram" in the Bible is called Syria today.

Syria has a narrow strip of fertile land along its Mediterranean coast. Inland is a mountainous region and east of that is the Syrian Desert.

WAR

For much of the last hundred years, Syria has been involved in wars and conflicts with its neighbors. Since 1971, the Assad family has ruled Syria. It's officially a secular country, but three-quarters of Syrians are Sunni Muslims, and there are several other Muslim groups too. The Assad family belongs to a Muslim group called the Alawites. Several smaller religious groups make their homes in Syria, including the Druze and the Yazidis. (You can read about them on pages 42 and 188 of this book.)

Syria claims to be a democracy, but the Assad family kept tight control of the country with the help of the army and secret police.

In 2011, people protested against the president's harsh rule. These protests led to a terrible civil war with several rebel groups fighting against the government and against each other. Other countries got involved, adding to the chaos and damage. Many major cities have been bombed into rubble, and almost half a million people have been killed. Nearly half the Syrian population has been forced to

Ancient Palmyra—damaged by war

FACT FILE

AREA: 71,500 square miles

POPULATION: 18.3 million

CAPITAL: Damascus

MAIN LANGUAGE: Arabic

MAIN RELIGION: Islam

CHIEF EXPORTS: Oil, minerals, spices, and fruits and vegetables

DO YOU KNOW?

You can still find and visit the "street called Straight" in Damascus, where Paul received his sight and because a believer in Jesus. (Read the story in Acts 9.)

leave their homes, many fleeing abroad. It will take a long time for the Syrian people to recover from the trauma of the war.

DISAPPEARING CHRISTIANS

For 1,300 years, Muslims and Christians lived together in Syria. Before 2011, there were Orthodox or Armenian churches in almost every Syrian town, as well as some Protestant churches. Christians made up only a small part of Syria's population, but they were allowed to go to church. National radio and TV stations broadcast Christian programs at Christmas and Easter. Christians were respected and many had good jobs as merchants, teachers, doctors, and lawyers.

But now Christians have been almost completely forced out of Syria. Some extremist Muslim groups want to get rid of all Christians. They bully, persecute, and even kill believers in Jesus. In some parts of Syria, no Christians remain. The only good news is that—even though the traditional Christian communities are disappearing—more and more Syrian Muslims are deciding to follow Jesus, especially Syrian Kurds.

NEW LIFE

"Sadiq, pull the cord! Do it now," his father said. Sadiq took the string in his hand, yanked, and the room went from darkness to light. The refrigerator began to hum for the first time in months. Sadiq's mother and sisters clapped their hands, and everyone smiled.

"Maybe life can start feeling normal again," Sadiq's mother exclaimed.

"Life will always be different—now we follow the way of Isa," his father said. ("Isa" is the Arabic name for Jesus.)

Sadiq's family lives in an area that was bombed time and again during the civil war. After the bombing, at first there was no electricity or water. Half the buildings were destroyed. A group of people brought in some generators and started to sell electricity at a fair price. They also gave out free bottles of water, blankets for cold nights, and useful things such as toothbrushes and batteries. When they gave out these things, they asked if they could pray for people in Isa's name. Sadiq will never forget the tears that fell from his father's eyes as these fellow Syrians prayed for God to protect and bless his family.

Afterwards, Sadiq's father gathered the family. "I always thought we lived in a way God wanted," he said. "But we Syrians have been fighting one another for years. These Christians have shown us another way—the way of the man of peace, Isa al Masih (Jesus, the Messiah)."

TO HELP YOU PRAY FOR SYRIA

YOU CAN THANK GOD FOR:

■ the growing numbers of new Syrian believers.

■ Christians who help refugees and displaced people, inside and outside Syria.

■ for the Bible in Arabic, the New Testament in the Kurdish dialect, and Christian satellite programs and websites.

YOU CAN ASK GOD:

■ for peace in Syria, so that people can return home and rebuild their lives.

■ to take care of children whose parents have been killed in the war.

■ to help Christians care for others, showing the love of God.

■ that many more Syrians will learn about Jesus and decide to follow him.

Refugees sleeping

TAI LUE
From the Land of Twelve Thousand Rice Fields

CHINA

VIETNAM

MYANMAR

LAOS

THAILAND

XISHUANGBANNA

In the Yunnan Province of southwest China, near the borders with Myanmar and Laos, there's a mountainous region called Xishuangbanna (pronounced *Shee-shwang-banna*). This is the ancient home of the Tai Lue people. Fifty years ago, monkeys, elephants, tigers, bears, deer, and even peacocks thrived in the thick green forests that covered the high mountains. Since then, almost half the forest has been cut down and replaced with plantations of rubber trees. Many more people—especially Han Chinese—have come to live in the area. Cutting down the forest has changed the climate. Rainfall has decreased and rivers have been drying up.

The Tai Lue people traditionally built houses on stilts, constructed with wood, bamboo, and thatch. Pigs and hens lived underneath. These days, concrete homes are more common.

The Tai Lue grow coconut palms, banana, papaya and mango trees, pineapples, and peppers around their houses. There are more rice fields than you can count: *Xishuangbanna* means "land of twelve thousand rice fields."

ANOTHER LIFE?

The Tai Lue people are Buddhists. There's a temple in every village. Most children go to a school run by the government. But seven-year-old Ai Kim's parents send him to the temple for lessons in their own language.

Ai Kim tried to be brave when he waved goodbye to his parents and left for the temple with his big brother. He was worried about what it would be like to live there for three long years.

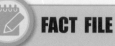

FACT FILE

NUMBERS: About 1.1 million, with around 790,000 in China

LOCATIONS: Yunnan Province of China, Myanmar, Thailand, and Laos

MAIN LANGUAGE: Dai or Tai Lue

MAIN RELIGION: Buddhism (but mixed with animism)

OCCUPATIONS: Farmers and traders; tropical crops such as pineapples are important, as well as rice

Forty other little boys were already at the school. "It's your turn to have your head shaved," a monk told Ai Kim. Once that was done, the monk helped Ai Kim put on the orange robe he now had to wear every day.

"Are you going to teach us how to read?" Ai Kim asked. "Yes, we start tomorrow," replied the monk. "You will learn to read the Buddhist scriptures. That will earn merit for you and your family, which will help you in your next life."

Ai Kim knew Buddhists believe that, when they die, they can be reborn as more important people if they are good, or as dirty animals if they are bad. This is called "reincarnation". Ai Kim believed all the good things he did would help him in his next life. But sometimes he felt frightened. If he did something wrong, what would happen to him in the next life?

DO YOU KNOW?

Early Western missionaries to the Tai Lue reached them by riding in on elephants from Thailand.

Songkran *(water festival)*

THE "GOOD GUY" WINS

"Tell us the story of the water-splashing festival, please!" the children begged their father after dinner one night. The Tai Lue people love to hear stories and—like many of their stories—this one is about how the good guy wins and the bad guy loses.

"Once upon a time a powerful demon-king ruled our people," said their father. "He made life very hard for them. He had seven wives. The youngest of them, Yu Xiang (*yoo shang*), had compassion for the people. 'I wish the demon-king would die,' she thought, 'so the Tai Lue people can be freed from his evil power.'

"The demon-king loved Yu Xiang very much. One day he told her his biggest secret. 'My power is in the single white hair on my head,' he said. 'I can be defeated only if it's pulled out and tied around my neck.' That night, while he was asleep, Yu Xiang pulled out the white hair, tied it tightly around his neck, and cut off his head.

"Everyone was happy that the demon-king was dead! But as soon as his head touched the ground, it burst into flames, burning everything it touched. Brave Yu Xiang managed to pick up the head. Immediately the fire stopped. But when she put the head down, the fire started again. 'Quick, quick!' the people shouted,

throwing water over Yu Xiang to put out the fire and wash away the blood.

"Each year, when we celebrate *Songkran*—the water-splashing festival—and have fun throwing water at each other, we remember this story. The water we throw makes us pure and clean, and keeps us safe for the coming year."

There have been Tai Lue Christians for almost one hundred years. They were persecuted at the start, and left to start a new village that's still Christian after all these years. But most Tai Lue people today don't know that doing good things, or throwing water, doesn't make their hearts clean, or help them after they die. There are only a few thousand Christian believers among the Tai Lue. Who is going to tell them that God sent his only son, Jesus, to defeat all the evil powers? Who will tell kids like Ai Kim that he doesn't need to worry about the bad things he does, if he tells Jesus that he's sorry?

TO HELP YOU PRAY FOR THE TAI LUE

YOU CAN THANK GOD FOR:

- the Tai Lue people, who have a strong culture that's survived many challenges.

- the few Tai Lue Christians who have passed on the faith across generations.

- all the people translating the Bible into Tai Lue. There is already a New Testament.

YOU CAN ASK GOD:

- for a church in every Tai Lue town.

- to set the Tai Lue free from the fear of evil spirits, and of not earning enough merit for the next life.

- that each person may know the love of Jesus, who washed away our sins once and for all.

- for the few Christians to boldly share the good news about Jesus with others.

- for many to learn about Jesus through the Tai Lue New Testament.

- for other Christians in Yunnan Province— minorities and Han Chinese—to show the Tai Lue how much God loves them.

THIRD CULTURE KIDS
Belonging to Two Worlds

"How do you speak like the English children?" Victor asked his friend.

"Hiding my Nigerian accent took practice," Seth replied. "At home, I still speak with a Nigerian accent like my father. But I got tired of the other kids in class making fun of me, so I learned to speak like them."

Victor nodded. He'd try to learn a new accent too. Nobody likes being teased for the way they speak.

In Victor and Seth's class of thirty, there were students from around twenty different countries. Many of them also spoke a different language at home. This was normal in their East London neighborhood. There seemed to be people from every part of the world.

But the neighborhood also had gangs. When older boys who were gang members came by, Victor felt scared. Sometimes they got younger boys to do bad things by threatening them, or paying them. His father said that if he didn't study hard, he might end up in a gang, and get into trouble with the police—or with his mother!

A UNIQUE GROUP OF KIDS

Third culture kids (TCKs) are children raised in a different culture from their parents. For example, a Nigerian boy growing up in England, or a Korean girl growing up in Japan. These days, millions of people move to new countries, so there are lots of TCKs. Sometimes their parents are refugees. Sometimes they work in business, or for their government. Sometimes they are missionaries.

No matter what jobs their parents have, all TCKs live between two worlds. They're part of the culture where they are growing up and part of the culture, or country, that their parents call home. They almost always speak two or more languages: their parents' language at home and the local language at school.

TCKs have a different experience of life from local children. They understand other TCKs best. Few feel as if they really belong to the country where they're growing up. But most don't feel they really belong in their parents' home country either. Sometimes they feel as if they don't belong anywhere. But TCKs often have a special skill: they can easily adapt to almost any place.

Many TCKs are good leaders. Nowadays, many of us live in places where different cultures mix, like in Victor and Seth's classroom. For some of us, getting along well with people who are different from us is hard to learn. But for TCKs, it's what they do best. They often find good jobs, because they're so good at getting along with people who are different from them.

NIGERIAN OR ENGLISH?

At the church where Victor's father was a pastor, they worshiped in the Nigerian

style. People wore their best clothes, and the music was loud, with joyful shouts of praise. His father preached long sermons and there were almost always several testimonies and offerings. Church would sometimes last four or five hours—just like Victor remembered from back in Nigeria. Victor loved the African style of music in church, but sometimes he wished the services were a bit shorter. Seth said that at the international church the services finished in only one or two hours!

Christian life in Victor's home was also African style. Every day, the family woke up early—often before sunrise—to pray together before breakfast. At night, they read the Bible and prayed some more before bed. Victor knew other Christian children, and none of them prayed as much as his family. He normally didn't mind, because he liked to pray. But sometimes Victor wished he could play video games and watch TV, like Seth or the English boys he knew.

Seth looked around the crowded room. His sisters Ivah and Michaela sat beside their parents, playing with their phones. There were more cousins, aunties, and uncles here than he even knew. How did he have so many Nigerian relatives living here in England?

The families were talking and laughing together in Yoruba, a Nigerian language. On TV, a Nollywood film—made in Nigeria—was playing while Afrobeat music blared from the kitchen. Seth liked both Nigerian music and Western music.

Seth's uncles were busy debating who had the nicest car while his aunties were setting out big bowls of *ogbono* (stew) and *fufu* (big, sticky balls of cooked dough from the cassava plant) next to cola and potato chips—Nigerian and Western food on the same table. Soon they would feast.

Victor would love it here! Seth imagined. But Seth wondered if *he* actually loved it here. Did he feel more comfortable with his schoolmates, or with his Nigerian family? Was he more like the Nigerians, or more like the English? Maybe when he was older he would figure it out—or perhaps he would move to another country and try something new!

TIBETANS
Following the God-King

TIBET
Autonomous Region

PAKISTAN

Dharamsala

NEPAL

Lhasa

BHUTAN

CHINA

INDIA

BANGLADESH

MYANMAR

A MYSTERIOUS WORLD

The Himalayan and Kun Lun Mountains surround the Tibetan plateau like a gigantic wall. This plateau, the highest and largest on earth, is often called "the roof of the world." It covers 714,300 square miles and averages more than 15,000 feet above sea level. For hundreds of years, few people visited—Tibet was a mysterious world. Today, visitors can fly to Lhasa, the capital city of Tibet, or travel through the country on roads and train tracks built by the Chinese.

In Tibet, the Buddhist religious leaders used to also be the political leaders. The Tibetan Buddhist officials and priests were treated as royalty, but most ordinary people were treated like servants. They even had to stick out their tongues when they met important people, to show their tongues were not black to prove they didn't practice black magic! In the Lhasa region, some Tibetans still do this as a sign of respect.

THE DALAI LAMA

The Dalai Lama is the most important priest, or *lama*, and leader of the Tibetan people. Tibetans believe the Dalai Lama is a god-king, and that when he dies his soul will always be reborn in a baby. As soon as the Dalai Lama dies, the search begins for the next Dalai Lama.

He has to be a baby boy born within eighteen months of the previous Dalai Lama's death.

The present Dalai Lama was born in 1935, in a farmhouse hundreds of miles from Lhasa. Although he wasn't yet two years old, he had to pass tests to see if he really was the new Dalai Lama. In one test, a number of things were put in front of him, some of which belonged to the previous Dalai Lama. Everyone watched anxiously. He pointed out exactly what had belonged to the last Dalai Lama. The new Dalai Lama had been found!

Thousands of very young Tibetan boys used to go to the monasteries to become monks and learn the Buddhist scriptures. When he was only five years old, the current Dalai Lama was taken to Lhasa to be enthroned in the Potala, the most important monastery in Tibet. Buddhist

 FACT FILE

LOCATION: About six million Tibetans live in China, mostly in central Tibet and the western Chinese provinces of Qinghai, Sichuan, Yunnan, and Gansu. Another 400,000 Tibetans live abroad, in India, Nepal, Bhutan, and Sikkim, and in North America and Europe.

MAIN RELIGION: Tibetan Buddhism

MAIN LANGUAGES: Tibetan, Mandarin Chinese

Potala Palace

Sand mandala

DO YOU KNOW?

The highest train in the world runs to Lhasa, the capital of Tibet. It has the world's highest train station, the world's highest train tunnel, and the world's highest section of track—at 16,640 feet above sea level!

monks taught him everything they could about Buddhism. He wasn't allowed to leave the Potala except to visit another monastery. Imagine how lonely he must have felt without his family or other children to play with!

LITTLE FREEDOM

In 1950, the Communist government in China took control of the land. They destroyed more than 6,000 monasteries and got rid of many ancient Buddhist scriptures. The Communists killed thousands and thousands of Tibetans. Many more fled across the high mountain passes into neighboring India and Nepal. In 1959, the Dalai Lama had to flee to Dharamsala, in India, where he still lives.

The Tibetans are devoted to their god-king. Some Tibetans—especially those living outside of Tibet—want Tibet to be a free and independent country. *Lamas* (priests) lead protests against the Chinese government, but the government works hard to stop them.

Many changes have taken place in Tibet. Priests no longer have the power they once had. Now, more Chinese people live in Lhasa than Tibetans. Chinese has become the official language. More Tibetan children go to school now than in the past, but all their lessons are in Chinese other than their Tibetan language classes at home.

There are very few Tibetan Christians. For nearly 150 years, missionaries have been telling Tibetans living in neighboring countries about Jesus. But their religion holds them powerfully and it is so different from Christianity that very few ever understand or believe in the gospel.

Prayer flag

Tibetan Lama

TO HELP YOU PRAY FOR THE TIBETANS

YOU CAN THANK GOD FOR:

■ the few Tibetans who follow Jesus instead of the Buddha or the Dalai Lama.

■ the modern translations of the New Testament in Tibetan.

■ using some Chinese Christians to bring a message of love and reconciliation to Tibetans.

■ Christians who help Tibetan people in times of need, like when extreme weather conditions (heavy snow, frost, earthquakes, floods) destroy their flocks, herds, or crops.

YOU CAN ASK GOD:

■ for the freedom to share Jesus with Tibetans. Neither the Chinese government nor the Tibetan Buddhist leaders want this to happen.

■ for Chinese Christians who live near Tibetans to love them with the love of Jesus, and to be humble and gentle. Tibetans have suffered much under Chinese rule.

■ to help many Tibetans find Christian resources through the internet, radio, and television so they can hear the good news about Jesus.

■ to free Tibetans from the powerful grip of their religion. Pray for them to understand the good news about Jesus, and to break free of fears and follow him.

TRINIDAD
Carnival and Calypso

Caribbean Sea

TRINIDAD AND TOBAGO

CARNIVAL

It's time for Carnival in Port of Spain, the capital of Trinidad! Thousands of men, women, boys, and girls crowd the streets. People are wearing colorful costumes that sparkle and glitter in the sun and dancing to the beat of the steel pans (drums).

People taking part in Carnival have spent weeks preparing to play *mas*, or masquerade. They've made fancy costumes, practiced their music, and written clever songs—calypso, soca, and chutney are popular local styles. It's all over at midnight because tomorrow is Ash Wednesday, the start of the Christian season of Lent.

MANY FESTIVALS

People in Trinidad celebrate lots of festivals. In October or November, they celebrate Divali, the Hindu festival of lights. Flames dance from thousands of little clay pots while people spend the night feasting with family and friends. The Hindu spring festival of Phagwa, or Holi, takes place in March. During this festival, people on the streets throw *abeer*, or brightly colored powder, at each other!

Muslims in Trinidad have their festivals too. On Hosay, they remember the murder of Hussein, the grandson of the prophet Muhammad. They carry paper models of mosques, called *tadjahs*, through the streets to the beat of drums and chanting. Then they feast all evening and dance all night. Afterward, they throw the *tadjahs* into the sea, as a sign of burial.

Some of these traditions may seem a bit strange, but different cultures have special ways of having fun and celebrating what's important to them.

TRINIDAD AND TOBAGO

Trinidad is one of the two main islands making up the Republic of Trinidad and Tobago. Trinidad is the farthest south of the Caribbean islands, only about seven miles from the South American mainland. Some of the people are poor. But money from oil, natural gas, and tourists has given Trinidadians a higher standard of living than most people in the Caribbean. Crime, particularly linked with drugs and poverty, is a problem on the islands.

MANY ROOTS

Although it was late, nine-year-old Earl

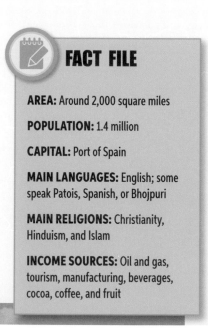

FACT FILE

AREA: Around 2,000 square miles

POPULATION: 1.4 million

CAPITAL: Port of Spain

MAIN LANGUAGES: English; some speak Patois, Spanish, or Bhojpuri

MAIN RELIGIONS: Christianity, Hinduism, and Islam

INCOME SOURCES: Oil and gas, tourism, manufacturing, beverages, cocoa, coffee, and fruit

164

Trinidadian dish: Bake and Shark

DO YOU KNOW?

The pitch lake at La Brea, in the south of Trinidad, is the biggest natural source of asphalt in the world. A legend says the lake was formed when a chief killed a sacred hummingbird. This made the gods so angry that they drowned his whole village in pitch.

Carnival costumes

was sitting outside with his father. He was too excited to sleep after Carnival. "I love festivals!" he said. "How come we have so many?"

"Because we Trinidadians come from many different parts of the world," said his father. "Most of us have roots in Africa, India, or Europe, but some come from the Middle East, China, and South America. When people arrived from all these different places, they brought their culture, religion, and festivals with them."

"Why did they all come to Trinidad?" Earl asked.

"It all started long ago," said his father. "When Christopher Columbus arrived from Europe in 1498, he took control of Trinidad for Spain. But the Tainos and Kalinagos had already been living on the island for centuries. Later on, French Catholics settled here too. They planted sugar and cacao plantations, and brought slaves from Africa to work for them. They tried to make the slaves forget their African religions and become Catholic. Then in 1797, the British captured Trinidad."

"What happened when the British came?" asked Earl.

"The government did away with slavery by 1838—but the plantation owners still needed workers. So they brought people from China, then later from India, as low-paid laborers. Many of these people stayed in Trinidad. Some were Muslims or Buddhists, but most were Hindus. They each kept their own religion and culture. Since that time, people have kept coming here from many parts of the world.

"Wherever we came from originally, we're all Trinidadians now. We got our independence in 1962 and we all love to join in the festivals! Our national anthem says, "Here every creed and race find an equal place." That's a great idea—but it's not always true. Sometimes there's tension between people of different ethnic backgrounds," his father said.

As Earl listened to his father, he thought of the church he went to each Sunday with his family. He loved singing hymns and learning stories from the Bible. There were many churches in Trinidad. But he knew that lots of people worshiped other gods, too. And many people who said they were Christian never went to church at all! Earl wished everyone in Trinidad would believe and follow Jesus. He wondered how that might ever happen.

TO HELP YOU PRAY FOR TRINIDAD

YOU CAN THANK GOD FOR:

- the beautiful diversity that makes Trinidad such a special and interesting place.

- the many churches in Trinidad.

- the freedom to follow Jesus and to share about him with other people in Trinidad.

YOU CAN ASK GOD:

- to help the different peoples of Trinidad live together in peace.

- that the government will be wise and fair to all people, no matter what their background or religion, and no matter whether they're rich or poor.

- for those who call themselves Christian to really get to know God and live a life that pleases him.

- that Christians will share the good news about Jesus with Trinidadians and other people now coming to the island for work.

TUAREG
Blue-Veiled Guardians of the Sahara

UNDER THE DESERT STARS

Augustine sat cross-legged on a large blanket spread out on the cool sand of the Sahara Desert. The moon and stars shone much more brightly out here than in the city where he lived. Several of the men sitting across from him had dark blue veils across their faces. These Tuareg men wanted to learn more about Jesus. They had only decided to follow him a few weeks earlier. Augustine told the story of how God revealed himself to the Old Testament herdsmen Abraham, Isaac, and Jacob. He shared that God loves every person, and that Jesus came so that people could know God. Augustine was thankful to God for this chance to share about Jesus with these unique people.

PROUD NOMADS

The Tuareg, or Kel Tamasheq (*tah-mah-sheck*), people live in the Sahara Desert. They are descended from the Imazighen (sometimes called Berbers) of North Africa. Hundreds of years ago, the Arabs drove them out of their homeland into the Sahara Desert and the Sahel—a semi-arid grassland area to its south. The name *Tuareg* comes from Arabic, and means "forsaken by God." Although badly treated by the Arabs, the Tuareg were powerful. Before long, they had forced the black Africans—who were living in the lands where they settled—to work for them as slaves.

The Tuareg spent their days raiding, trading, and herding. They moved through the desert, with their herds of camels, cattle, sheep, and goats. Traders and explorers traveling across the Sahara paid the Tuareg to guide and protect them. Everyone was afraid of these guardians of the desert, but they were afraid of no one.

In the nineteenth century, France took control of large areas of West Africa. They banned raiding, which had always been a part of the Tuareg way of life. They also created boundaries between countries, so the Tuareg could no longer move so freely from place to place. The proud Tuareg became much less powerful.

FAMINE

The Tuareg inhabit a wide area, stretching from southwest Libya to southern Algeria, Niger, Mali, and Burkina Faso,

including the Sahara Desert and the Sahel. If the Tuareg area were a country, it would be one of the largest in Africa.

Although the Sahara and Sahel are huge areas, there's never much rain there. Since the "famine of no hope"—between 1968 and 1974—there have been many droughts and famines, and thousands of people have died. Many Tuareg were forced to abandon their nomadic life and had to move into refugee camps or large cities to survive.

TENT LIFE

Under the hot sun Amud tugs on his hoe, weeding between millet plants.

"Slaves used to work in our gardens, while we traveled across the desert with our camels, herds, and families," he says. "But now we're poor and have no slaves. We have to grow our own millet and vegetables. At least I still have a tent."

Although poor, Amud wears a silver cross around his neck. It's been part of his family for generations. It's common for the Tuareg to wear, or decorate their things, with crosses. Many think this shows that the Tuareg were Christian before they converted to Islam more than a thousand years ago.

Amud's ragged, oval tent is made of leather. It's about ten feet long and twelve feet wide.

"This tent has been my home for a long time," he says. "My parents used to carry our tents and belongings on the backs of our camels as we moved from place to place. They were proud that the Tuareg were called 'the lords of the desert.'"

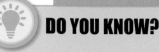

DO YOU KNOW?

The blue turban and veil or *tagelmust* that Tuareg men wrap around their head can be almost twenty feet long. They cover their mouth with the veil when they meet someone they respect. When a Tuareg man eats, he uses his left hand to lift the veil from his mouth.

ABANDONED?

The Tuareg are Muslims. Because they moved around so much, they didn't usually build mosques. But when the Tuareg moved to a new place, a Muslim holy man traveled with them to pray for them.

Until recently, most Tuareg had never heard about Jesus.

When Biga decided to follow Jesus, people laughed at him for following the white man's religion. But soon they saw how much God had changed him. There are very few Tuareg Christians, but they want to show others that God loves them, and would never forsake them.

When Christian organizations started to send food and other aid to the Tuareg, the Christians made sure that the neediest people got their share.

"How can we follow Jesus, too?" some of them wanted to know. "Life is very hard—but now we know God hasn't abandoned us."

Tamasheq New Testament

TO HELP YOU PRAY FOR THE TUAREG

YOU CAN THANK GOD FOR:

- the few—but increasing—numbers of Tuareg who follow Jesus.

- the New Testament translated into Tamasheq, the Tuareg language.

YOU CAN ASK GOD:

- to help the Tuareg people in their struggle against poverty and famine.

- to send more Christians to the Tuareg, to show God's love, and teach them how to follow Jesus.

- for more stories from the Bible in Tuareg dialects, especially in audio format. The Tuareg love storytelling.

- to show the Tuareg that they can follow Jesus and still remain Tuareg. They don't have to lose their culture to follow him.

TURKEY
One Country, Two Continents

EARTHQUAKE!

Several years ago, a terrible earthquake in Turkey destroyed many homes. Thousands of people died or were badly hurt. For several days, rescuers dug into the rubble. Finally, they gave up hope of finding anyone else alive. But, as bulldozers started to clear the rubble, rescuers discovered a seven-year-old boy named Murat trapped deep under a huge pile of bricks. He'd been buried for nine days.

"It's a miracle!" said doctors who examined Murat. "It's so hot, we don't know how anyone could live so long without water."

"But I did have water," Murat insisted. "Every evening, a nice man brought me bread and water."

The boy's family was puzzled. No one could have visited him because he was buried under the rubble. Was it a miracle? Did an angel visit Murat?

BETWEEN TWO WORLDS

Turkey is a rectangular-shaped country whose center is a wide plateau surrounded by a ring of hills and mountains. Most people live near the coast, which surrounds Turkey on almost three sides.

Istanbul, Turkey's largest city, is the only city in the world in two different continents. Half of Istanbul is in Europe, and the other half in Asia. A narrow channel of water called the Bosphorus divides the city. It is through the Bosphorus that you can sail from the Black Sea to the Mediterranean Sea. Every day, more than two million people cross this waterway—by bridges, ferries, and tunnels—on their way to and from work and school.

There is a big difference between life in the city and in the traditional countryside. Schools, hospitals, houses, and jobs are all much better in the cities. But the countryside is fertile and grows many crops. Turkey leads the world in

growing cherries, apricots, hazelnuts, figs, and pomegranates, and is near the top in growing watermelons, cucumbers, tomatoes, chickpeas, and pistachios.

Most of the population are ethnic Turks, but there are also many other groups. The Kurds are the largest ethnic minority. They have a long and difficult history of their own. (You can read about the Kurds in this book, on page 86.)

Today, Turkey itself is like a bridge between Europe and Asia—a mix of Western and Middle Eastern culture. But Turkey's people are facing challenges to their freedom, and many worry about the country's future.

VISITORS AND REFUGEES

Tourism is very important to Turkey. Millions of people visit Turkey every year for its beaches, history, and delicious food. Meanwhile, millions of Turks have moved to Europe for work—especially to Germany, where there are more jobs. They send home some of their pay to

FACT FILE

AREA: 300,948 square miles

POPULATION: 81.9 million

CAPITAL: Ankara

MAIN LANGUAGES: Turkish; Kurdish and others also used

MAIN RELIGION: Islam

CHIEF EXPORTS: Cars and auto parts, clothing and textiles, machinery, minerals, food

DO YOU KNOW?

Turkey is a land full of Bible history. The Tigris and Euphrates rivers start in Turkey. Some people say that its highest mountain—Mount Ararat—is where Noah's ark came to rest. Many of the cities mentioned in the New Testament are in modern Turkey. You can even visit the ruins of buildings mentioned in Acts and Revelation.

Ancient theater, Ephesus

support their families.

Because of the wars in nearby Syria and Iraq, many refugees have come to Turkey. Many also flee into Turkey from Iran. At one point, there were more refugees in Turkey than in any other country: nearly three million from Syria alone. Many hope one day to return to their own country, but some are settling in Turkey, and some are trying to reach Europe to start new lives there.

"TO BE A TURK IS TO BE MUSLIM"

For more than a thousand years, this part of the world was strongly Christian, but after the invasion of Turkish tribes from the east it gradually became almost entirely Muslim. There is a saying, "To be a Turk is to be Muslim." Today, almost every Turk is a Muslim, although many don't take their religion too seriously.

There are very few Turkish Christians, but they are slowly growing in number. Even though the law allows people to become Christian, some Turkish Christians have been prevented from meeting to worship. Some have been thrown out of their families or lost their jobs for following Jesus. A few who chose to leave Islam and follow Jesus have even been murdered.

Christians in Turkey from different backgrounds—Turkish, Kurdish, Armenian, and Assyrian—meet together to pray and study the Bible. This shows people that following Jesus brings peace and turns enemies into friends.

There are two Christian TV channels as well as Christian radio stations, websites, phone hotlines, online chatrooms, and several Christian publishing houses—all in Turkish—helping tell Turks more about Jesus. But Turkish people have been slow to receive the gospel. Only through persistent prayer and sharing God's love will hearts become open to Jesus.

TO HELP YOU PRAY FOR TURKEY

YOU CAN THANK GOD FOR:

- the whole Bible and many Christian materials that are freely available in the Turkish language.

- Christians in Turkey who keep on sharing the gospel, even when it's difficult.

YOU CAN ASK GOD:

- to open the hearts of Turkish people to receive Jesus.

- to encourage Turkish Christians who suffer for following Jesus.

- to help Turkish pastors teach the Bible and serve their churches well.

- to give Christians the courage to reach out in love to Turkish people and to the millions of refugees who have come to Turkey.

Istanbul

UKRAINE
Where Easter Bells Ring

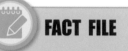

"Khrystos Voskres!" (Christ is risen!) the priest called out to the crowd of people.

"Voistynu Voskres!" (He is risen indeed!) they shouted in reply.

The sun was just rising, but a big crowd had gathered at the church. It was Easter morning—Resurrection Sunday. The people walked three times around the building singing to remember the walk the women in Jerusalem made to Jesus' tomb. Then the priest struck the church doors with his cross, and they opened. Jesus defeated death and opened the doors of heaven! The people went inside to worship joyfully.

Black Sea

Marichka was filled with wonder. The church here in Kyiv was so much bigger than the one back home. Inside, it glittered with decorations and icons. The big choir of priests sounded like angels singing! She was so glad her parents had brought her to Kyiv for Easter.

After church, they walked back to her Uncle Yuri's home. He was carrying a large wicker basket. Families had brought baskets of special Easter food to the sunrise service to be blessed. Uncle Yuri's basket contained *paska* (bread decorated with dough crosses), *pysanky* (decorated

hard-boiled eggs), ham, bacon, sausage, *hrudka* (special Easter cheese), *khrin* (horseradish and beets), and even butter shaped like a lamb. Soon they would taste these delights.

"What language were the priests singing in?" Marichka asked her *babusya* (grandmother) as they walked. "It sounded beautiful, but I only understood bits of it."

"It's Church Slavonic," her babusya replied. "It's an old language we use only in traditional church services now. These days many churches use Ukrainian, so

FACT FILE

AREA: 233,090 square miles

CAPITAL: Kyiv or Kiev

POPULATION: 44 million

OFFICIAL LANGUAGE: Ukrainian

MAIN RELIGION: Christianity (Ukrainian Orthodox are the largest group)

CHIEF EXPORTS: Metals, fuels, chemicals, machinery, and food

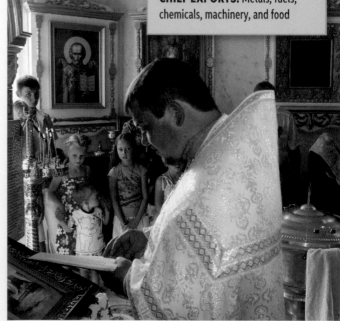

St. Andrew's Church, Kyiv

people can understand the words. We are Ukrainian Catholics. Different from Catholics in Western Europe—although we're all part of the Catholic family."

"Most Ukrainians belong to Orthodox churches that have been around a long time," Marichka's mother added. "Some follow religious leaders here in Kyiv, but others follow leaders in Russia. Some people belong to newer Protestant churches, mostly started by Germans and Americans."

Uncle Yuri smiled. "We Ukrainians once had our own radical Christian groups, with names like the 'Spirit Wrestlers' and the 'Icon Fighters.' They practiced a simpler Christianity, without fancy buildings, paintings, or priests in robes."

Marichka was impressed. Her family knew so much about all the different churches.

STANDING FOR PEACE

"This is where the protests happened," Uncle Yuri told them, as they walked past a big open space in the city center. In Kyiv, thousands of people had fought over who should be Ukraine's leaders and whether to have strong links with Western Europe or with Russia.

"It doesn't really matter who our leaders are," Uncle Yuri continued. "If we can't live honestly and get along with each other, our country will never progress."

He pointed to another spot in the square. "During the protests, they set up a church in a tent there. They had prayers every hour, and priests from different churches took turns to lead—Orthodox, Catholic, and even Protestant. It was beautiful. When the police attacked the protesters, some priests stood between the two groups. That day, no one got hurt! Those brave priests gave me hope for our country's future," he said.

FASTING TO FEASTING

Back at Uncle Yuri's, they set the food basket on the dinner table and lit a candle. During Holy Week—the week before Easter—there had been lots of fasting and prayer. Now it was time to feast. Yuri broke open a beautiful painted egg and gave everyone a piece. *"Khrystos Voskres!"* he said. *"Voistynu Voskres!"* they responded, and ate their piece of egg. Breaking the egg symbolized Jesus' breaking open his tomb when he rose from the dead.

Lots of other food followed. Bible stories and family stories were told. They sang favorite hymns and played games. Easter is the most special time in Ukraine—even more special than Christmas!

TO HELP YOU PRAY FOR UKRAINE

YOU CAN THANK GOD FOR:

- the majority of Ukrainians who know about Jesus and believe in him.

- the religious freedom that all the churches enjoy.

- the different churches and priests standing united during the protests.

YOU CAN ASK GOD:

- to bring peace, healing, and reconciliation to a land torn by conflict.

- to get rid of corruption in the government and raise up leaders who do right.

- to help Ukrainians who know about Jesus to get to know him better.

- to help Ukrainians who would like to become missionaries.

UNITED ARAB EMIRATES
More Foreigners Than Locals

At one time there were seven Arab sheikhs in the Arabian Gulf, each ruling his own independent sheikhdom, or emirate. In the early 1970s, these sheikhdoms joined to form the United Arab Emirates, or UAE. Each sheikh still rules his own state, but they all meet regularly to make decisions that affect the whole country. Abu Dhabi is the largest emirate by area, and its capital is also the capital city of the UAE. However, Dubai has the most people.

In the 1950s, oil was discovered in the UAE, and the money earned from oil has completely changed the country. What were once simple villages in the desert are now busy, modern cities, such as Dubai and Abu Dhabi, with huge air-conditioned shopping malls filled with luxury stores. They have the world's tallest skyscrapers and biggest indoor waterparks—even an indoor ski hill, in the desert! Harbors that were once the haunt of pirates, smugglers, and trading boats called *dhows* are now ports for massive oil tankers and super-yachts owned by Arab billionaires.

Traditional pastimes in the UAE included camel racing, bullfights, and hunting with falcons.

Some people still enjoy these, but today the UAE is crazy about technology. There are plans for large-scale projects such as skyscrapers that rotate, jet packs for firefighters, and drones to fly people to work. But even on a smaller scale, nearly every Emirati has a smartphone, and many have several. If you're rich, you can even buy smartphones and tablets made of solid gold.

A FOREIGN LAND

The UAE depends heavily on foreign workers. For every one Emirati, there are seven foreign workers. More than half come from South Asian countries, such as India, Bangladesh, and Pakistan. Some do lowly jobs, like cleaning toilets, while others run major companies from their gleaming office towers.

For a foreign worker, a job in the UAE can be a hard experience. He or she will earn enough money to send some home for their family, but will probably work extremely hard and feel very homesick. Foreign workers are often treated unfairly—even cruelly. Sometimes bosses act as if their workers are unimportant and don't matter. But God thinks they matter.

A PLACE TO MEET GOD

The discovery of oil has made the UAE rich—but it hasn't made people happy or given them hope for the future. Even the best Muslims can't be sure God has

Dubai

FACT FILE

AREA: 30,000 square miles

POPULATION: 9.5 million

CAPITAL: Abu Dhabi city

MAIN LANGUAGES: Arabic (official); widely spoken languages include Bengali, English, Farsi, Hindi, Mandarin, and Urdu

MAIN RELIGIONS: Emiratis are almost all Muslim. Most foreign workers are Muslim, but others are Hindu, Christian, or Buddhist, or follow no religion.

CHIEF INDUSTRIES: Oil, natural gas, tourism, and investment

forgiven their sins. But Christians know Jesus has taken away all our sins.

Some foreign workers who come to the UAE are Christian. Others meet Jesus while they are working here. This is true for Arabs, South Asians, East Asians, and Africans—and even for people from Europe.

Christians working in the UAE are allowed to worship together. There are dozens of groups, usually meeting with other Christians from their own country or language group. Even Muslims are allowed to go to church services, but it's illegal for them to become Christians.

The official punishment for leaving Islam is death. Despite this, some Muslims are deciding to follow Jesus.

GIRLS AND BOYS AT HOME

Sharifa adjusted her headscarf. She was nine years old, and this was the first time she would wear it in public.

"It's not long till I'll have to wear a black cloak and veil when I go out," she told her friend. That was part of growing up as a girl in the UAE.

"Boys have all the fun," said her friend. "My mom just texted that our driver is coming to pick me up to visit with her sisters—but my brothers are going out to play soccer with their friends."

"At least we can go to school, like the boys. They may get to have more fun outside, but I have top marks in all my classes— and better marks than my brothers!" Sharifa said. "I'm going to study at a good university and become a scientist."

TO HELP YOU PRAY FOR THE UAE

YOU CAN THANK GOD FOR:

- the many guest workers who come to know Jesus as their Savior while they're in the UAE.

- freedom for Christians to openly worship together and have church meetings.

- Christian radio, satellite TV, and internet programs that can be accessed in the UAE—in Arabic and many other languages.

YOU CAN ASK GOD:

- to give every Emirati and foreign worker the chance to hear about Jesus.

- to help Christian guest workers live in ways that show what it's like to follow Jesus, especially when they're treated badly.

- to show people that wealth can't bring happiness, but Jesus offers joy and peace.

URUGUAY
Where Christmas Day Is "Family Day"

TOURISTS AND COWBOYS

Uruguay is a small country, sandwiched between two bigger countries: Brazil and Argentina. It's known as an easy and peaceful place to live. Tourists from around the world come to enjoy Uruguay's white, sandy beaches and pleasant climate.

Away from the coast, there are rolling grassy plains and low hills known as the Pampas. Here, cowboys raise cattle and sheep on huge farms called *estancias*. Uruguay exports a great deal of meat, wool, and cowhides. But a lot of people leave the countryside because they think they can get better jobs and earn more money in the cities.

South Atlantic Ocean

Carnival

TAXICAB EVANGELISTS

Ricardo slumped down on the back seat of the taxi. He'd just been fired from his job, and he felt very miserable. What could he do now? There weren't enough jobs to go around. He should never have left his father's farm to work in the city.

The taxi driver switched on the radio. "Whatever problem you have right now," the voice on the radio was saying, "God is ready to help you. He loves you and sent Jesus to die on the cross for you and take away your sins. Trust in him, and you'll find a friend who's always with you."

Ricardo sat up and listened.

"It's true!" said the taxi driver, when he saw Ricardo was listening. "Since I accepted Jesus as my Savior, my life has completely changed."

The driver explained how his life, his family, and his attitudes had all changed.

He had discovered that God answered his prayers. With Jesus in his life, he felt new hope.

The driver gave Ricardo a Bible, and he agreed to read it. "Maybe there's hope after all," he thought.

FACT FILE

AREA: 68,037 square miles

POPULATION: 3.5 million; almost half live in the capital city

CAPITAL: Montevideo

MAIN LANGUAGE: Spanish

MAIN RELIGION: Christianity, mostly Roman Catholic; many Uruguayans don't follow any religion

MAIN EXPORTS: Meat, leather, wool, textiles, and rice

AN EMPTY PLACE

Most Uruguayans are descended from the Roman Catholic settlers who came from Spain and Italy centuries ago. Around a hundred years ago, many turned their backs on the Catholic Church. Even Christmas Day lost its name, becoming known as "Family Day." A lot of people thought God didn't matter and chose not to follow any religion. Today, Uruguay is the least religious country in South America.

Everyone in Uruguay goes to school, and many go on to university. Most people think a good education, a good job, and a good retirement are the most important things in life. And many people do live quite comfortably. But there isn't enough work for everyone, and some Uruguayans live in poverty—both in the countryside and in the slums of Montevideo, the capital city.

About half of all Uruguayans would describe themselves as Catholic, and more than half believe in God—but few people actually go to church. When they need help with problems or decisions, a few turn to "spiritists"—people who contact the spirits for guidance. Some children wear charms, believing they will stop evil spirits from harming them. But most people pay no attention to spiritual matters at all. People in Uruguay are finding there's an empty place in their lives when they don't believe in God.

ANSWERED PRAYER

One day twelve-year-old Gonzalo heard a man talking about Jesus, and he decided to follow the Savior. He wanted to learn all he could about God, Jesus, and the Bible. For the next two years he went to a Christian club.

But Gonzalo's father was an atheist and didn't like Christians. One day he got angry with Gonzalo and told him he could never go to a church again. Gonzalo decided he should obey his father, even though he didn't want to. But the boys at the Christian club prayed for Gonzalo.

Three weeks later, his father changed his mind, and Gonzalo returned to the club. The boys thanked God for answering their prayers so quickly!

Christians in Uruguay often work with missionaries—usually from other South American countries—running ministries like Gonzalo's club in order to share the gospel. *Fútbol* (soccer) is the most popular sport in Uruguay, so *fútbol* clubs are a good way for Christians to share with local communities, especially young people. Some Christian groups also plant new churches: Uruguay has more than twice as many evangelical churches today as it had thirty years ago.

TO HELP YOU PRAY FOR URUGUAY

YOU CAN THANK GOD FOR:

- the peace and stability many people in Uruguay experience, and the opportunities they have for education and good care.

- Christians from Uruguay and missionaries from other countries who boldly share about Jesus with others.

- *fútbol* programs and other Christian clubs that give young people a chance to enjoy sports and learn about Jesus.

YOU CAN ASK GOD:

- to awaken the people of Uruguay to their need for God, showing them that life is empty without him.

- to show people that having nice cars, houses, gadgets, and lots of money won't make them truly happy or bring them peace.

- for good programs to help new Christians follow Jesus and to train pastors and leaders for the new churches.

UZBEKISTAN
Dried Up Sea—Thirsty Souls

WHO IS JESUS?

Akmal and Timur were bored. "It's too hot to play soccer," grumbled Akmal. "And it's too far to go to the river for a swim. There's nothing to do!"

"Let's go over to my uncle's house and watch a DVD or something on YouTube," suggested Timur. "He's got air-conditioning, so we can stay cool."

The two boys wandered down the dusty road. Timur's aunt gave the boys cold green tea. "You can watch a video while I finish my baking," she said.

"This one's called *JESUS*. It's in Uzbek. I wonder what it's about?" They watched in silence for a few minutes.

"I don't like movies without gangsters or gunfights," Akmal said doubtfully.

"Hey! Look! That guy who was paralyzed can walk now," Timur said.

"Yeah! And the girl who was dead is alive again. Wouldn't it be great to be able to do that? I wonder who this Jesus guy is. Is he real?" Akmal asked.

"Oh, look! Why are they putting him on a cross? What's he done? Go back—I want to find out why they're trying to kill him," Timur exclaimed.

"He just said he was king."

"Why doesn't he do another miracle and get down from the cross?" Akmal asked. "I can't believe they let him die in the movie. I thought he was a god who couldn't die. Wait . . . here he is. He's alive again!"

"But why did he die in the first place?" Timur asked.

"Well, they said he had to die to take away the guilt and punishment for all the things everyone ever did wrong. Do you think that includes us?"

"It said everyone," said Timur thoughtfully. "Do you think it's true? I wish it was."

That night Timur told his dad about the film. He asked if he knew who Jesus was.

"Oh, he's the Christians' prophet," his father replied. "But I don't know much about him. If you're so interested in religion, go ask your grandfather about our prophet, Muhammad. We Uzbeks are Muslims—not Christians."

Timur decided to go back to his uncle's the next day to watch the video again. He wanted to know more about Jesus.

A SHRINKING SEA

Uzbekistan means "land of the Uzbek people." About eighty percent of its people are Uzbeks. But many Russians also live in the towns and cities. Cities such as Samarkand and Tashkent are on an ancient trade route called the

FACT FILE

AREA: 173,350 square miles

CAPITAL: Tashkent

MAIN LANGUAGE: Uzbek; Russian also used

POPULATION: 32.4 million

MAIN RELIGIONS: Islam among Uzbeks and most ethnic groups; Orthodox Christianity among Russians

CHIEF EXPORTS: Gold, natural gas, cotton, and chemicals

Dried-up Aral Sea bed

Silk Road. In centuries past, the traders and their goods passing through made these cities rich. But Uzbekistan is no longer a rich country. A small number of people control most of the wealth. Health standards are low, schooling is poor, and good jobs are hard to find. As a result, thousands of young Uzbek people go to Russia and other countries to find work.

Uzbekistan is one of the biggest cotton-growing countries in the world. Children were forced to work in the cotton fields at harvest time, even missing school to pick cotton. But then the president changed the law, and now children can't be made to work.

Cotton farming needs good supplies of water. The Aral Sea, in northern Uzbekistan, was the fourth largest lake in the whole world, so the government used its water for their huge cotton plantations. But they used so much that most of the water is gone. One of the world's biggest lakes is now almost completely dry!

CONTROLLING RELIGION

For nearly seventy years, Uzbekistan was part of the Soviet Union, controlled by a communist government. In 1991, when the Soviet Union broke up, Uzbekistan became an independent country again. People hoped the new freedom would bring a better life. But it can be dangerous to speak against the government. In 2005, government troops killed hundreds of people at a demonstration.

After Uzbekistan became independent again, many Uzbeks returned to the Muslim faith. But the government tries to control the mosques and Muslim preachers. Muslims are often arrested for being "too religious."

The government also tries to stop people from telling Uzbeks or other Muslims about Jesus. Almost every Christian who wasn't originally from Uzbekistan was kicked out of the country. The government persecutes churches, especially those attended by Uzbek people. They burn Bibles, expel Christian students from college, fire Christian employees, and have sometimes arrested people who trust Jesus. Christians meet mainly in secret house churches. Even though there is so much persecution, the number of Christians is growing. There are at least 10,000 that we know of.

TO HELP YOU PRAY FOR UZBEKISTAN

YOU CAN THANK GOD FOR:

- the growing number of Uzbek Christians.
- Christian resources in Uzbek, such as the Bible, the *JESUS* film and other videos, and Christian radio.

YOU CAN ASK GOD:

- for leaders who will rule the country justly and fairly.
- for Uzbeks to search for the peace that Jesus gives.
- to help Christians be unafraid when they share Jesus' love.
- that every Uzbek will get to hear about Jesus, and many will choose to follow him.

Sher-Dor Islamic school, Samarkand

VENEZUELA
Land of Grace

Venezuela sits at the top of South America. As the story goes, Christopher Columbus told the king and queen of Spain that he'd found a "Land of Grace" after he first saw beautiful Venezuela. This country has miles of sandy beaches in the north, snow-capped mountains in the west, and the Amazon jungle in the south.

Venezuela also has one of the largest lakes in South America, Lake Maracaibo. The local Goaro Indians built houses on stilts in the water of Lake Maracaibo. When the first European explorers saw these villages, they called this region *Venezuela*, or "Little Venice," because the Italian city of Venice is also built on water.

Caribbean Sea

LOOKING FOR PEACE

Today most Venezuelans live in cities. Some people are very rich and live in huge houses, with barred windows, alarms, and guard dogs to protect them from thieves. But millions of Venezuelans live in cramped conditions, in shacks put together from sheets of metal, bits of wood, and plastic. Schooling—and even university—is free in Venezuela, so most children go to school. But kids from poorer families may have to drop out early to start earning money for their family.

Venezuela has more oil than any other country, and the government has used the money from selling oil to help the poor. But Venezuelans are divided over how best to run the country, and now the oil money is less than before. There have been huge protests and violent clashes. Millions have fled to nearby countries. Those who remain are suffering: there isn't enough food in the stores to feed everyone or enough medicine to care for the sick. Even children who can go to school are often hungry, without enough food to eat.

MISSIONARY IN ACTION

Carmen and her family live in a neighborhood of Caracas. They aren't rich, but they get by. One day Jacinto, a Venezuelan missionary working with indigenous (original) groups in the Amazon rainforest, came to visit after Sunday service. Carmen had loads of questions for him.

"How did you become a missionary? What's it like living in the jungle?"

Jacinto smiled. He was always glad to meet young Christians who want to know about life as a missionary.

"I heard about Jesus at university

Hillside homes in Caracas

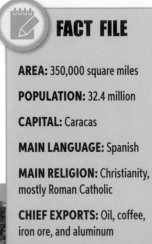

FACT FILE

AREA: 350,000 square miles

POPULATION: 32.4 million

CAPITAL: Caracas

MAIN LANGUAGE: Spanish

MAIN RELIGION: Christianity, mostly Roman Catholic

CHIEF EXPORTS: Oil, coffee, iron ore, and aluminum

DO YOU KNOW?

The highest waterfall in the world is in Venezuela. The Caroni River drops 3,212 feet over the edge of the Auyán-tepui plateau to form the Angel Falls.

Toucan

and decided to follow him," he said. "Then a friend took me to a camp where I met missionaries working among tribal groups in our country. The government doesn't normally allow in missionaries from other countries. But as a Venezuelan, I can easily live with tribal people. I wanted to help the poor, so I moved into one of their villages.

"I'm just one of the many Christians living there. We use Christian audio recordings and the *JESUS* film in different local languages to tell people about God's love. We're translating the Bible into those languages too. Some of the groups don't really trust people from outside their own tribe. But others are peaceable and gentle. In this remote part of Venezuela, people know little or nothing about the world beyond their thatched houses, vegetable plots, and the wild pigs, monkeys, and birds living in their part of the forest. They have little to no internet access. Most have never seen a car or television. But, to be fair, until I moved there I did not know much about their way of life either," he said.

TELLING THE GOOD NEWS

"We Venezuelans are odd when it comes to religion," Jacinto continued. "Almost everyone believes in God and Jesus, but few people attend church. At Easter, people parade through the city streets carrying statues of Jesus on the cross and singing sad songs. But people believe that a good job, money, and health are the most important things, so they look for ways to try to get them. Some try to make bargains with dead saints.

Rich and poor alike visit witch doctors and buy charms—but the charms rarely work. Few people understand who Jesus is: that he didn't just die—he also rose from the dead and has the power to help everyone who trusts in him."

Carmen's dad had been listening too.

"Churches like ours are small—but look how fast they're growing," he said. "We're praying that many more people will hear the good news about Jesus."

"And now we're sending missionaries to other countries too," said Jacinto.

"When I grow up I want to be a missionary," said Carmen.

"Amen, little sister!" he said, smiling. "You know, many people have come to Caracas from other nations. Why not start right here, making new friends and sharing Jesus with kids from other parts of the world? There are many Lebanese, Chinese, Indians, and Haitians who now call our country home."

TO HELP YOU PRAY FOR VENEZUELA

YOU CAN THANK GOD FOR:

- Venezuelan Christians who live and work in Amazon villages, sharing the good news of Jesus.

- Venezuelan missionaries who go to other countries to share the good news.

- the fast-growing churches of Venezuela.

YOU CAN ASK GOD:

- that many people in Venezuela will decide to follow Jesus—both Venezuelans and immigrants.

- that Venezuelan Christians will care for the poor.

- to help people see that charms, witch doctors, and promises to dead saints won't give them the help they seek.

- to bring peace to Venezuela. Pray for the government to make good decisions for its people.

Seaside resort

VIETNAM
God Is Faithful

NOT AFRAID

One by one and as silently as possible, the believers climbed the notched pole to Nai's bamboo-and-thatch house to pray and teach the Bible to new Christians. They knew they would be punished if officers of the communist government caught them leading Bible studies in a private home without permission. But they weren't afraid.

Suddenly, two men burst into the house and grabbed Nai. They marched him away into the darkness. "You're under arrest!" they shouted. "This meeting is illegal."

The other Christians slipped home in the darkness, wondering who had betrayed them by telling the police about their meeting.

Although the law says people are free to follow whichever religion they choose, the Vietnamese government often persecutes Christians. Throughout the mountains of Vietnam, thousands of tribal people, called *Montagnards* (French for "mountain people"), have become Christians. Their homes and churches have been burned, and many of them—even children—have been put in prison. But they haven't stopped telling other people about Jesus. The main Vietnamese ethnic group, called the Kinh, also has a growing number of Christians that are spreading the good news. Pastors who are imprisoned share about Jesus with other prisoners—and even with the prison guards!

The shape of the country on a map is unique. The Vietnamese say it looks like a long pole with a basket of rice hanging on each end. That fits, since the main crop is rice. Vietnam is also among the world's leading growers of cashews, black pepper, and coffee. For years Vietnam was poor, but today its wealth is increasing fast.

MIXED BELIEFS

Many Vietnamese still worship their ancestors, while also practicing Buddhism, Taoism, or Confucianism. Some newer religions that exist only in Vietnam mix together local traditions, Buddhist ideas, and Catholic beliefs. Many younger people focus more on making money and buying nice things and follow no religion at all.

Hundreds of years ago, missionaries told the Vietnamese about Jesus. There

Ho Chi Minh City

FACT FILE

AREA: 128,000 square miles

POPULATION: 96.5 million

CAPITAL: Hanoi

MAIN RELIGIONS: Buddhism, animism, and Christianity; some Vietnamese practice folk religions, and many follow no religion.

MAIN LANGUAGES: Vietnamese; also Chinese, Khmer, Thai, and nearly one hundred other languages

CHIEF EXPORTS: Electronics, machinery, shoes, clothing, rice, oil, and coffee

![lightbulb icon]

DO YOU KNOW?

Vietnamese is a tricky language. There are six different tones, so the same word can be said six different ways, each with a different meaning. For example, the word *ma* can mean mother, ghost, tomb, but, a young rice plant, or horse—all depending on the tone used.

were Christians in towns and villages throughout the country. But after World War II, the communist government in Vietnam demanded complete loyalty. It became very difficult to be a Christian, and many Vietnamese fled the country.

Recently, the government has taken a more mixed approach to Christians. It has allowed some Bibles to be printed again in Vietnamese and in some tribal languages, and some training programs for pastors and Christian leaders are allowed. Christians have more freedom to meet for worship in the big cities, but not in smaller cities or mountain areas. The government still tries to control the churches and doesn't like Christians to hold church meetings in their homes. Christians continue to be arrested, imprisoned, and beaten. Tribal peoples and people who convert from their traditional religions often face the most persecution.

Many Christians have suffered for their faith, yet the church in Vietnam goes on growing bigger and stronger. There are new Christians in Catholic and Protestant churches, in new and old churches, in official "registered" churches that have government approval, and in unofficial churches. More and more Vietnamese churches want to send missionaries to other countries too.

FREELY GIVE

Danh felt a bit embarrassed. His father had told him they wouldn't be going to the beach for the weekend after all, and

he'd gotten upset and shouted. Swimming in the sea would have been fun. Instead, Danh was sitting at a ceremony with some pastors in his dad's office.

Danh's father owned the small office building. His company was moving to a new, bigger building, and he was giving this one to a young and fast-growing church. Danh's father was always saying, "God gives us all different talents, and we must use them for him. My gift is not to preach but to run businesses and be generous to God's people."

When Danh saw the joy on the pastors' faces, he wasn't upset about the beach any longer. Instead, he felt proud of his father. Danh thought to himself, *I wonder what talent God will give me to use for him?*

Ha Long Bay

TO HELP YOU PRAY FOR VIETNAM

YOU CAN THANK GOD FOR:

- the growing church in Vietnam, among both the mountain tribal groups and the Vietnamese.

- the faithfulness of many Christians who follow Jesus—even in prison.

YOU CAN ASK GOD:

- that every Vietnamese tribal group will hear about Jesus.

- for all Vietnamese to be able to worship God freely in the ways that are best for them.

- to help the government understand that Christians can follow Jesus and be good citizens too.

- for good training programs to help prepare new leaders for the growing churches.

- to help churches in Vietnam work in unity and send out many missionaries to other countries.

WODAABE
Beautiful Nomads of the Sahel

NIGER

CHAD

NIGERIA

CENTRAL AFRICAN
REPUBLIC

CAMEROON

TEACH US ABOUT JESUS

One Sunday morning, two young men from the Wodaabe tribe walked into a church. Everyone wondered what would happen next. Wodaabe were known as a proud people who would never enter a church. But there they were, looking very humble. Although the service had started, they walked right to the front and turned to face the congregation.

"Will you show us how to follow the Christian way?" they asked the worshipers. "We want you to teach us and our children about Jesus."

The people in the church became very excited. Some church members went back with the visitors to their camp and told everyone there about Jesus. Several Wodaabe—including these men—decided to follow him.

ALWAYS ON THE MOVE

Life can be challenging for the Wodaabe. They live in Niger, in the Sahel region of Africa, south of the Sahara Desert. The Wodaabe belong to a bigger group, called the Fulani, and are also known as the Bororo, which means "those who live in the cattle camps."

The Wodaabe are nomads, traveling from place to place with their cattle, sheep, and goats. During the long dry season, the men often have to walk up to five hours each day to find water and pasture. When the Wodaabe move camp, they pack all their belongings on the backs of their donkeys—or if they're wealthier, their camels.

"We're like birds in a bush," a village elder explained. "We never settle down or leave any trace where we've been."

Their food is simple. The Wodaabe usually eat porridge made from millet, and milk is the most important part of their diet. If their cows don't get enough food, they become weak and have no milk. If the people have no milk to drink, they become hungry and ill. When there's no rain for several years, the cattle die, and the people starve.

As well as looking after cattle, the Wodaabe are traders. They sell their dairy products and famous dyed cloth in West Africa and elsewhere in the world.

TABOOS

The Wodaabe are almost all Muslims, but they mix many of their own traditions and beliefs with their Islamic faith. By tradition, there are a lot of things the Wodaabe aren't supposed to do; these are called "taboos." Some may seem strange. When a mother gives birth to a baby, she is described as

Fulani silver ring

> ### FACT FILE
>
> **HOMELAND:** Niger
>
> **MIGRATION RANGE:** Nigeria, Cameroon, Central African Republic, and Chad
>
> **NUMBERS:** Very hard to count, because they move around so much; estimates are up to 3 million
>
> **MAIN LANGUAGE:** Wodaabe dialect of Fula or Fulfulde
>
> **MAIN RELIGION:** Islam
>
> **OCCUPATION:** Nomadic herders

DO YOU KNOW?

boofeydo, which means someone who has made an error. The Wodaabe aren't supposed to name a child until he or she is twelve years old. Mothers aren't supposed to talk to the oldest child in their family. And the Wodaabe aren't supposed to look people in the eye when they talk to them. These are just a few of the many taboos they follow. The word *Wodaabe* actually means "people of the taboo."

BEAUTIFUL

The Wodaabe think they're the most beautiful people on earth. Every year, they hold celebrations to show off their good looks.

Like the other young men, Jebbi wanted to look really handsome on the day of the Wodaabe festival. He rubbed yellow powder into his skin to make it look lighter. Then he tried to make his eyes and lips look bigger, drawing around them with a black powder called *kohl*. The Wodaabe think a high forehead is very beautiful, so Jebbi shaved the hair

from the front of his head. After this, he painted a line down his nose to make it look longer. Because he wanted to do everything possible to look beautiful, he hung some little bags of magic powder around his neck.

Jebbi put on his hand-embroidered robe, turban, ostrich feathers, and copper and brass jewelry hung with beads and cowrie shells. Then he checked his appearance in the pocket mirror that every young Wodaabe man carries. Now he was ready to dance and sing with the other men before an audience of admirers. Perhaps he would be judged to be the most beautiful young man. Such an honor was sure to get him a good wife! Nothing is more important to a young Wodaabe man than for his tribe to think he is beautiful.

FOLLOWING THE NOMADS

How can we tell people about Jesus if they are constantly on the move?

A few Christian Wodaabe travel from camp to camp telling people about Jesus. Others are at Bible school learning more about Jesus and how to tell their people about him.

Hundreds of Wodaabe have decided to follow Jesus and want others to know him too. Wodaabe Christians hope that whole families will come to know Jesus together, so they can encourage one another when life gets difficult.

Since 2015, the Wodaabe have had the New Testament in their own language.

TO HELP YOU PRAY FOR THE WODAABE

YOU CAN THANK GOD FOR:

- every Wodaabe Christian—they are a minority in their tribe.

- Wodaabe Christians who are learning how to reach their own tribe with the gospel.

- the New Testament, which is available in their language in print and audio.

YOU CAN ASK GOD:

- to free the Wodaabe from the fear of breaking their taboos.

- to show the Wodaabe that Jesus thinks they are all beautiful and that he loves them all.

- that whole families will decide together to follow Jesus.

- that the Wodaabe will find ways to follow Jesus and have a church as they move around with their animals.

XINJIANG
Along the Silk Road

Xinjiang, a province in northwest China, contains the huge Taklamakan Desert—one of the loneliest places on earth. Fierce winds howl across its massive sand dunes and rocky outcrops, whipping up whirling clouds of sand. In winter it's freezing cold, in summer it's scorching hot—and there's almost no water to be found. The name Taklamakan means "once you get in, you'll never get out."

Yet this desert has rich deposits of coal, gas, oil, gold, and gemstones. A number of companies work on its outer edges, accessing these resources.

But Xinjiang is more than just desert. The Taklamakan Desert is surrounded by spectacular mountain ranges. Rivers flow from the mountains and water the broad pastureland, so the people of Xinjiang can raise sheep, cattle, and horses. There are also fertile oases in the desert, where fruit and vegetables grow well.

RUSSIA
KAZAKHSTAN
MONGOLIA
Urumqi
KYRGYZSTAN
XINJIANG
Autonomous Region
TAJIKISTAN
Kashgar
AFGHANISTAN
CHINA
PAKISTAN
INDIA

SUNDAY MARKET

At the western edge of the Taklamakan Desert is the ancient city of Kashgar. Every Sunday morning, Ayshem and her brother Aziz load their flat donkey cart with fruit and vegetables to take to the market there. People come from far and wide on bicycles, motorcycles, tractors, and donkey carts to sell their produce and buy things to take back home.

As soon as they arrive at the friendly, noisy marketplace, Ayshem and Aziz set out a blanket and display their produce on it. There's plenty to buy at the market: fruit and vegetables, flowers, beautiful Atlas silk, blankets, flat naan bread, chickens, horses, and even camels. Everyone wants a bargain!

Ayshem wanders off to meet her friends, leaving her brother to sell their fruit and vegetables. She's wearing a colorful knee-length dress, long trousers, and an embroidered cap. Her long black hair is neatly plaited. She's glad she doesn't have to wear a heavy, brown veil, like some of the women traditionally wore.

MUSLIMS AND CHRISTIANS

More than half the people living in Xinjiang are Muslims. The Uyghur (wee-gur) are the most numerous of the nine Muslim groups living there. The government used to give money to rebuild mosques, print Muslim books, and even open an Islamic college. But this policy has changed, and today it's very hard for Muslims to practice their faith in Xinjiang. Some Muslims in Xinjiang pray five times a day, but publicly practicing Islam and wearing Muslim clothing has become much more difficult.

Christianity first came to Xinjiang in the sixth century. When the famous thirteenth-century traveler Marco Polo passed through Xinjiang along the Silk Road, two Catholic friars went with him to tell people about the Christian faith once again. The Silk Road was an ancient trade route, connecting Europe and the Middle East with China. Today, many Christians travel the ancient Silk Road as tourists.

FACT FILE

Xinjiang is officially considered a self-governing region of China.

AREA: 640,000 square miles

NUMBERS: 22 million—nine Muslim people groups live in Xinjiang, including Uyghurs, Kazakhs, Kyrgyz, Hui, and Tajiks. More than half the population of Xinjiang come from these Muslim groups.

MAIN RELIGIONS: Islam and Buddhism, and some follow Chinese religions

MAIN CITIES: Urumqi, Kashgar

PRODUCTS: Silk, cotton, wool, fruit, oil, gas, and minerals

Naan bread

In the early twentieth century, there were still some Christian Uyghurs. But during a time of persecution and violence, most of them were killed or fled to other countries. Now, Uyghurs are hearing about Jesus again, and the church is small but growing. There are several hundred Uyghur Christians in Xinjiang, and the New Testament has now been published in Uyghur.

DISTRUST

The government sent many Han Chinese to Xinjiang to help settle the province. The Han and the Uyghurs haven't always gotten along well. Even though there are many Christians among the Han, the Uyghurs—even Uyghur Christians—don't always trust them. This has started to change, however, as some Han Christians build good relationships with their Uyghur neighbors.

The Chinese government increasingly treats religious groups—especially Muslims—harshly in Xinjiang. An alarming number of Uyghur Muslims have been imprisoned for "illegal religious activities." Christians face challenges also. Some Uyghur

Urumqi

Christians were sentenced for three to five years in prison, just for planning a Bible study.

EATING NOODLES FOR JESUS

Chen slurped up the noodles with delight. Uyghur food was so tasty! She was eating *laghman*, made from soft noodles with fried lamb and vegetables on top. Chen and her family moved to the city of Urumqi (ur-oom-chee) a year ago. Her father was sent by the Chinese government to help improve the hospitals. Chen's family are Han Chinese Christians. She loves Jesus and wants to share about him with Uyghurs, most of whom know nothing about him. But it's hard for Uyghurs to trust or be friends with Han Chinese. So what could she do?

Chen's family decided to start by learning about Uyghur food and about the exciting Uyghur music and dances. They even learned to speak Uyghur. As the Uyghur cook watched them enjoying the noodles, Chen smiled and said to him in his own language, "*ohshaptu!*" (delicious!).

TO HELP YOU PRAY FOR XINJIANG

YOU CAN THANK GOD FOR:

- Christians in Xinjiang who share the good news of Jesus' love.

- the Uyghurs, Kazakhs, and Kyrgyz who follow Jesus.

- the New Testament in Uyghur and the full Bible in the Kazakh and Kyrgyz languages.

YOU CAN ASK GOD:

- to bring peace and forgiveness between the Muslim people of Xinjiang and the Han Chinese.

- that Chinese Christians would be good friends to their Muslim neighbors and tell them about Jesus.

- to help Christians from within China and abroad to learn the local languages of the Muslim peoples of Xinjiang, so they can share the good news with them.

- to help Uyghurs—both Christians and non-Christians—find and read the New Testament, which is now in their language.

- to help Uyghur Christians find strength in God's Word to face persecution.

- that many people in Xinjiang listen to Christian radio programs and use Christian websites and mobile apps in Uyghur and the other local languages.

YANOMAMI
Children of the Forest

HOLDING UP THE SKY

The Yanomami live deep in the rain forests of South America. They occupy part of the region called Amazonia, along the border between Brazil and Venezuela. There are between two and three hundred Yanomami communities, and they've lived here for thousands of years.

As the legend goes, one day the sky fell down, pushing earth's inhabitants into the underworld. Only the Yanomami's god, Oman, protected himself and survived. The back side of the "old" fallen sky became the forest for the Yanomami, and a new sky was put in place. It is constantly under threat from the world's chaos, and the shamans (priests) must work hard with the spirits to keep it held up. If they don't, the sky will fall again, this present world will come to an end, and another will start again on the back side of the fallen sky.

VENEZUELA

BRAZIL

ONE BIG HOUSE

A traditional Yanomami village is like one big, circular house with a courtyard in the middle. It's called a *shabono*. Every family brings trees, vines, and thatch from the jungle to help build the shabono and cover the roof of their own section. The outside wall of the shabono separates the village from the jungle, but there are no inner walls. The inner courtyard is used for feasts, celebrations, and other gatherings. People go in and out of the village through little holes in the outer wall. The size of the ring can vary, but some are home to as many as four hundred people.

Some years ago, gold was discovered on Yanomami land. Suddenly thousands more outsiders rushed in, hoping to get rich from gold mining. Some shot and killed the Yanomami, or badly damaged their villages. They brought more diseases and more Yanomami died.

FACT FILE

COUNTRIES: Southern Venezuela, northwest Brazil

NUMBERS: Estimates range between 35,000 and 45,000 Yanomami; more live in Brazil than in Venezuela

MAIN RELIGION: Animism

OCCUPATIONS: Farming, hunting, and collecting fruits in the forest

MAIN LANGUAGES: Four related languages—Yanomae, Yanõmami, Sanima, and Ninam

HARM AND HELP

Until the 1940s, the Yanomami had little contact with the outside world. Once contact was made, the Yanomami learned about metal pots and pans, tools, and other useful things. Some missionaries and government workers started to bring education and health care. Sadly, contact with outsiders also brought diseases— such as measles, influenza, and malaria— and many Yanomami died as a result.

DO YOU KNOW?

The Yanomami traditionally wear very little. The rainforest is hot, and they've lived this way for thousands of years. For special occasions, ceremonies, and battles they sometimes cover parts of the body with paint, flowers, or feathers. They sleep in hammocks to stay cool—some still use hammocks made of tree bark.

Brazil and Venezuela have now set aside areas of Amazonia for the Yanomami where it's illegal to mine. But some mining continues, and miners use mercury, which contaminates the rivers and leads to even more deaths. The Brazilian army sent soldiers to stop the illegal mining, but while they brought some help, these soldiers also brought yet more diseases.

People around the Yanomami territory are cutting down many trees, which is harming the jungle and making the Yanomami way of life even more difficult. When the Yanomami try to interact with the outside world, selling their handcrafts and other goods, people often deceive them and take advantage of them. You can see why the Yanomami believe their "sky" is in danger of falling again!

Today, some Yanomami have moved to cities in Brazil and Venezuela and some have traveled abroad. But most still have never traveled outside of Amazonia or even beyond their village.

THE GREAT SPIRIT

Missionaries first came to Amazonia to tell the Yanomami about Jesus in 1950. When people got sick with diseases, the missionaries tried to help and prayed with them.

At first, only a few Yanomami seemed interested in hearing about God, the Great Spirit, who loves them. Their shamans are deeply involved with the spirits, and people have always gone to them for help. Many Yanomami still need to hear that God has power over nature and all the spirits. When Jesus told the storm on the Sea of Galilee to stop, a sickness to be gone, or an evil spirit to leave, they all obeyed him.

Today there are Yanomami Christians in Venezuela and Brazil.

Early missionaries wrote down the difficult Yanomami language, and there's now a printed Yanomami New Testament. Because not all Yanomami can read, there's also an audio version. Some Yanomami teach their own people to read and write and some provide health care.

Others, like Maloco, want to share the good news about Jesus. He was only a small boy of eight when he decided to follow Jesus.

"Don't laugh at me because I'm small!" he said. "I want to tell everyone about Jesus."

It's not always easy for Christians to live for Jesus. Some Yanomami see Christianity as a religion for the white people, but not for themselves.

TO HELP YOU PRAY FOR THE YANOMAMI

YOU CAN THANK GOD FOR:

■ creating the Yanomami and caring for them over thousands of years.

■ the New Testament in the Yanomami language.

■ people who bring health care and education to the Yanomami.

YOU CAN ASK GOD:

■ that Yanomami Christians will tell others about Jesus.

■ that when the Yanomami fight with one another, Christians will show the way that brings peace.

■ to help Yanomami Christians respect women and girls as made in God's image.

■ to protect the Yanomami from people who try to take advantage of them.

■ that leaders in Brazil and Venezuela will ensure the Yanomami are treated fairly.

YAZIDIS
A Mysterious People

SYRIA

IRAQ

RELIGION, RULES, AND RITUALS

Khansa faced toward the rising sun, kissed the neck of her shirt, and said the words of the Sunrise Prayer. It was Wednesday, the holy day when Tawsi Melek first came to earth. Khansa decided she would say all five of the daily prayers on Wednesdays—not just the two prayers most Yazidis said at morning and night. She felt grateful to still be alive, so she would honor God by praying more.

Khansa belongs to the ancient Yazidi people, who come from the mountains of northern Iraq and nearby parts of Syria and Turkey. The Yazidi religion and culture is a sort of secret. Nobody is allowed to become a Yazidi: you have to be born of Yazidi parents. The Yazidis have no holy book such as the Bible. Their religion is passed on by a group of men called the "Talkers" or "Elders," who learn their stories and rules by heart, then pass them on to the next generation.

FACT FILE

HOMELAND: Iraq has 450,000 Yazidis; smaller groups are in Germany, Russia, Iran, Armenia, Georgia, and Syria

NUMBERS: Up to 1 million globally, but that number is decreasing

MAIN LANGUAGE: Kurmanji Kurdish

MAIN RELIGION: Yazidi

The Yazidi religion is a mix of an ancient religion, called Zoroastrianism, with Islam, Christianity, and other religions. They believe there is one God, who used seven great angels to create the world. The first and greatest of these, Tawsi Melek, was in the form of a peacock. But this peacock angel disobeyed God and was thrown out of heaven. He cried for seven thousand years, and his tears put out the fires of hell. When he repented, God forgave him. The peacock angel taught Adam and Eve how to worship and pray. Yazidis respect him as a representative of God.

Muslims often think the Yazidis worship the devil, and in the past some groups, such as Da'esh (the so-called Islamic State), have attacked them for this reason. Yazidis say they don't worship the devil. They aren't even allowed to speak their word for the devil!

MOUNTAIN OF MEMORIES

In the distance, Khansa could see Sinjar Mountain. She remembered the day when she ran with thousands more Yazidis to escape the fighters of Da'esh. Old people, women, and children left everything to get away. For days they were trapped on that mountain, without food, water,

or shelter. There was no way of escape. Khansa remembered how hot it was. She thought she might not survive. Then Kurdish soldiers from Syria arrived and helped them get away. Not everyone made it. Khansa's father and brother were killed by their attackers.

She still cried most days because she missed them so much. Yazidis believe that when their bodies die, their souls move to a different body—a person or an animal. Each soul goes through many lives until it becomes pure enough to

Yazidi freedom fighter

Sharing Jesus with Yazidi children

enter heaven. Khansa wondered how many lifetimes that would take.

Khansa hated the fighting. But her mother told her that seventy-two times in Yazidi history other peoples attacked them and tried to destroy them. Khansa's cousin, Ayma, was part of a group of Yazidi women fighters. They were as good at fighting as the Yazidi men!

God gave us our religion, Khansa thought. *Why can't they let us live in peace?*

BELONGING TO THE TRIBE OF JESUS

Marwan couldn't wait to get home to tell his family what he had heard. His American friend, Jack, had a Bible. It had many stories in it about Jesus—who is considered to be a prophet in Marwan's Yazidi tribe. The Yazidis believe in one supreme God and honor Jesus as a prophet—but don't accept him as Savior of the world. Now with the Bible, the hundreds of families in Marwan's tribe could learn much more about Jesus, the prophet their tribe was meant to know about!

Yazidis don't usually mix with other people, but sometimes Marwan's parents let him play with Jack. They lived in Duhok, where Marwan's family took refuge after they escaped Da'esh. Jack's parents helped them and other refugees find shelter and food when they arrived with nothing.

Today Jack had read him a story from the Bible about the despised Samaritan people. "The Samaritans sound like the Yazidis," Marwan said. "The religious people around us despise us and misunderstand our beliefs the same way."

He was amazed that Jesus chose to visit the Samaritans, the least important people in the whole region. Jesus spent time in their village, ate with them, and taught them about God. If Jesus cared enough about Samaritans to visit them, would he visit a people like the Yazidis too?

Ancient Yazidi holy site, Lalish, Iraq

TO HELP YOU PRAY FOR THE YAZIDIS

YOU CAN THANK GOD FOR:

- Yazidis who follow Christ in Armenia, and now also in Iraq, and in the West.

- the soldiers who helped save the Yazidis from the so-called Islamic State (Da'esh).

- Christians who have been good neighbors to the Yazidis.

- the many Christians around the world who pray for the Yazidis, now that more have heard about them.

YOU CAN ASK GOD:

- to protect the many Yazidi people who live in war zones.

- to show the Yazidi people that, although others hate them, Jesus loves them.

- to reveal the truth about God and about Jesus to the Yazidis.

- for many Yazidis to meet Jesus and give their lives to him—a hard decision for any Yazidi.

Water tanks in refugee camp

YEMEN
Land of the Queen of Sheba

TERRACES AND TALL HOUSES

Yemen, at the southern tip of the Arabian Peninsula, was once one of the world's most mysterious places. Few people were allowed to visit.

It's a beautiful land, with rugged mountain peaks and steep valleys. The mountainsides are often terraced to make small fields where crops can be grown. Some of these terraces are more than a thousand years old, but they still grow sorghum, potatoes, fruit, and coffee. Yemenis also grow a lot of the plant called *khat*. The khat leaves are a mild drug. Many Yemenis chew them for hours each day.

The towns of Yemen have colorful markets and beautifully decorated mud houses, sometimes six or seven stories high. Several generations of the same family often live in one house. Most of the families in Yemen belong to tribal groups, each with its own leader. Family and tribe are very important in Yemen. But some people are without a tribe. They are called *achdam* or *abid* and are descended from servants and slaves.

DINNER GUESTS

Hassan was only eight years old the first time he wore a *jambiya* (a ceremonial dagger) tied around his waist, outside his *thawb* (a white, ankle-length tunic). He remembered watching his father greet arriving guests. Yemeni people are traditionally very hospitable.

In the kitchen, his sister was kneading dough and slapping it against the side of the mud oven. A fire blazed at the bottom of the oven. If she wasn't careful, the flatbread would slip into the fire.

Hassan's father led his guests up the stairs to the *mafraj*—the special room with carpets and cushions on the floor used to entertain visitors. The guests left their shoes at the entrance. An old television stood in the corner, and a gun hung from a nail in the wall. The Qur'an rested in a niche in the wall, neatly wrapped in a clean cloth.

A plastic tablecloth was laid on the floor, and they served a generous meal. Delicious dishes of vegetables, sauces, and freshly baked flatbread were brought in, followed by rice with meat. The men ate from the serving dishes, using their right hand. The leftovers were taken back to the kitchen, where the women and children ate them.

After the meal, the men washed their hands in a bucket of hot water, and Hassan carefully poured them cups of coffee. They talked about how

FACT FILE

AREA: 203,850 square miles

POPULATION: 28.9 million

CAPITAL: Sana'a

MAIN LANGUAGE: Arabic

MAIN RELIGION: Islam

CHIEF EXPORTS: Oil products and fish

Khat leaves

hard it was to water the fields and the high price of food at the market.

Hassan is a few years older now, and sadly these kinds of visits and meals don't happen anymore. War, violence, and famine have interrupted normal life for almost every family.

A LAND OF SUFFERING

For hundreds of years, different tribes in Yemen had rivalries with one another. Sometimes they fought. Then there were civil wars between the north and the south of Yemen. In 2015, fierce fighting erupted between two different groups of Muslims, the Shias and Sunnis. Neighboring countries got involved, bombing cities and towns in Yemen. Muslim extremist and terrorist groups sent fighters to join in.

Even before this war, Yemen was the poorest country in the Arab world. Now things are far worse. Millions of people have fled their homes to escape the fighting. There's nowhere near enough food or water to go around, and terrible diseases such as cholera are spreading quickly.

Many Yemeni children have never learned to read and write. Most would love the chance to go to school, but because of the fighting, almost all schools

DO YOU KNOW?

Have you heard of the Queen of Sheba? You can read in the Old Testament about how she gave wise King Solomon expensive gifts. She may have come from what is now the land of Yemen.

are shut down. How can kids learn when their schools are closed and their homes bombed? Most children can't even get enough to eat or drink each day. May God have mercy on the children of Yemen!

BETRAYAL AND FAITH

For many years, Christian workers have tried to show Jesus' love to the Yemeni people. It's difficult because Yemenis are very proud of their Muslim faith. If a Yemeni were to choose another religion, their family would feel it was a great dishonor. That person would be seen as a traitor who deserves to be killed.

Christians have to meet in secret, in small groups that won't be noticed. But as the war and violence in Yemen worsens and the suffering increases, more and more Yemenis want to follow Jesus. They see Muslims fighting other Muslims and believe Jesus is their only hope for peace.

Even though following Jesus is very dangerous, there are more Christians from Yemen than from all of the six other countries of the Arabian Peninsula combined.

Rock Palace, Wadi Dahr

TO HELP YOU PRAY FOR YEMEN

YOU CAN THANK GOD FOR:

- the growing numbers of Yemeni Christians.

- Christian radio, TV, and internet available in Yemen.

YOU CAN ASK GOD:

- for peace in Yemen.

- to protect Yemeni believers and give them courage.

- to bring whole families to Jesus, so they can learn to follow him together.

- for more Yemenis to hear about Jesus through Arabic Bibles, Christian radio, TV, internet, and dreams and visions.

ZIMBABWE
A Man-Made Disaster

ZAMBIA
MOZAMBIQUE
HARARE
ZIMBABWE
Bulawayo
BOTSWANA
SOUTH AFRICA

ZIMBABWE

FORGIVEN!

Stephen Lungu couldn't believe his ears.

"Some people are so mixed up inside that they even kick paraffin stoves!" said the preacher.

How could he possibly know? That very morning, Stephen had been so mad when his stove wouldn't light that he'd kicked it across the floor.

Stephen and his friends had gone to the gospel meeting to make trouble. Instead, he discovered Jesus was real. He asked Jesus to forgive his sins and change his heart. And what a change there was!

When Stephen was only a little boy, his mother had left him. He stayed with his grandmother, but she was so poor that he had to scavenge for food. By the age of eleven, he was living on the streets. Then as a teenager he joined a violent gang.

Stephen hated his mother for abandoning him. But now Stephen knew Jesus and began to live like him. He knew he needed to forgive his mother.

One day Stephen met his mother again. He told her how God had helped him forgive her for leaving him. She felt very sorry for what she'd done and asked Stephen for forgiveness. She also asked God to forgive her. Stephen helped her to trust in Jesus too.

THE SMOKE THAT THUNDERS

Some parts of Zimbabwe are spectacular. The national parks are full of elephants, lions, cheetahs, hyenas, and rhinos. The Zambezi River in the northwest forms the border with Zambia. As it pours over the Victoria Falls, there's so much spray and noise that local people call the falls "the smoke that thunders." Downstream the Zambezi has been dammed to form Lake

Kariba, one of the largest man-made lakes in the world. It provides hydroelectric power for both Zambia and Zimbabwe.

TIME FOR CHANGE

Zimbabwe has many problems. Fewer tourists go there now because of the country's poverty and political troubles. White people ruled Zimbabwe for much of the twentieth century. They made the country wealthy by mining gold and nickel and by farming. But they treated black Africans unfairly. In 1980, after

FACT FILE

AREA: 150,873 square miles

POPULATION: 16.9 million

CAPITAL: Harare

MAIN LANGUAGES: Sixteen official languages. English is used for business. Shona is most commonly spoken.

MAIN RELIGIONS: Christianity, animism

CHIEF EXPORTS: Tobacco, platinum, gold, nickel, steel, iron, and diamonds

DO YOU KNOW?

At one point, Zimbabwe's own money became worth so little that it was no longer used. One US dollar could buy you 750,000,000,000 (750 billion) Zimbabwe dollars.

Victoria Falls

years of fighting, the country gained independence from Great Britain. The black Africans who had been the rebels now became the new leaders.

The new government promised people land of their own to farm. They divided up most of the big farms and gave many of their own people plots of land. But the plots are small, and many of the farmers can grow barely enough food for their families to eat. At one time, Zimbabwe grew so much food that it could send food to help other countries. Today it cannot feed its own people.

This country's problems are complicated and very painful for all its people. Huge areas of land are unused. No one is helping poor farmers to grow crops well, and in the towns it's hard to find work. Ninety percent of the people have no job. Millions have left the country; those who stay are often very poor. The terrible disease HIV/AIDS has killed many Zimbabweans. More than one million children have lost one or both of their parents to this disease. Many of these kids now live on the streets.

A new president came to power in 2017—the first new leader in thirty-seven years. Zimbabweans are hoping for changes that will improve the current situation of their country.

HELPING OTHERS

A lot of Zimbabweans have become believers through Christian meetings at university, school, and youth camps—ministries that are still going strong in Zimbabwe. Others are learning to follow Jesus in church and through Christian friends.

When Macmillan went to agricultural college, his friends laughed.

"You're wasting your dad's money," they said. They aren't laughing now, because his crops grow better than theirs. Macmillan has forgiven their teasing, and he's helping improve their farms.

"God loves them as much as he loves me," he says. "I can show them his love by helping them."

Despite the problems, Zimbabweans such as Stephen and Macmillan have come to know Jesus and are helping others. Some Christians in Zimbabwe are praying for a new beginning that will bring hope to the people. Many new churches have started up in the last few years. Zimbabwean Christians want a government that will rule wisely, so everyone will have enough and people will forgive one another for the wrongs of the past.

Rural kitchen—an open fire

ANIMISM

Animism is a term that has been used for those religions that existed before the coming of major world religions such as Hinduism, Buddhism, Christianity, and Islam. Usually they don't have written scriptures or a holy book. Each animist tribe or people group has its own unique set of beliefs and rituals.

In the Old Testament, the Egyptians, the Philistines, and the Babylonians each had their own gods and religions. So did the Greeks and Romans we read about in the New Testament. Many of the groups in this book, such as the Bijagos (page 24), Dogon (page 40), Navajo (page 104), and Yanomami (page 186), were animists, but some have become Christian.

A WORLD OF SPIRITS

The gods and spirits of these animist groups are generally invisible, but people often make pictures or sculptures of them. These gods and spirits are usually associated with places, such as a forest, river, or mountaintop. They can sometimes be linked with a specific tree, cave, or rock.

Some of these spirits are seen as friendly, but others are evil and can make bad things happen to people. For this reason, people live in fear of these evil spirits and make special offerings and sacrifices so that the spirits won't hurt them and their families. At other times, they make offerings and sacrifices to get what they want from the spirits—perhaps placing food before an idol to get success when they go out hunting, or sacrificing a chicken to get a good harvest. Disasters, such as droughts, famines, sickness, fires, earthquakes, storms, and floods, are usually believed to be the work of evil spirits.

Animists often wear special bracelets or charms, sometimes called "fetishes." They believe these give them magical protection from harm or supernatural powers over others.

A CREATOR-GOD

Many animists believe there is a great creator-god or sky-god. He is not a god they can know, because he's mysterious and so far away that they can't reach him. They think that, after this god created them and their world, he forgot about them and isn't interested in what happens to them. So they are more concerned with the spirits that affect their everyday life.

ANCESTOR WORSHIP

Animists often believe that, when a person dies, their spirit goes on living.

Masked shamans of the Mah Meri people, Malaysia

Medicine men, Lesotho, Southern Africa

194

This spirit can help or harm them. That means it's very important for animists to respect their ancestors. They do this by building shrines, making offerings, and asking for their help. Yet troubles still come. When they do, people may believe that someone else in the family has made the spirits of the ancestors angry.

PRIESTS AND RITUALS

As in other religions, there are people who perform special roles or have special knowledge of spiritual things. Different animistic groups use different names for these people, such as "shamans," "medicine men," or "witch doctors." Their task is to help people understand omens and signs, and to tell them what they must do to keep on the good side of the spirits. There are also priests, who look after the shrines and help organize important festivals and activities. These rituals and festivals are sometimes strange and scary, but often have interesting and colorful costumes, masks, dances, and songs. How wonderful it is when these tribes start using that kind of creativity to worship the true Creator-God!

FREE IN JESUS

Since Christianity began, animist tribes have usually been those most open to the good news of Jesus. Almost all the tribes and peoples of Europe were animist before they became Christian. Through the teachings and lives of missionaries, such as St. Patrick in Ireland, many animists started to follow Jesus. They found that the God of the Bible was much more powerful than their ancient gods and local spirits.

Animists who decide to follow another religion often stay stuck in their old way of thinking about the spirits, and try to mix their old and new beliefs together.

Vodun dance, Togo, Africa

Christians from an animist background might visit the pastor on Sunday and the witch doctor on Monday. They will pray to Jesus, but also give sacrifices to the spirits, just to make sure their prayers are heard by someone, or something, with the power to answer.

As Christians, we know Jesus is greater than any spirit. We learn in the Bible that he told storms and waves to stop and evil spirits to leave—and they all obeyed him. In fact, Jesus gave us—his disciples—his own authority over the spirits. They have to submit to the power of Jesus, whose Spirit lives in us. Those who follow Jesus can live free from the fear and power of the spirits. As Jesus said in John 8:36, "If the Son sets you free, you will be free indeed"!

Shaman, Peru, South America

BUDDHISM

THE BEGINNING OF BUDDHISM

Prince Siddhartha Gautama was born in India about 2,500 years ago. At his birth, it was foretold he would conquer the world—perhaps as a great military leader, or perhaps as the first to find the meaning to life. His father—a king—wanted him to be a great military leader and ensured he lived in luxury. Gautama married a beautiful woman, and they had a son. On a hunting trip, Gautama saw four sights that shocked him: a man who was sick, a man who was old and frail, a dead man, and a holy man who had given

Golden Buddhas, Bangkok, Thailand

up everything to seek the meaning of life. Gautama left his parents, wife, and child and wandered throughout India for six years, trying to understand the meaning of suffering, life, and death.

Gautama had been taught that everyone dies many times and has thousands of lives. This is called reincarnation. How a person lives in this life affects his next life. If a person has done a lot of good deeds, he or she may be reborn as a wealthy or wise person, or as a monk. People who do bad things will probably be poor and suffer a lot in their next life. They might even be reborn as an animal—or worse, an insect. Gautama wanted to know how to escape this cycle of birth and rebirth. He studied with different Indian holy men, but found no answers, not even through fasting and giving up all his luxuries. He finally decided to look within, through meditation— thinking very deeply about things. His mind was enlightened, and he saw everything in a totally new way. Gautama became known as the Buddha. In his language, this means "enlightened one."

Ceramic Buddha

THE WAY OF ENLIGHTENMENT

The Buddha spent the rest of his life traveling around and teaching this way of enlightenment. He taught that suffering is the result of our desires and our ignorance—we are always seeking satisfaction in things. True satisfaction can come only when we realize that the world is an illusion—like a movie that seems so real, but when it has ended is nothing but memories. He taught his followers, called Buddhists, how to live as monks and meditate. That would allow them to reach *nirvana*, or emptiness—nothingness, and an end to this cycle of birth, death, and rebirth.

Buddhist shrine, Tokyo, Japan

GAINING MERIT

Not everyone will become a monk and live a life of meditation. Ordinary Buddhists can gain merit by becoming monks or nuns for a few weeks, by giving food or money to the monks, and by making offerings in the temples. Earning merit is like getting points to help a person reincarnate into a life that is closer to enlightenment.

As Buddhism spread to other Asian countries, different cultures came to practice it differently. In southern countries such as Thailand, Myanmar, and Sri Lanka, the monks wear yellow robes and seek to follow the original teaching of the Buddha. Northwards, in China, Korea, and Japan, the monks wear gray robes, and the temples contain images of enlightened beings. People pray to these beings for help when they are in need.

In central Asian places, such as Tibet and Mongolia, the monks wear deep red robes and practice chanting as well as deep meditation. The people place prayer flags on the roofs of their houses and on the mountainsides. They spin small prayer wheels as they walk or sit, and outside the temples are much bigger prayer wheels that people spin as they pass by. On the prayer wheels is a mantra, or holy saying, which the people believe carries their prayer to the farthest part of the universe.

A DIFFERENT ENDING

The Dalai Lama is the most respected Buddhist leader. According to Buddhists, he gained nirvana through enlightenment, but came back to this world to guide others. He is reported to have said that Buddhism and Christianity are the same. They do have some things in common—such as telling the truth, seeking wisdom, and living in the right way. But in reality, they are very different.

Buddhists hope to end the pain and suffering of existence and reach the emptiness of nirvana. But Jesus promises abundant life now and in eternity. The images of heaven in the Bible are not of emptiness, but of feasts and celebrations. Most Buddhists try to reach nirvana through meditation and by building up enough merit to eventually achieve enlightenment. Christians know that our own efforts will never be enough to earn eternal life, but that Jesus gives it freely to everyone who believes in him.

Incense burning

CHRISTIANITY

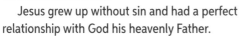

JESUS: SENT FROM GOD

For centuries, the Jewish people had been waiting for their Messiah (the Savior from God) to come and be their ruler. This Messiah would bring peace and justice, and save them from their enemies. Two thousand years ago, God told a pure-hearted young Jewish woman named Mary that she would have a baby who was God's very own Son, the promised Messiah. She gave birth to this baby in Bethlehem and named him Jesus.

Jesus grew up without sin and had a perfect relationship with God his heavenly Father.

When he was about thirty years old, Jesus chose twelve men to be his first followers. For three years, Jesus traveled around with them, healing the sick and teaching people about the kingdom of God and how God wanted people to live. More men and women followed him, and some began to realize that Jesus was the Messiah the Jews had been waiting for.

A lot of people loved to listen to Jesus and see the miracles he did; but some of the Jewish religious leaders were envious of this. Jesus claimed to be the Messiah and Son of God, but they did not believe him—they arrested him and accused him of saying things against God. The Roman rulers saw this was causing a lot of disturbance in Jerusalem, so—even though they didn't think Jesus was guilty of any crime—they allowed him to be killed.

Jesus was nailed to a big wooden cross, and he hung there until he died. But that wasn't the end. Three days later, Jesus rose from the dead, by the power of God. Over the next forty days, many people saw him and spent time with him. Then Jesus returned to heaven. Before he left, he gave his followers instructions: to go throughout the world doing as he had done, teaching people about the kingdom of God and showing people how to follow him.

Jesus also promised to send his Holy Spirit to be with them always. Ten days later, this Holy Spirit appeared like fire among Jesus' followers—Christians call this the "Day of Pentecost." Now, every person who follows Jesus can have his Holy Spirit in them to encourage them, to teach them how to please God, and to give them power to witness boldly about Jesus and do the same work he had done.

WHAT CHRISTIANS BELIEVE

In the beginning, when God first created man and woman, he made them perfect. He wanted them to be his friends and promised to look after them. But because people didn't believe God and disobeyed him, sin came into God's perfect world. All of us sin—we say and do things that go against what God wants and insist on our own way instead. Our sin is like a huge wall that stops us from reaching God. But God loves us too much to leave it that way!

Jesus was without sin, so when he died on the cross, his sacrifice took away all the sins of the world. Through this sacrifice, Jesus destroyed that dividing

Cristo Redentor, Rio de Janeiro, Brazil

wall. Now the way to God is open to everyone who trusts in Jesus. Because Jesus was perfect, he also broke the power that sin and death had over the world. Evil was defeated, and Jesus rules the entire universe.

THE BIBLE

The Bible is a collection of sixty-six books about God's relationship with humanity and his plan for us all. It was written by as many as forty different people, across about 1,500 years. The Bible includes history, stories, poetry, prayers, songs,

prophecy, and letters full of teaching. Christians believe the whole Bible was inspired by God, and that all of it is useful for helping God's people to know him and serve him. Through the Bible, we learn how God loves all people, how he wants us to live, and how he is at work restoring the whole world to the way he meant it to be.

CHURCHES

Christians meet together to worship Jesus in every country in the world. There are many kinds of church, including many varieties of Orthodox, Catholic, Protestant, Anglican, and independent churches. With so many cultures, nationalities, and traditions, there is naturally a lot of variety in how Christians worship. They sing different songs in different styles of music. Some dress very simply; others wear their best clothes. Some churches are led by priests, some by pastors, and others by the congregation itself. Most gather on Sunday, others meet on Saturday or Friday, and some meet every day.

Some Christians worship God in huge cathedrals, with beautiful statues and decorations, while others meet in very simple buildings, in a room, or even under a tree. But the real church is not buildings. It's all the people who believe in Jesus and follow him.

Most churches around the world do similar things when they meet together. They pray to God, hear his Word (the Bible), and sing songs to praise him. Jesus taught his disciples to baptize in his name (Matthew 28:19) and remember him by taking Communion together (Luke 22:19).

The first churches sent people as missionaries to travel throughout the world, sharing about Jesus and God's kingdom. Many churches through history have done the same.

Christmas and Easter are the most well-known Christian holidays. Christmas celebrates Jesus' birth, and Easter his resurrection. But other days are important too, such as Good Friday, when Jesus was crucified; Ascension Day, when he was taken up to heaven; and Pentecost. Churches around the world celebrate these holidays in ways specific to their own culture or region.

ETERNITY

Christians know that Jesus is alive today. Even though we can't see him, he lives in us through his Holy Spirit. He is always ready to help, in bad times and good times. Christians believe life doesn't end when our body dies, because Jesus has promised that anyone who believes in him will in the end be resurrected, to live forever as part of God's family.

Jesus said that he will one day come back to earth to rule the world as the King of Kings. He will bring justice and make everything fair, the way God originally meant it to be. The Bible says that heaven will be like a wonderful party, where we will celebrate together. It also talks about how all people who believe in Jesus will worship him before his throne, and we will be from every tribe, nationality, and language—that's a lot of variety!

Ethiopian Orthodox pilgrims, Jerusalem

HINDUISM

Hinduism grew out of the way people in India lived and worshiped more than 3,500 years ago. They passed on their beliefs in stories, hymns, poems, and prayers collected over centuries. Many of these have been recorded in Hindu scriptures. They passed on their traditions and rituals from generation to generation, within the family and community.

About 75–80 percent of the people who live in India are Hindus. India is one of the world's biggest countries, and the people of India belong to hundreds of different language and ethnic groups. Hindus who live in different parts of the country worship in different ways and keep different festivals. Temples in north India often look quite different from those in the south.

WHO IS GOD?

Understanding what Hindus believe can be very hard for people from other religions. In one sense, Hindus believe in millions of gods and goddesses. But at the same time, Hindus also say they believe in only one supreme being, and all the gods and goddesses are different versions of one god. Only a handful of gods and goddesses are written about. Among the most popular are Vishnu, the protector of the world; Kali, the destroyer of evil; the fun-loving Krishna, who is often thought of as an older brother; and Ganesh, the elephant-headed god of good fortune. Hindus believe that every

person has an eternal soul, or *atman*. Some Hindus say that all atman and all life is part of one supreme being. But others say the supreme being is separate from living things on earth. Some Hindus say there is really no god at all.

So, you could believe in no god, one god, or many gods, and still be a Hindu! You can see how Hinduism can be difficult for others to understand.

WORSHIPING IDOLS

Hindus can choose which gods or goddesses they want to worship—and many stay devoted to their chosen gods for their whole lives. Everywhere you go

Pilgrim, Nepal

Pilgrims at the Ganges river, Varanasi, India

in India, you'll see temples and shrines, where people worship their gods and goddesses. You'll also see shrines in offices, stores, and houses. These shrines usually include an idol—a statue of a god or goddess. Taxi drivers may even have a tiny shrine inside their vehicle.

Hindus often bathe the statues of their gods, before dressing them in fine material or in gold. They then offer prayers, perfume, flowers, incense, and food to the statues or pictures of their gods and ask for their help in daily life.

CASTE

Every Hindu is born into a social group called a *caste*. Some castes are considered better than others. At the top is the priestly caste, then come rulers and soldiers, and then merchants and farmers. The people in the lowest castes may be the servants of the higher castes. The Dalits, or "Untouchables," are regarded as so low that they're beneath even the lower castes. They usually have to do the jobs that nobody else wants to do—such as sweeping the streets and cleaning toilets.

A person can't do anything to upgrade to a higher caste. Your parents' caste will be your caste for your whole life.

Higher-caste Hindus don't usually mix with people from lower castes, because they consider them impure. This way of thinking is deeply rooted in Hindu life and culture. But young people in India today, with modern lives in big cities, mix across castes more than people of previous generations.

LIFE AFTER THIS LIFE

Hindus believe that, when people die, they come back to life again as another person, or even as an animal. This is called *reincarnation*. Hindus also believe in *karma*, which means that the way people behaved in their past life affects their place in this life—and what they do in this life will decide their place in the next. If they behave in all the ways they are supposed to, they believe they'll have a better rebirth.

Hindus burn the dead bodies of their loved ones. They believe this will help the dead person's soul move on more quickly to its next life. They scatter the ashes in one of the holy rivers.

Rebirth may go on forever, as people can never be sure they've done everything the right way. Some Hindus give up everything—home, family, and possessions—to spend their lives in meditation and prayer. The ultimate goal of every Hindu is to achieve *moksha*—freedom from this cycle of reincarnation.

PILGRIMAGE

The largest festival gathering on the planet is for a Hindu festival called *Khumb Mela*. Hindus go on a pilgrimage to a holy site, usually gathering on the banks of a river, such as the sacred Ganges. The main event of the festival is a day of bathing in the river. One year, more than thirty million people visited the festival on just one day. But the festival can last many days—even months.

A Hindu may go to worship a particular god or goddess, or to give thanks for something good that has happened. Most pilgrims bathe in the river as they pray and worship to purify themselves from bad deeds. They even take some water home in bottles, to sprinkle over their loved ones and possessions to purify them.

Christians know that only the blood of Jesus can wash our bad deeds away forever, and only faith in him can make us truly pure.

ISLAM

Muslims believe that God gave revelations to the prophet Muhammad 1,400 years ago, near Mecca, in what is today Saudi Arabia. Muhammad claimed that the archangel Gabriel gave him messages from Allah (the Arabic name for God). These messages began as a call to turn away from sin and to worship only Allah. The messages expanded to include a mix of history, teaching about Allah, and instructions on how Muslims should live. Muslims believe these messages are the completion of all that God revealed through their prophets—including Abraham, Moses, David, and Jesus. After Muhammad died, his closest followers collected these messages to make the Qur'an, the Muslim holy book.

There are nearly two billion Muslims in our world today. There are two main sects, Sunni Muslims (80–90 percent) and Shi'ite Muslims, as well as many other smaller groups.

PRAYERS

Muslims can pray anywhere, but they mostly worship in mosques. These mosques are often beautifully decorated, but they have no pictures or statues because Muhammad thought people might worship the images instead of Allah. Five times every day the call to prayer comes from the minaret, the tall tower by the side of the mosque. The chant includes sayings like "God is great" (*Allahu Akbar*) and "Hurry to prayer." It also includes the *shahada*, which says there is no god but Allah and Muhammad is the messenger of Allah.

Wherever they pray, Muslims have to face toward Mecca, the holiest city of Islam. On Fridays, the Muslim holy day, they pray in the mosques just after midday. All women must wear a headscarf or veil, and many men wear a cap, to show their respect to Allah. They wash before they pray. They kneel on a special mat, and some use a string of beads to help them remember the ninety-nine names of Allah in the Qur'an.

THE FIVE PILLARS OF ISLAM

There are five important duties that every Muslim is supposed to keep, called the "Five Pillars of Islam." First, they must say the *shahada*, the Muslim confession of faith. They are required to pray five times every day. They are to give money to

Islamic holy site, Dome of the Rock, Jerusalem, Israel

Prayers at Jama Masjid, Delhi, India

charity. Every year, in the month of Ramadan on the Islamic calendar, Muslims should fast during the day, and eat and drink only between sunset and sunrise. Old people and children, sick people, pregnant women, and travelers are excused from fasting. Finally, all Muslims are expected to go to Mecca on a pilgrimage (*haj*), at least once in their life, if they are able.

CHILDREN

As soon as a baby is born, it is washed, the *shahada* is whispered in its right ear, and then a little honey or a soft date is put on its tongue by a respected family member. On the baby's seventh day, the hair is usually shaved.

At around seven years old, many Muslim boys (and in a few places, girls too) begin to learn to read the Qur'an in Arabic. They also learn how to pray and how to behave in the mosque. At home, they learn what foods they can eat, how to cook them, and how they should behave and dress.

DRESS

All Muslims are supposed to be modest in their clothing. Clothes that show off a person's body are considered improper, especially for women. Women often wear ankle-length trousers covered by a skirt, and a long-sleeved top or dress, and cover all or part of their heads. In some countries, women cover themselves completely in long veils whenever they leave home.

MUSLIMS AND THE BIBLE

Muhammad taught that there is only one God, Allah. Christians also believe in only one God; but Muslims find it hard to understand how one God can exist eternally as Father, Son, and Holy Spirit.

Muslims are taught to respect the Bible, but most also claim the original Bible has been changed and corrupted. They're often willing to read the stories about Jesus in the New Testament, which they call the *Injil*.

We can tell Muslims about the wonderful things Jesus said and did, and how we can be close to God through him. Muslims recognize Jesus as prophet, Messiah, and Word of God, but don't understand how Jesus could be both fully human and fully divine. Unlike Christians, who believe Jesus gave his life for the sins of the world and rose again to conquer death, most Muslims believe Jesus did not die on the cross.

Muslims believe that Allah will judge each person according their good and bad deeds at the end of their life. Many Muslims try hard to have enough good deeds to outweigh their bad deeds, and they hope Allah will be merciful when he decides whether he will let them into Paradise or send them to hell. Christians also believe in heaven and hell, but the Bible teaches that we can be fully confident that Jesus made the way for all those who trust in him to join him in Paradise.

JUDAISM

Judaism, the religion of the Jewish people, is based on Torah, which means wisdom, instruction, or teaching. Jewish people also use the word *Torah* for the first five books of the Hebrew Bible.

The Jews believe that God is the Creator of everything, that he created all peoples in his image, and that he called Israel—the Jewish people—to be in a special relationship with him.

THE BEGINNING

God made the world good, but sin made it imperfect. God called Abraham and his family to be his people. He told Abraham to leave his own country (Genesis 12:1-3) and go to a new place that God would show him. God promised Abraham that he would bless him, give him a new land and many descendants, and bless all the peoples of the world through him. Abraham obeyed God.

A CHOSEN NATION

Hundreds of years passed, and some of Abraham's descendants, the Hebrews (another word for Israel or the Jewish people), became slaves in Egypt. God chose Moses to lead them out of Egypt to the Promised Land. (You can read the story in Exodus chapters 1–19.) God told Moses that Israel would be his special people. He wanted them to worship him alone and to be different from all the other nations, who worshiped lots of gods.

God wanted them to be holy, like himself, so he gave them the Law, which included the well-known set of rules we call the "Ten Commandments." Following the Law would give the people good relationships with one another and with God. God promised to bless and help the people if they were obedient. If they did

Jewish boy prepares for his bar mitzvah

not keep God's rules, they would be punished. But God would never abandon them.

Throughout their long history, Jewish people have seen everything that has happened to them as the work of God. He has given them his love and care, guided, helped, and also punished them. God has allowed them to thrive, but he has also allowed them to suffer. Wherever they have lived and whatever they have suffered—and they have suffered a lot—the Jewish people have survived.

THE PROMISED MESSIAH

Jewish people have always expected God's promised Deliverer, or Messiah, to bring peace and justice on earth and to lead them back to their own land. Religious Jews pray daily

Jewish kippah (headgear) and prayer shawl

for his coming. Some Jewish people in Jesus' day recognized that he was the promised Messiah and followed him. In time—together with Jesus' followers from other nations—they all became known as "Christians."

WORSHIP

The first prayer a Jewish child learns comes from Deuteronomy 6: "Hear, O Israel: the Lord our God is one Lord; and you shall love the Lord your God with all your heart, and with all your soul, and with all your might." Many Jews say this every morning and evening.

The Jewish people have lots of festivals during the year that remind them of their history. Those who keep the faith usually keep the Sabbath every week. The Sabbath starts at sunset on Friday and ends at sunset on Saturday, and is very special to Jewish families. It's their holy day, a day of rest. The family may go to a service in the synagogue on Friday evening and again on Saturday morning.

There's a special Sabbath meal on Friday evenings. Before sunset, the mother lights two candles and blesses God, then the father takes a cup of

Lighting the Hanukkah menorah

wine and says a blessing for his family. Everyone eats a piece of bread with salt to remind them how God provided his people with manna for food on their way out of Egypt to the Promised Land.

ALL AROUND THE WORLD

There are over 16 million Jewish people living in countries all around the world. Many are very religious. Some may believe in God but don't practice their faith. And some no longer believe in God or his Messiah. About 6.5 million Jews live in Israel—a similar area to the Promised Land—but Jewish people come from many places to pray in Jerusalem. They consider Jerusalem to be God's holy city.

Hebrew scripture scroll

WHAT'S NEXT?

GET TO KNOW JESUS

God loves you and has a special purpose for your life. He already knows the good things he has planned for you and what he wants you to do. So why don't you ask him to show you?

Perhaps you are thinking, *But I'm not sure if I really know Jesus.* Since God is the Creator who made the whole world—including you—he already knows all about you. He longs for you to ask him to be your friend. Jesus loves you and died for the whole world—including you—because that was the only way to take away all the wrong things that get between us and God. Tell him that you want to get rid of them all. Then tell him you want to live his way and do what he wants you to do. You can be sure that he will help you.

Spend time getting to know Jesus. Talk with him, listen to what he says, and learn to obey him. Read the Bible and learn his Word by heart. God's Holy Spirit can speak to your heart, and will help you to pray and tell others about him. You can be sure that no matter what happens, Jesus will never stop loving you and will help you every day of your life.

READ

- Get books from your library or school about the countries you've read about. Find out what people's lives are like there, who the Christians are in that in that country and how they worship, whether they are persecuted—or the answers to any other questions you might have.
- You can find lots of interesting stories about missionaries. Some have been written for children. There are plenty of wonderful books about the adventures of missionaries around the world.

- Mission organizations also post stories and updates online so you can learn about what they do. They will help you understand more about what it's like to be a Christian or a missionary in different parts of the world from yours.
- You can also find out more about different people groups. Find mission agencies that work in the countries where that people group lives. Ask them about the people group you are thinking of.

LOOK

- Watch the news, travel programs, or videos about the world on TV or YouTube.
- Watch Prayercast videos to pray along with the narrator as you watch a video about a country.
- Look for pictures of the countries and people you have been learning about. Try to find pictures that show life both in the cities and in the countryside or villages. Try to find pictures that show life for those who are rich and those who are poor. Find pictures of famous landmarks and sites for the country.
- Go to the websites of mission agencies working in the countries you have been learning about. They have lots of interesting information, prayer requests, and sometimes special resources for children and families. Countries often have their own websites to share with the world about all the interesting people and places there.

LISTEN

- Almost every country has interesting music, using different rhythms, melodies, instruments, and languages. Often there are dances that go with the music too. You might discover songs you enjoy even more than music from your own country! There is also a lot of good Christian music from other countries.

TASTE

- Try foods or visit food markets from different countries or regions. You will be amazed at the variety of flavors and foods. You won't like everything you try, but we're sure you'll love some of them.
- Learn to cook at least one of the dishes you like with your family.

MAKE FRIENDS

- If missionaries come to your church, listen to what they say. Ask them questions, and find out how you and your church or Sunday school class can help them or pray for them. If the missionaries have children,

make friends with them, and try to stay in touch while they are living away.

- There may be people in your church or school who have recently come from another country. Be a friend to them, and help them to feel at home in their new country. If they are trying to learn your language, help them. Maybe you can try to learn how to say a few things in their language too.

- If there are people in your neighborhood who have recently moved there from another country, get to know them. Maybe they will teach you some things about their home country, their religion, or their culture. Perhaps you will have a chance to tell them about Jesus.

Are there Christian churches from other cultures in your own city or town? Visit their church service sometimes and get to know them, we are all God's family!

You may know some missionaries who have been sent from their home church overseas to help tell people about Jesus in your country. You can pray for them and help them in their work too.

PRAY
God wants to share his work with us, and he does this by asking us to pray! Sometimes it's hard for us to keep on praying, but here are a few ideas to help you.

- Choose seven different topics, countries, people groups, or individuals. Write them down, and pray for one of them each day of the week.

- When you know a prayer has been answered, write that down too.

- Get a world map. Mark on it the places you pray for. Add pictures of the people you are praying for.

- It helps to pray with someone else—a friend, your family, or your Sunday school class. Maybe even start a Pray for the World club.

- There are lots of good ideas on the internet about how kids can pray in fun ways. Search online for "children in prayer" and "kidsprayer."

GIVE
- Missions often have special projects. Find one you really like, and give some of your money to help that project. Your family, friends, or Sunday school class may want to help support a project, and your parents or teachers may have ideas to help you raise money.

- Find missionaries working in some of the places in this book, and give a little money to them each month. Remember that missionaries come from many countries all over the world, not just your own. Most of them need

the support of other Christians to pay their way.

GO!
- Some missionary organizations have summer camps for children (for example, WEC International in Great Britain) where you can have a lot of fun, meet missionary families, and learn about their work.

- You or your whole family might even be able to visit missionary friends who live in a different culture, to find out what it's like to be a missionary.

- Some organizations have special mission trips for teenagers.

- If you take a vacation in another country, pray for the people in that country—especially for those you meet personally. Think about how you could share Jesus' love with them. Pray for the Christians there. If you can find a church, go attend a service with your family. Christians worship God in so many different and interesting ways.

Remember to ask your parents before you try these ideas. You will need their permission, and they might have some good ideas too.

WORD LIST

agnostic: a person who believes we can't know anything about God, or even if he exists.

alpaca: a South American animal that looks like the llama and is related to the camel; usually raised for its fine wool.

altar: 1. the Communion table in a church; 2. a flat-topped block of stone or wood for making sacrifices and offerings to gods (including to God in Old Testament times).

ancestor: anyone from whom you are descended. Your parents, grandparents, and great-grandparents are all your ancestors.

animist: see Animism, p. 194.

Ash Wednesday: the first day of Lent (the forty-day period before Easter). Some churches put ash on the foreheads of worshipers as a sign that they're sorry for their sin.

atheist: a person who believes there is no God or gods.

Bible school: a college where people study the Bible and can also sometimes learn to be a pastor or missionary. Some Bible schools offer degrees or diplomas. Churches sometimes hold Bible schools for a week or several weeks.

Buddhist: see Buddhism, p. 196.

bullock cart: (sometimes called ox cart) a cart with two or four wheels, used to transport goods, pulled by oxen. It has been used since ancient times, and is still used in some parts of the world, especially South Asia.

caste: a group into which a person is born, often related to Hinduism or to some countries in South Asia. The most important caste is the priestly caste, then rulers and soldiers, then traders and storekeepers. There are other lower castes, and "outcastes" (sometimes called "untouchables"), who sometimes have to do jobs such as sweeping streets, cleaning toilets, and washing clothes to serve people from higher castes.

Catholic: 1. the word *catholic* means "universal," and sometimes the "catholic church" refers to all the Christians in the world; 2. the Roman Catholic Church is a denomination, and there are Roman Catholic churches (usually just referred to as Catholic churches) in almost every country. Like other Christians, Catholics believe that Jesus is the Son of God and the Bible is the Word of God. But they also believe that other traditions are important and honor Mary as the Mother of God. They believe that Jesus gave the apostle Peter special authority, which was handed down to the bishops of Rome. The Pope is the Bishop of Rome, the head of the Roman Catholic Church.

charm: something worn to bring good luck.

church: 1. the whole body of Christ, or all Christians in a place, no matter what denomination or ethnic group they are part of; 2. part of the name of a tradition or denomination (for example, the Orthodox Church or the Lutheran Church); 3. a fellowship of Christians that form a local body of Christ, usually meeting together on Sundays for worship, caring for one another day by day, serving their local community, and sending people to tell others of God's love.

civil war: a war between groups of people in the same country.

colony/colonize: an area taken over, settled, and ruled by another country. People who colonize a country sometimes force their foreign cultures, religions, and values onto the people already living there.

communism: a political movement. The original idea was for a society in which there would be neither very rich nor very poor people, but where everyone shared equally in the work and in the wealth. This became the form of government in countries such as Russia, China, Vietnam, and Cuba, where the state controlled everything. Today most communist countries are changing and allow for some people to own their own business.

continent: one of the seven big land masses in the world. The continents are Africa, Antarctica, Asia, Oceania, Europe, North America, and South America.

coup: a sudden, often violent, takeover of a government by a small group of people.

cult: a religious group, usually smaller than other religious groups, that often has its own objects of worship and its own ceremonies, which are frequently secretive. Cults can consider themselves part of religions such as Christianity or Islam, but usually are considered "false religions" by the larger religious group.

culture: the customs, traditions, values, and way of life of a people.

customs: opinions or beliefs passed on from one generation to the next; the usual ways of doing things.

democracy: a system of government in which the adult population of a country elects people to govern them.

descendant: a person who is descended from another. You are a descendant of your parents, grandparents, and great-grandparents.

dialect: the way people in a particular part of a country speak their language. This includes the words they use and the way they pronounce them. One language can have many dialects.

dictator: a ruler who has total power over all that is done in his or her country.

drought: a long period of time without rain, so that there is a shortage of water.

emigrate: to leave one's own country to go and live in another country.

evangelical: a person who believes that the Bible is God's Word and tells us about Jesus' birth and sinless life, that he died for our sins so God could forgive us, and that he rose again from the dead. Evangelical Christians believe that only by having faith in Jesus can we be forgiven for our sins and have our relationship with God restored. We cannot earn our way to God by doing good things. The actual word *evangelicals* means "good news people" or "gospel people."

evangelist: a person who shares the good news of Jesus' love with others.

exile: 1. a person sent away from his or her own country and forced to live in another country; 2. the period of time a person or group is forced to live in another country.

export: anything people in one country grow or make to sell to another country.

extremism: having very strong views, and acting them out in ways that most people think is wrong. Extremists usually have these views about religion or politics.

famine: a time when food is so scarce that people and animals go hungry and sometimes die from starvation.

to fast: to not eat for a while, often for religious reasons. Usually fasting is combined with prayer.

fetish: an object that is supposed to have spiritual powers or to have a spirit inside of it. Fetishes are used mostly in animist religions.

Hajj (or haj): the Muslim pilgrimage to Mecca, the holy city in Saudi Arabia. All Muslims are expected to go on this pilgrimage at least once in their lifetime.

Hebrew: the language in which the Old Testament was originally written. A modern form of Hebrew is spoken in Israel today.

heretic: a person who believes things that are different from the accepted teachings of his or her religion.

Hindu: See Hinduism, p. 200.

Holy Trinity: God the Father, God the Son, and God the Holy Spirit together are called the Holy Trinity, three persons in one God. The Father, Son, and Holy Spirit are all equally God; they are all eternal and never change. They all took part in the work of creation. Jesus is the Son of God who came to earth to live and die to save us from our sins. After Jesus returned to heaven, God sent the Holy Spirit to work in the lives of Christians and to be with them always.

icon: a sacred piece of art, often a painting. Christian icons are often paintings of Jesus, his mother Mary, a saint, or angels.

idol: a statue or image of something that is worshiped as a god.

incense: a substance—such as spices, wood, or oil—that is burned for the fragrance and smoke it makes, usually as an act of worship.

Jain: a follower of Jainism, a small, ancient religion from India. Jains believe they must not hurt or kill any living thing and are strict vegetarians.

***JESUS* (film):** a movie from 1979 that has been translated and shown in more than 1,500 languages. It shows the life of Jesus from Luke's Gospel. Millions of people have seen it. It is used in many churches and homes around the world to help people understand who Jesus is. A lot of people have come to know him through watching this film.

Jewish: See Judaism, p. 204.

jinns: supernatural creatures in the Muslim world. The English word for it is "genie." Jinns are not humans or angels, and they can be good or evil.

legend: a story passed down from one generation to the next about something that happened long ago. The story may or may not be true.

Lent: Forty days of fasting and repenting for sin, observed between Ash Wednesday and Easter in the church calendar. Many branches of the Christian church observe Lent. Some people skip one meal a day during Lent or give up something they really enjoy, such as chocolate, and give the money they would have spent to charity.

looting: stealing things from houses or stores during a riot, battle, or other disaster.

malaria: an illness spread by mosquitoes, in which a person has high fevers and chills, and sometimes dies.

martyr: a person who is killed for his or her beliefs.

mass: the main service in some forms of Christianity (especially in the Roman Catholic Church), usually including Holy Communion.

medicine man: in animism, a person who has powers of healing. This may be through contact with the spirits or through their knowledge of plants and other natural things that can help healing. (See also: shamanism; witch doctor.)

meditation: in some religions this means thinking deeply about things, and in others it means emptying your mind from any thoughts.

merit: a reward in the future that comes from doing something good. Buddhists believe that, if they gain enough merit, they will be reborn into a better life when they die.

Messianic Jews: Jews who follow Jesus. They believe Jesus is the Messiah sent by God and have accepted him as their Savior.

missionary: a person who is sent to another place to share with others about his or her faith.

monastery: a building or buildings where monks live, work, worship, and study their religion in peace.

monk: a man belonging to a religious group, usually living in a monastery.

mosque: Muslim place of prayer, fellowship, and worship.

Muslim: a follower of Islam (see Islam, p. 202).

noble: a person of high rank by birth, such as a duke or duchess.

nomad: a member of a tribe that moves from place to place to find food or pasture for their animals.

offering: something given as a gift and sign of devotion, usually to a god or a religious congregation.

omen: something that happens and is taken as a sign that something else will happen. Some omens mean good things will happen, others that bad things will happen.

Orthodox Churches: branches of the Christian church found in many countries. The largest are from Russia, Greece, Armenia, Ethiopia, and Egypt. They base their beliefs on the Bible, the creed (a statement of faith), and traditions. They have many icons of saints in their churches. There are often no organs or musical instruments, but the services are chanted or sung. Often the only seats in churches are around the walls. People may stand during services, or move around to pray in front of icons.

peasant: person who lives and works on the land, often as a hired worker.

Pentecost: the day in the church calendar when Christians celebrate the coming of the Holy Spirit (Acts 2). It's sometimes called

Whitsun, or Whitsunday, and takes place on the seventh Sunday after Easter.

persecution: attacking, killing, or driving people from their homes or places of worship because they have different political or religious beliefs or come from a different ethnic group.

pilgrimage: a journey to worship at a holy place. People who go on pilgrimages are called "pilgrims."

plantation: a large farm, or area of land, planted with trees or crops, such as tea, coffee, cotton, or sugar. A number of people are hired to work on plantations.

plateau: area of high, level ground. Sometimes called a "tableland."

poncho: a garment, rather like a cape, worn in some South American countries. It is made from a piece of cloth with a hole in the middle, so it can be put on over the head.

poverty: the situation people live in where they don't have enough money to meet their basic needs.

prayer beads: string of beads used to help a person repeat prayers. Many religions use them, including some Christians.

prayer wheel: a cylinder-shaped box with prayers written inside and on the outside. Small ones are held in the hand, and bigger ones spin around a central shaft. It's thought that, as the wheel spins, the prayers go out into the universe. They are used by Tibetan Buddhists.

Protestants: members or followers of Christian churches that broke away from the Roman Catholic Church during the Reformation in sixteenth-century Europe.

Qur'an: (or Koran) the Muslim holy book.

raid: a sudden attack on another group of people.

Ramadan: a month of fasting in the Islamic calendar, during which Muslims don't eat or drink from sunrise to sunset.

ration: 1. to divide something so everyone has the same amount; 2. to restrict how much of something someone can have—for example, food during a famine.

rebel: a person who refuses to obey those in authority and fights against them.

refugee: a person who has been forced to flee from his or her home or country because of war, famine, or persecution. Refugees often go to camps, where they hope to find food, shelter, and safety until they can return to their own homes or settle in another country.

revolt/revolution: a rebellion that attempts to overthrow a government.

Sabbath: the seventh day of the Jewish week, from sunset on Friday to sunset on Saturday. It's the Jewish holy day and day of rest.

sacred: something that's holy and precious to followers of a religion.

sacrifice: 1. killing an animal as an offering to a god or goddess; 2. an offering of food or an object to a god or goddess.

saint: a holy person.

savior: a person who saves another from harm or difficulty. Jesus is our Savior because he died to save us from our sins and the power of evil.

sect: a group of people who have a different set of beliefs from the majority group of a religion.

secular: 1. not sacred or holy, but dealing with the ordinary things of this world; 2. considered not religious or related to a religion in any way.

settler: someone who goes to live in a new country, sometimes in an area that they believe hasn't been developed. Sometimes there are already people living in the places settlers move to.

shamanism: a form of animism mainly found in Siberia and other parts of Asia and among peoples native to the Americas. The word *shaman* means "one who knows," and a shaman keeps in touch with the spirits so he can guide his people to do what the spirits want them to do. (See also: medicine man; witch doctor.)

sheikh: (pronounced like "shake") the chief of an Arab tribe or village.

Shi'ite Muslims: (also called Shi'as) Muslims who believe their leaders must be descendants of Ali, Muhammad's cousin and son-in-law.

shrine: a building or place where sacred objects are kept.

Sikh: a follower of Sikhism, a religion founded about five hundred years ago in what is now part of North India and Pakistan by a man called Guru Nanak. Sikhs believe in one God and that all people are equally important. Sikhs often don't cut their hair. Men keep their hair in place with a wooden comb and wear a turban. The Sikh place of worship is called a *gurdwara*, and their holy book is the Guru Granth Sahib.

slum: an overcrowded—often dirty—area of a city, usually without the basic services other neighborhoods have, such as sanitation, water, electricity, garbage collection, schools, and clinics. Most people living in slums are too poor to live elsewhere.

spirit: a supernatural being. Ghosts and fairies are spirits. Animists believe that objects and places in nature have spirits. The Bible says that angels are spirits (Hebrews 1:13-14) and that God is spirit (John 4:24).

spiritist: a person who believes it's possible to make contact with some spirits, usually with the spirit of a dead person.

Sunni Muslims: Most Muslims belong to the Sunni branch of Islam and closely follow the teachings of the prophet Muhammad.

superstition: an idea or action based on a belief in ghosts, lucky and unlucky signs, and supernatural happenings.

taboo: something that's forbidden or not acceptable for religious or social reasons.

temple: a building used for worship.

terraced fields: level fields made on a hillside, with the outer edge of each field kept in place by a wall. Terraced fields go up a hillside like a series of large steps.

terrorism: the use of violence to create fear to achieve political or religious goals. Terrorism is used to attack ordinary people, not just soldiers or police. A person who uses terrorism is a terrorist.

thatch: straw or reeds used to cover a roof.

traditional religion: a religion or way of worship that has been handed down from one generation to another within a tribe or people group, and is considered to be the original or native religion of that group.

traditions: opinions, ways of doing things, or beliefs that have been passed on from one generation to the next.

translate/translation: to put the words of one language into the words of another language so that both have the same meaning. A person who does this is called a translator. A Bible translation is a Bible put into the words of another language to mean the same as its original languages (Greek, Hebrew, and Aramaic).

tribe: people belonging to the same race or group, and often ruled by a chief.

United Nations: an international organization of more than 190 countries who try to work together for world peace. It was founded in 1945 at the end of World War II. It tries to settle quarrels between countries or within a country; to develop friendship between nations; and to help overcome some of the world's major problems, such as poverty, terrorism, and climate change.

visa: an official government document, sometimes stamped in a passport, that gives someone permission to enter or leave another specific country.

voodoo: a religion in the West Indies that evolved from beliefs brought over by African slaves.

witch doctor: in animism, a person who has contact with the spirits and can understand signs and omens. (See also: medicine man; shamanism.)

yak: a long-haired Tibetan ox.

ACKNOWLEDGMENTS

A great many people and Christian ministries have helped in the production of this update to *Window on the World*, and we want to thank each one who volunteered time to help make a resource that families can use to pray. We believe that God hears and answers prayer, and we are convinced that children have a special part to play in praying for the world in which they live.

We want to thank all who have prayed for this project: our own families and friends, our fellow Operation World team members (especially John Bardsley, who provided the early drafts), our colleagues in WEC and the Lausanne Movement, and our faithful Operation World prayer team scattered around the world.

We wish to particularly thank those from the countries and people groups included here who have provided us correction and guidance, especially where our information or tone needed to be reconsidered. While we aim to balance between local and global perspectives, we no doubt fall short in a number of instances. These friends old and new have graciously answered our questions; provided information, stories, and photographs; and have checked the results. Our interactions with them have often been a great source of inspiration. Many encouraged us as they shared the impact of earlier editions on their families and churches.

All Nations Christian College has welcomed us into their community. We are grateful for the use of our office space on campus, and for the warmth of fellowship experienced here.

We continue to be grateful for Pieter Kwant (of the Piquant Agency), our long-time agent and partner in the work of mission. And we count ourselves blessed to again have benefitted from the expertise, partnership, and friendship of Jeff Crosby, Al Hsu, Justin Lawrence, and the rest of the team at InterVarsity Press.

The greatest encourager of all is God himself, whose mercies have indeed been new every morning (Lamentations 3:22-23). As we worked, we discovered that God has answered many of the prayers included in the previous editions, which were so thoughtfully written first by Jill Johnstone and then Daphne Spraggett. We praise God for his love and faithfulness, and thank him for the privilege of being invited to change the world through prayer!

Molly Wall and Jason Mandryk

IMAGE CREDITS

p. 4   (boy) Pixabay / (monks) Pixabay

p. 5   (girt-paint) Pixabay / (child) Pixabay / (girl-book) Pixabay

p. 8   (children) Pixabay

p. 9   (city) Pixabay / (mountains) Pixabay

p. 10   (wagon) By Andrey Shevchenko on Dreamstime / (bullock) By malik 5 on Dreamstime

p. 11   (Mother Teresa) by Meunierd on Megapixl

P. 12   (Baku) Dreamstime

p. 13   (schoolgirls) by Bazruh on Dreamstime / (flame) by dinozzaver on 123RF / (mud volcano) Pixabay

p. 14   (boy) Vilondo.com / (ploughing) by TatianaMorozova on Dreamstime

p. 15   (dancer) by Denis Voskvinov on Dreamstime / (statue) Vilondo.com

p. 16   (family) by Smandy on Dreamstime / (food) by Haseeb Qasim on Dreamstime /

p. 17   (market) Paop on Dreamstime / (mountain) by Shahbanobaloch on Dreamstime / (suroz) Diego Mor

p. 18   (boy) Pixabay

p. 19   (bride) Pixabay / (river) Pixabay

p. 20   (boy) Carsten ten Brink, (tent) by Bertramz on Wikimedia Commons/ (desert) Pixabay

p. 21   (girl and woman) Carsten ten Brink Carsten, (man) by Anonymous/Joshua Project, (shield) by Walters Art Museum on Wikimedia Commons,

p. 22   (family) Pixabay / (children) Pixabay / (city) Pixabay

p. 23   (monastary) Pixabay / (idol) Pixabay

p. 24   (village) Pixabay / (girl) Pixabay

p. 25   (woman) Rea Finlay, (girls) Rea Finlay

p. 26   (Rio de Janeiro) Pixabay / (father son) Pixabay

p. 27   (soccer boys) Pixabay

p. 28   Dreamstime, Pixabay

p. 29   Pixabay

p. 30   Megapixl

p. 31   Megapixl

p. 32   Megapixl

p. 33   (market) Megapixl / (caravan) iStock.com/giancarlo salvador

p. 34   Dreamstime, Creative Commons

p. 35   Dreamstime, Allfree

p. 36   (children) Norlen Perez

p. 37   Tim Dowley Associates, Creative Commons, Pixabay

p. 38   USAFE

p. 39   Megapixl, Francisco Anzola

p. 40   Dreamstime, Pixabay

p. 41   Wikimedia Commons: Ferdinand Reus

p. 42   Dreamstime

p. 43   Dreamstime, visitisrael

p. 44   Antoine Vasse Nicolas, Pixabay

p. 45   Pixabay, Megapixl

p. 46   Pixabay, Allfree

p. 47   (rock church) Dreamstime / (AU hq) Jason Mandryk

p. 48   Dreamstime

p. 49   Pixabay, Allfree

p. 50   (parrot) Pixabay / (parade) IMG00591 © Ted Obermayer

p. 51   Dreamstime

p. 52   Wikimedia Commons, Dreamstime

p. 53   (people) flikr / (tiger) Pixabay

p. 54   Pixabay

p. 55   Tim Dowley Associates, Pixabay

p. 56   Allfree

p. 57   Dreamstime, Pixabay

p. 58   Pixabay, Wikimedia Commons

p. 59   (mosque) Jenny Koelbing / Arnoldmm Wiki

p. 60   Megapixl

p. 61   Allfree, Pixabay, Creative Commons

p. 62   Wikimedia Commons

p. 63   Megapixl, Wikimedia Commons

p. 64   Dreamstime

p. 65   Megapixl

p. 66   (church) Pixabay / (boats) Pixabay

p. 67   Pixabay

p. 68   Dreamstime

p. 69   (children) royalkids.org / (schoolgirls) Pexels

p. 70   (building) Pixabay / (boy) Dreamstime

p. 71   (saris) Pixabay / (pottery) Dreamstime

p. 72   Mehmit Canli, Wikimedia Commons

p. 73   Allfree, Wikimedia Commons

p. 74   Pixabay, Allfree

p. 75   (ziggurat) Anonymous, (tree) (mosque) Allfree, Megapixl

p. 76   Allfree

p. 77   (father and son) Pixabay / (children) Pixabay

p. 78   Pixabay

p. 79   Pixabay, Wikimedia Commons

p. 80   (girls) Allfree, Pixabay / (Tokyo) by Jazeal Melgoza on Unsplash

p. 81   (schoolkids) Pixabay / (sushi) Pakutaso / (restaurant) Allfree

p. 82   flickr izicono

p. 83   (mountain) Ali Arhab / flickr izicono

p. 84   Megapixl, Pixabay

p. 85   (mosque) Pixabay, (eagle hunter) by Edwardje on Dreamstime

p. 86   Dreamstime

p. 87   Pixabay, Megapixl

p. 88   Pixabay

p. 89   Allfree, Dreamstime

p. 90   Wikimedia Commons

p. 91   (child) (idol) Dreamstime / (granary) Dilwyn Roderick

p. 92   (girl) Faly Ravoahangy / (city) Pixabay

p. 93   (lemur) Allfree / (lady) Faly Ravoahangy

p. 94   (cooking) Allfree / (minaret) iStock.com/vau902

p. 95   (plane) Allfree / (beach) Pixabay / (coral) Pixabay

p. 96   Dreamstime

p. 97   (kora) © nathalie_r Neverdie225/ Wikimedia Commons

p. 98   Pixabay, Pixagram

p. 99   (mask) Pixabay / (children) Pixabay / (city) Pixabay

p. 100 Dreamstime, Pixabay

p. 101 Allfree, Pixabay

p. 102 (boy) S & A Biro / (city) Pixabay

p. 103 (ger) Elizabeth Benn

p. 104 Pixabay, Allfree

p. 105 Allfree, Pixabay, Dreamstime

p. 106 (men working) Allfree / (girl) Pixabay

p. 107 (mountain) Pixabay / (holy man) Pixabay / (children) Pixabay

p. 108 Tourism New Zealand

p. 109 (sheep) Pixabay / (geyser) Chris McClennan/Tourism New Zealand / (kiwi) iStock.com/GlobalP

p. 110 Dreamstime

p. 111 (cemetery) Pixabay / (mosque) Dreamstime, Pixabay

p. 112 Megapixl

p. 113 (monument) Wikimedia/Bjørn Christian Tørrissen, (children) Anonymous

p. 114 Pixabay

p. 115 Pixabay, Allfree

p. 116 (mountain) Allfree, Pixabay / (boys) Pixabay

p. 117 (wedding) Anita Azeem / (mosque) Pixabay

p. 118 Pixabay

p. 119 Pixabay

p. 120 Pixabay

NB Every effort has been made to acknowledge sources accurately. If any inaccuracies have occurred, please let us know.

OTHER RESOURCES FROM OPERATION WORLD

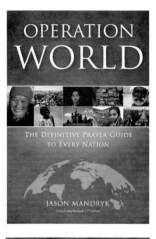

OPERATION WORLD

Operation World (OW) is widely regarded as the definitive volume of prayer information about the world. First published in 1964 and now in its seventh edition, OW is the recipient of the ECPA Gold Medallion Award for Excellence in Evangelical Christian Literature and was listed in *Christianity Today*'s Top 50 Books That Have Shaped Evangelicals.

INDIVIDUAL TITLES CURRENTLY AVAILABLE

Operation World (7th Edition)
Operation World (with CD) (7th Edition)
Operation World Personal CD (7th Edition)
Operation World Prayer Map (7th Edition)
Operation World Prayer Map (UV Coated) (7th Edition)
Operation World Professional DVD-ROM (7th Edition)

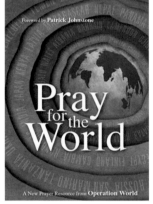

PRAY FOR THE WORLD

This timely and accessible prayer guide is an abridged version of *Operation World*, the leading resource for people who want to impact the nations for Christ through prayer. *Pray for the World* includes challenges for prayer and specific on-the-ground reports of answers to prayer from Christian leaders around the world.

THE FUTURE OF THE GLOBAL CHURCH

In *The Future of the Global Church* Patrick Johnstone, author of six editions of the phenomenal prayer guide *Operation World*, draws on his fifty years experience to present a breathtaking, full-color graphical and textual overview of the past, present, and possible future of the church around the world.

THESE TITLES ARE AVAILABLE FROM IVPRESS.COM

For updates on future products, please visit operationworld.org.

Follow Operation World:

 Operation World    @OperationWorld   OW Operation World App